Palgrave Studies in Classical Liberalism

Series Editors

David F. Hardwick, Department of Pathology and Laboratory Medicine, The University of British Columbia, Vancouver, Canada
Leslie Marsh, Department of Economics, Philosophy and Political Science, The University of British Columbia, Okanagan, Canada

This series offers a forum to writers concerned that the central presuppositions of the liberal tradition have been severely corroded, neglected, or misappropriated by overly rationalistic and constructivist approaches.

The hardest-won achievement of the liberal tradition has been the wrestling of epistemic independence from overwhelming concentrations of power, monopolies and capricious zealotries. The very precondition of knowledge is the exploitation of the epistemic virtues accorded by society's situated and distributed manifold of spontaneous orders, the DNA of the modern civil condition.

With the confluence of interest in situated and distributed liberalism emanating from the Scottish tradition, Austrian and behavioral economics, non-Cartesian philosophy and moral psychology, the editors are soliciting proposals that speak to this multidisciplinary constituency. Sole or joint authorship submissions are welcome as are edited collections, broadly theoretical or topical in nature.

Eliana María Santanatoglia

An Evolutionary Account of Law

The Role of Evolutionary Thinking in Legal Theory and Philosophy

palgrave
macmillan

Eliana María Santanatoglia
Law School
University of Buenos Aires
Buenos Aires, Argentina

ISSN 2662-6470 ISSN 2662-6489 (electronic)
Palgrave Studies in Classical Liberalism
ISBN 978-3-032-12161-5 ISBN 978-3-032-12162-2 (eBook)
https://doi.org/10.1007/978-3-032-12162-2

Cover credit: Pattadis Walarput/Alamy Stock Photo

This Palgrave Macmillan imprint is published by the registered company Springer Nature Switzerland AG
The registered company address is: Gewerbestrasse 11, 6330 Cham, Switzerland

To Federico, my husband and to Eugenio, my son.

Thank you for your unwavering support.

To Federico for his intellectual contribution, discussion and support. We thought many of these ideas together, so a large part of this book belongs to us both.

To Eugenio, for giving meaning to this and every other enterprise I undertake.

Competing Interests The author has no competing interests to declare that are relevant to the content of this manuscript.

Preface & Acknowledgements

This book is the result of many years of study, reflection and writing, since it is an English version of my Ph.D. dissertation presented at the Law School of the University of Buenos Aires. It aims to propose an evolutionary account of law, tending bridges between the realms of philosophy of social sciences and legal theory. It follows a path that starts with the analysis of the ideas of the authors of the Scottish Enlightenment, continuing with the work of F. A. Hayek, and ending with the evolutionary authors of the late twentieth and early twenty-first centuries. In turn, it explores several seminal debates on the epistemological and methodological assumptions of the social sciences, on decision theory, the rationality of agents and the unit of study of law. In addition, the proposal includes thinking about the evolution of legal orders from three parallel evolutionary processes: biological, social and individual, considering and combining the ideas of various theories such as evolutionary psychology, evolutionary game theory, co-evolutionism and the concept of homo heuristics, among others.

The process of producing this work over the years has been a long one, fuelled by many people and debates.

I would like to express my gratitude to two key mentors who have instilled confidence in me and provided guidance over the years. Firstly, I would like to thank Professor Dr. Martin Diego Farrell, my Ph.D. dissertation director at the Law School of the University of Buenos Aires, for his support, good advice and motivation over the years. Thanks to his erudition, guidance and patience, I was able to present such an unusual perspective within the Argentine academic realm.

This work is also dedicated to the memory of the late Dr. Ezequiel Gallo. I first encountered the Scottish Enlightenment through one of his papers many years ago. He was a prominent advocate of evolutionary ideas and a key supporter of the David Hume Institute Foundation, serving as a source of inspiration for many. I will always be grateful for his tremendous social grace, generosity and support throughout the process of establishing an institute inspired by David Hume in Argentina, as well as for the memorable conversations about Hume and other intellectual interests in common.

The genesis of this book can be traced back to my dissertation for the M.Sc. in Philosophy of the Social Sciences at the London School of Economics and Political Science in the UK. I would like to express my gratitude to Professor Jason McKenzie Alexander, the programme and thesis director, for introducing me to contemporary schools of evolutionary thought in the social sciences and for his guidance. I would also like to thank all my fellow mates and friends, with whom I engaged in deep and passionate debates about many of the philosophical underpinnings of the notions discussed here during that year: Esha Senchaudhuri, Catherine Herfeld, Mark Stanford, Ivan Sandoval Cervantes, Roberto Fumagalli, Paolo Mantovani, Joelle Abid-Rached, Erwin Dekker and many others. I apologise to everyone I forgot to mention here.

Moreover, the chapters of the book especially devoted to 'Classicl Evolutionism' were discussed at length in seminars in which I participated as a researcher both at the ESEADE University Institute and at the Friedrich A. von Hayek Foundation. I thank its authorities, professors and some of my colleagues at those years, on behalf of all those who collaborated in the formation of these ideas: Delia Ferreira Rubio, Martín Krause, Gabriel Zanotti, Carlos Newland, Enrique Aguilar, Eduardo Zimmermann, Ricardo Rojas, Osvaldo Schenone, Alejandra Salinas,

Eduardo Stordeur and Juan Ramos Mejía and frequent assistants such as Marina Carbajal and Eleonora Urrutia.

I would also like to express my gratitude to Liberty Fund Inc. for providing me with repeated opportunities to discuss the ideas of the Scottish Enlightenment, Hayek and other thinkers of the liberal tradition, both as a participant and as a director of their colloquia. I am also grateful to the Institute for Humane Studies, which supported my studies and participation in conferences abroad where I was able to present part of the work that makes up this book.

I would also like to thank all the colleagues and seminar participants of the David Hume Institute Foundation who, in recent years, have contributed to understanding and refining the notions of contemporary evolutionism and have accompanied Federico Sosa Valle and myself in this adventure of working with ideas.

I would like to express my gratitude to Leslie Marsh, the editor of the Palgrave Studies in Classical Liberalism series, and to Ellie Duncan, my editor at Palgrave Macmillan, for providing me with this invaluable opportunity to present my research to an international audience. I also would like to thank Leonie Sittner for the guidance and patience during the last months, and I would also like to acknowledge Gideon Parry for his willingness to work under pressure and for his meticulous proofreading.

Finally, I would like to express my gratitude to my family and friends, especially my mother, for her invaluable intellectual and moral guidance and for her daily support. And, as stated in the dedication, I would like to express my eternal gratitude to my husband Federico and my son Eugenio for their constant support and love, which have made this endeavour possible.

Buenos Aires, Argentina — Eliana María Santanatoglia, Ph.D.

Praise for *An Evolutionary Account of Law*

"*An Evolutionary Account of Law* is a landmark contribution bridging classical evolutionary thought and cutting-edge social science. Santanatoglia masterfully integrates insights from the Scottish Enlightenment and Hayek with evolutionary game theory and cognitive science, presenting legal rules as stable strategies emerging from individual interactions rather than top-down constructs. This genuinely novel framework is essential reading for anyone seeking to understand how normative orders emerge, stabilize, and change."

—Jason McKenzie Alexander, *Professor of Philosophy, Department of Philosophy, Logic and Scientific Method at the London School of Economics and Political Science, UK*

"This very well argued book offers firstly a complete examination of the theories of justice of classical philosophers, as David Hume, Adam Smith and Friedrich von Hayek. Secondly, and more important, brings a thought provoking examination of the often neglected thesis about the influence of evolution in the sphere of law. A mandatory book for everyone interested in legal and political philosophy."

—Martín Diego Farrell, *Professor Emeritus, Law School of the University of Buenos Aires, Argentina*

About the Author

Eliana María Santanatoglia holds a Ph.D. in Philosophy of Law from the Law School of the University of Buenos Aires (UBA, Argentina). She also holds an M.Sc. in Philosophy of the Social Sciences from the London School of Economics and Political Science (LSE, UK), a MA in Economics and Political Science from ESEADE (Argentina), and is a Lawyer graduated from the University of Buenos Aires Law School (UBA). At the UBA Law School, Eliana is a regular Adjunct Professor of Legal Theory and the Deputy Director of the Department of Philosophy of Law. She is also co-founder and Executive Director of the David Hume Institute Foundation—Centre for Research in Normative and Institutional Evolution. She currently serves as the Director of Global Affairs of the Honourable National Senate of Argentina. She is currently President of the Board of the LSE Alumni Association of Argentina and Co-Chair to the Programme Committee of the University Women's Club of Buenos Aires.

In the academia, she was Director of the Master's degree in Economics and Political Science and the Bachelor's degree in Social Sciences at ESEADE (2011–2012). She directed two DECyT research projects

(2020–2022, 2022–2024) at the UBA Law School. She has directed two and attended numerous Liberty Fund Inc colloquia. She has worked as a professor—at both the undergraduate and postgraduate levels—and as a researcher at the University of Buenos Aires Law School (UBA), ESEADE, the University of Belgrano (UB), the Hayek Foundation and other institutions (2002–2017). She has received a scholarship from the European Union's AlBan programme and a Fellowship of the Institute for Humane Studies, among others. She was Vice-President of the LSE Hayek Society (2006/2007).

In the public sector, she worked as an advisor and programme coordinator at the Institute for Political Training and Public Management of the Ministry of Government of the City of Buenos Aires (2020–2023). She has served as advisor to the Undersecretary of Government, Ministry of Government of the City of Buenos Aires (2016–2019), coordinating the Virtual School of the Undersecretary of Government and Attorney General of the City of Buenos Aires.

Her main areas of research are legal theory, constitutional law, moral and political philosophy, the philosophy of social sciences and the interrelations between these disciplines, with special interest in the evolutionary view of rules and institutions. She has published numerous papers in academic journals and book chapters, and she has lectured and participated in colloquia and seminars in these areas of thought in Argentina, Brazil, Uruguay, Guatemala, Chile, the United States and England.

General Introduction

This work attempts to introduce an evolutionary account of law. This conception implies the idea that the legal order is not the deliberate creation of an individual or a group, but rather the unintended, gradual and cumulative result of interactions between individuals over time. Thus, individuals and rules interdefine and co-evolve.

This evolutionary view of rules and institutions is not new. Its main antecedent is the eighteenth-century Scottish Enlightenment, whose representatives include David Hume, Adam Smith or Adam Ferguson. Before them came the precursors of this school of thought, including Shaftesbury, Hutcheson and Mandeville. It also has its representatives in the twentieth century such as Friedrich Hayek or Douglass North.

This proposal is inspired by a current and widespread debate, particularly—but not exclusively—in the Anglo-American academic world. Among the most recent and widely discussed schools and theories in the social sciences, a new perspective has appeared that presents evolutionary accounts on social phenomena, with a particular focus on rules and institutions. This theoretical framework proposes diverse insights into the processes by which these institutions emerge, stabilise, change or disappear.

There are a number of new schools and theories that propose evolutionary conceptions of rules and institutions. Among these theories, some propose that biological adaptation is the underlying cause of all forms of social behaviour in 'homo sapiens'. In other words, they explain the emergence of certain regular behaviour—later established as a rule or social institution—as sophisticated strategies of biological survival.

Then, some propose that cultural evolutionary explanations are the best means of understanding the specific way in which particular institutions or rules emerge, change, stabilise or disappear. Among these are those that refer to the search for the genesis of institutions and the 'competition' between different institutional strategies. Many of these theories are supported by sophisticated mathematical models, which are used to predict the emergence of rules and institutions. These models are designed to identify the most stable or dominant strategies in situations involving repeated games and a specific framework of incentives.

Finally, there are those that combine biological and cultural arguments to provide co-evolutionary models of explanation. The co-evolutionary view has brought a new level of rigour and detail to the explanation of individual and social learning processes, as well as the emergence, stabilisation and change of rules and institutions. It has also clarified the mutual influence between biological and cultural evolutionary processes.

The work is divided into three parts: First Part (Chapters 1–3) corresponds mainly to a presentation from the history of ideas, where we analyse what we will refer to as 'classic evolutionism', mainly represented by the eighteenth-century Scottish Enlightenment and Friedrich Hayek in the twentieth century. This part is further divided into three chapters. In the first chapter, we will review the main contributions of the Scottish Enlightenment thinkers to the notions of law and justice, with particular reference to David Hume, Adam Smith and Adam Ferguson. In the second chapter, we will examine Friedrich Hayek's proposal in relation to his evolutionary view of law. The third chapter of the First Part analyses the contributions of 'classic evolutionism' to the study of law.

In Second Part (Chapters 4–7), we will carry out a detailed analysis of the contributions of the new schools of thought that propose an evolutionary approach in the social sciences. The second part of the book is divided into four chapters. The first chapter provides an introduction to these new evolutionary schools, offering a classification of them and an account of 'biological turn' and the 'revival' of Hume within this school of thought. The following three chapters will be devoted to the following topics, in order of appearance: firstly, the most 'biologistic' theories of cultural phenomena, which explain them as sophisticated mechanisms of biological adaptation, especially in current evolutionary psychology. Secondly, we turn to the perspective of cultural evolutionism, which posits that the emergence of rules and institutions is rooted in cultural evolutionary processes, particularly within the domain of evolutionary game theory. Finally, the last chapter of the Second Part will be devoted to co-evolutionary proposals that try to unravel the weight that both cultural evolution and biological evolution may have on the emergence of certain behaviours or social regularities.

In the Third and final part of this work (Chapters 8–10), we will present our own proposal of an evolutionary view of law that combines elements of 'Classic Evolutionism' and other new evolutionary perspectives on social phenomena. The third part of the book is divided into three chapters. The first two provide the 'bricks' necessary for the construction of the theory. In this regard, the primary current debates on the methodology required to understand these phenomena from this perspective (methodological individualism vs. methodological holism, *homo economicus* vs. *homo sociologicus*) and the potential responses to these tensions as outlined by the evolutionary perspective will be introduced. The debate on the rationality of agents, i.e. whether they make decisions based on the principles of rational choice theory or by a bounded rationality, will also be analysed. In addition, we propose an analysis of evolution of law at three levels—biological, social and individual—and we discuss what is the unit of study to be considered by this evolutionary account of law.

Finally, in the last chapter, we will synthesise all these elements to set out our account of the legal order as the permanent result of the emergence, stability and change of legal rules, which emerge in turn from repeated interactions between individuals. Finally, we will attempt to draw parallels with other theoretical schools and highlight what we consider to be the strengths of this particular legal perspective.

Contents

List of Figures

Part I

Classic Evolutionism

1

Justice and Law for the Eighteen-Century Scottish Enlightenment

1.1 Introduction

This work attempts to formulate a theory that proposes an evolutionary account of law. That is, a view that understands rules and institutions as the unintended outcome of individual interactions, in a particular context, over time. This proposal is inspired by a widespread debate, especially in the Anglo-American academic realm, about the way in which social and moral rules emerge and how they stabilise, change or disappear.

These new evolutionary theories in the social sciences are based, explicitly or implicitly, on evolutionary conceptions of the social that have a long tradition, namely those inspired by Darwin and his conception of biological evolution based on the mechanism of natural selection. To this mechanism of natural selection, these new evolutionary theories add elements of twentieth-century biology, in particular genetics, and the latest findings of current neurosciences, to provide ultimate explanations of regular human behaviour from a biological point of view.

But, it is worth remembering that Darwin himself offers a culturalist—and non-biological—explanation of the evolution of human social institutions, in the work that deals specifically with the evolution of man:

E. M. Santanatoglia, *An Evolutionary Account of Law*, Palgrave Studies in Classical Liberalism, https://doi.org/10.1007/978-3-032-12162-2_1

"The Descent of Man" (Darwin, Darwin, 2004), a subject considered briefly in the second part of this book. Even those who believe that the ultimate explanation of regular human behaviour lies at the biological level recognise that there were authors before Darwin, who provided evolutionary insights into rules and institutions.

The eighteenth-century Scottish School—or Scottish Enlightenment—is now recognised as the group of authors who proposed the first evolutionary views of morality, political institutions, rules of justice and the price system, among other social phenomena. Darwin—who is generally regarded as the father of this view—referred to the notion of sympathy when discussing the moral sense, quoting abundantly from authors such as David Hume (Darwin, 2004, ch. 4, p. 132) and following Hume's vision of the evolution of human behaviour.

Likewise, Friedrich A. Hayek (Hayek, 1983, ch. 1, p. 23) who continued this school and brought it closer to the twentieth-century debate, insisted on pointing to these authors and ideas as the initiators of the evolutionary view of social phenomena, long before the work of Charles Darwin, proposing a kind of 'pre-Darwinian Darwinism'.

The Scottish Enlightenment is usually associated with thinkers such as Adam Smith, David Hume or Adam Ferguson. These authors are recognised in the history of ideas not only for their contributions to philosophical thought, but also as the 'fathers' of several of today's social science disciplines, such as political economy or institutional analysis. Today, these authors have been rediscovered and recognised as inspiration for current evolutionary theories in the social sciences and philosophy, such as Ken Benmore's view on "Natural Justice" (Binmore, 2005, ch. 3, p. 39), i.e. when he refers to the 'scientific tradition' in philosophy.

In order to introduce some of their ideas, we find Argentinean historian and intellectual Ezequiel Gallo who places us in the scenario where these authors conceived and presented their ideas:

"Scotland at the beginning of the 18th century unfolded before the restless spectator a landscape of contrasts as sharp as they were striking. In its Lowlands were beginning to emerge the first signs of that great commercial and industrial revolution which was to shake the foundations of the world for centuries to come. The region was bustling with activity, with a multiplication of businesses and jobs, contacts with the farthest corners of the earth, and a bustle that reflected increasingly optimistic expectations. In the lowlands, the spectacle of wealth creation was incessantly striking the most alert minds of the time. You didn't have to travel far in that Scotland to find a diametrically opposed world. The Highlands offered a geography as attractive as it was rough, a suitable setting for that virile and haughty world of the clans, a world isolated, poor and powerless to contribute to the multiplication of the species. An abyss separated the two regions, the contrast between wealth and poverty, between progress and stagnation. A contrast that not only reflected an easily verifiable contemporary reality, it also reflected, in miniature, the history of a humanity that had only for brief periods and in restricted areas, known the bustle of the lowlands. A world, in short, that had almost always stumbled, if not retrogressed, in its attempts to make possible the survival and growth of its inhabitants. Centuries and not just kilometres separated the lowlands from the highlands. It was against this background that the questions that the Scottish authors addressed arose. First, what are the steps and institutional mechanisms by which men are leaving the previous rustic society and integrating into the complexities of the new society (polished society)? Secondly, how can we ensure that this transition is not permanently frustrated and continues to advance on solid foundations?" (Gallo, 2008, pp. 34–35, our translation).

These authors, in turn, drew on the debates of their time and were inspired and influenced by several figures who acted as their teachers or guides. Among them, we will name only a few to illustrate the intellectual environment of the time that may have given rise to the emergence of the particular view of law and justice later held by authors such as David Hume and Adam Smith.

1.2 The Antecedents of the Scottish School: Mandeville, Hutcheson and Shaftesbury

Three of the thinkers considered 'fathers' of the Scottish Enlightenment were, paradoxically, not Scottish. Mandeville, Hutcheson and Shaftesbury, to whom we refer, were professors in Scotland and represented an important influence on second generation authors such as David Hume,

Adam Smith and Adam Ferguson. We will review only some of their main ideas that will allow us to better understand the contribution of this school to the debate of their time and to their disciples.

Bernard de Mandeville (1670–1733) was a Dutch physician who in 1714 wrote the renowned "The Fable of the Bees" (Mandeville, 1732). This work—the meanings and conclusions of which are still debated to this day—is considered a kind of satire of the customs of the time, together with a moral critique. Mandeville describes a society in which individuals are driven by their basest passions, thus indulging in vicious behaviour and excessive consumption of harmful goods such as alcohol and gambling. But what Mandeville observes is that in these 'vicious' communities there is, paradoxically, an effect of economic growth that is not observed in the same way in those 'puritan' communities composed of virtuous citizens. In his famous line about 'private vices, public benefits', Mandeville is not extrapolating from the moral value of conduct to material consequences and vice versa (i.e. he does not say 'private vices, public virtues' as some argue) but he does observe that the virtue of citizens does not necessarily guarantee their progress and material well-being.

What we would like to highlight is Mandeville's introduction of the notion—which, in Hayek's view (Hayek, 1978, p. 253), was completely original for the time—of the 'unintended consequences of intentional individual actions' that will be much discussed in the twentieth century. Mandeville identifies beneficial social effects of individual behaviours that were not only not designed to produce such effects but were not even planned to produce beneficial consequences in individual terms, since they were 'guided' by vicious inclinations. It seems to show, then, a paradoxical and unexpected effect whereby individuals motivated by negative or destructive inclinations produce unintended public wealth or social welfare effects.

Following this observation, we can identify the first indications of the idea of an emergent social order, independent of the intentions or plans of the particular individuals who compose such order. We will see later how Friedrich Hayek, an author who, in the twentieth century, continues thinking in evolutionary terms, especially values Mandeville's 'anti-rationalism' (Hayek, 1983, p. 20). He was one of the first to explain the emergence of social phenomena as the product of a gradual evolution of advantageous habits and practices and not as the product of a rational contract or deliberate decision by individuals.

On the other hand, there is **Francis Hutcheson (1694–1749),** one of the founding fathers of the Scottish School, of Irish origin and descended from a Scottish Presbyterian family. Among his best-known works are "An Inquiry into the Original of Our Ideas of Beauty and Virtue" (1725) and "An Essays on the Nature and Conduct of the Passions and Affections, with Illustrations of the Moral Sense" (1728). In 1729, he was teaching at the University of Glasgow, having been being the first to teach in English; he had Adam Smith as a student, who would later be recognised as one of the most important exponents of this school. He engaged in several disputes with Hobbes and Mandeville and, as we shall see, had several points of contact with the views of his contemporary, Lord Shaftesbury.

Lord Shaftesbury (Anthony Ashley Cooper, 3rd Earl of Shaftesbury) (1671–1713) was himself an English politician, philosopher and writer. He was heavily influenced by Locke in his education, and he debated with Hobbes and in 1711 first published "Characteristicks of Men, Manners, Opinions, Times" (Shaftesbury, 2001) in which he reunited most of his mature work. Both Hutcheson and Shaftesbury agreed on some main points that were the basis for the debates of their disciples and students, such as David Hume and Adam Smith.

Among these common positions propounded by Hutcheson and Shaftesbury were the following:

(a) The notion of 'moral sense', that is, the idea that all individuals innately possess a moral sense, just like the other senses such as sight, touch or smell. This sense has a fundamental function, which is to enable us to perceive virtue and vice in ourselves as well as in others. In other words, the ability to distinguish between good and evil is, for these authors, a constitutive part of human nature.
(b) The idea of Benevolence or Generosity: both authors hold that benevolence is an original and irreducible part of human nature. This position is clearly opposed to other conceptions of human nature, such as the Hobbesian one, which could be described as

'pessimistic'. Thus, this first generation of Scottish School thinkers present an 'optimistic' view of human nature and conceive generosity as a fundamental element of human nature. They also draw an analogy between virtue and beauty.

(c) In addition to the moral sense, there is what is called 'common sense', which refers to public sense. Based on a naturalistic view of individuals and their social context, this perspective on common sense also allows them to understand other social and psychological phenomena such as honour, guilt and pride. For these authors, these senses (or feelings) are intimately related to the approval or gratitude of others. This insight, which delves into how moral standards are based on an intersubjective regard or approval, had a significant influence on the foundations of both David Hume's and Adam Smith's moral philosophies.

(d) As noted, Hutcheson and Shaftesbury depart from observation and take a naturalistic view of their object of study. In this case, they start from an empirical psychological stance, which is interesting to note, given the current resurgence of empirical psychology (which is addressed in the second part of this work).

(e) Finally, it is worth noting the complete separation that operates between Morality and Theology for these authors. This theoretical position also explains the subsequent theoretical developments of their disciples and the implications of such a division within the wider panorama of political and moral philosophy.

1.3 The Notion of Justice for David Hume

1.3.1 David Hume on Human Nature

For the evolutionary account of law proposed in this book, we consider a 'minimal' notion of human nature, as presented by David Hume. For Hume, human nature has an objective aspect and two subjective aspects. The 'objective' aspect of human nature consists in the scarcity represented, in this case, by the 'innumerable wants and needs' that individuals experience, while at the same time having to satisfy them with 'scarce means'.

Hume adds to this objective aspect two subjective characteristics (Hume, 2000, p. 309): (a) self-interest or egoism of individuals and (b) their limited generosity. Self-interest, in Hume's terms, does not refer to a purely negative disposition or a base selfishness; rather it refers to the fact that individuals naturally and generally care more for themselves than for other human beings, although there is a natural concern for other people close to them, such as family and friends. The second subjective aspect—limited generosity—is related to the first and it is the tendency of men to be more generous to the people closest to them than to strangers.

On the other hand, Hume introduces what are the main problems that people would have to face in a 'natural state' or 'pre-social' community. Broadly speaking, individuals would have to face three fundamental limitations: (a) the limitation of their own strength, (b) the impossibility of attaining perfection in any particular art and (c) the lack of security. In Hume's view, these three difficulties could be solved by society. Society thus appears as the means to providing a remedy for each of these drawbacks through (a) the conjunction of forces, which permits the increase of strength; (b) the division of labour which permits the increase of individual capacities; and (c) mutual succour, which remedies the lack of security.

We believe that Hume's vision of human nature is accurate and useful with regard to real life. Human beings seem to be confronted with the scarcity of nature's provision of goods to satisfy all their needs and desires. At the same time, they generally show more concern for themselves, and the people close to them than for complete strangers.

At the same time, Hume does not show us a picture in which selfish humans, in their natural state, are completely isolated and must create artificial bonds with each other, but, on the contrary, he shows us a picture in which humans have feelings towards each other, such as sympathy, and can form small groups such as families and communities.

As we will see in the next title, the element of sympathy and other natural virtues, then, implies offering a 'mixed' and—we understand—more complete view of human nature—neither completely pessimistic nor completely optimistic, neither totally selfish nor totally generous. Individuals are not just self-interested subjects strenuously seeking to overcome the problem of resource scarcity but are subjects who, on grounds of sympathy and interpersonal relationships, constitute communities that enable them to overcome the initial difficulties of the state of nature.

The limitation that might be observed in Hume's view is whether it is possible to establish common rules with other people who are not part of each individual's close circle. The question is: how can a cooperative order emerge between individuals who do not share their immediate contexts and who may even be strangers to each other? This problem—that of the 'Great Society'—was posed and, we believe, solved by Adam Smith.

The theoretical proposal of this book combines this conception of human nature proposed by Hume with other aspects or features of human nature—such as limited rationality or limited knowledge—proposed later by other authors and schools in line with this tradition. We will consider these other aspects in following chapters.

1.3.2 Hume and His Naturalistic View of Morals

Hume conceives morality not as a creation of reason but as a result or effect of our natural feelings and inclinations. When an individual is judged in moral terms as 'vicious' or 'virtuous', his actions are not analysed in themselves but as the sign or manifestation of his individual character. The dispositions of his character to act out of a natural vice or virtue produce pleasure or displeasure in other individuals, and these feelings are the source of moral distinctions. Hume says, "If any action be either virtuous or vicious, ′tis only as a sign of some quality or character. It must depend upon durable principles of the mind, which extend over the whole conduct, and enter into the personal character" (Hume, 2000, p. 367).

In Hume's view, all men share a common nature which implies a certain propensity to the same feelings and affections, though in varying degrees. **Sympathy** is a feeling that connects the experience of others with one's own and enables one to feel certain sensations in relation to the passions of another.

The process of sympathy works with different types of perceptions. The spectator has, first, an impression of sensation. In the case of the moral sphere, the spectator first observes the pleasure that the actor feels when he acts in a virtuous way or other similar feelings (the spectator does not always feel the exact same sensation as the actor does). Then, the spectator has an idea of the virtuous disposition of the character that motivated such pleasure. Finally, the spectator will have an 'impression of reflection' and will also feel pleasure. The feeling of pleasure that this action produces, and the moral judgement regarding the virtues that could have motivated it, cannot be distinguished, both are part of the same 'sense of virtue' experienced by the observer when he contemplates a character (Hume, 2000, Book 3, Part 1, Sect. 2).

Since all individuals share these feelings, they may also share moral judgements about certain actions and, consequently, about certain characters. Hume also proposes the introduction regarding the point of view of the 'judicious spectator' from which we could reach a general and 'shareable' judgement.

However, Hume observes that human action can be motivated by different kinds of virtues and vices and thus distinguishes between natural and artificial virtues. This distinction is based on certain characteristics. We can, thus, distinguish natural and artificial virtues in relation to the following properties (Hume, 2000, p. 307):

(a) In the case of **natural virtues**, good arises from each individual act motivated by these virtues. We can take pleasure in seeing every virtuous act originating from a natural virtue. In the case of **artificial virtues,** the good does not arise in each individual act, but through the established system of rules. Moreover, individual acts may even have bad results and even appear vicious; their virtue derives from the virtue of the whole social scheme.
(b) The good that results from natural virtues is the object of a natural passion or instinct, not the result of social convention. This means that a virtuous character possesses this natural disposition to behave in good and virtuous ways. On the other hand, artificial virtues are

the product of convention, which do not respond directly to natural inclinations. In this sense, the character that possesses the disposition to respect the rules imposed by artificial virtue, out of a sense of duty, will be judged as virtuous.

(c) Acts motivated by natural virtues have a tendency towards the common good, e.g. charity and clemency. Hume draws attention to the fact that also artificial virtues, such as justice, may have this tendency to the common good, but the benefit is produced by the whole system and not by each virtue-motivated act. Moreover, the benefit is social and not individual in this case.

(d) '**Moral taste**' with respect to natural virtues is universal. All men will regard acts motivated by these virtues as 'virtuous', regardless of their historical or social context. Since these virtues are appreciated by our senses and not by our reason, all people 'feel' them in a similar way, since we all share the same nature. Finally, in the case of actions motivated by artificial virtues, we approve of the action because of other reasons, such as a sense of duty or the long-term beneficial consequences that might have motivated this action.

1.3.3 The Origin of Justice

Hume considers that all human acts are provoked by a motive other than a sense of duty (Hume, 2000, p. 307). However, Hume observes that certain acts are considered virtuous despite not being motivated by a natural virtue and that this could be the case with regard to respecting the rules of Justice.

Thus, Hume raises the question of what the origin of justice could be, since the sense of duty is proper to educated and civilised men, but not to men in a 'natural condition' or state of nature. *"Wherein consists this honesty and justice, which you find in restoring a loan, and abstaining from the property of others?"* (Hume, 2000, p. 308). In considering what might be the reason for such respect for the rules of justice in the state of nature, Hume systematically rejects several possible answers:

(a) Virtue cannot derive from an external action since the **virtuous motive** is what makes an action virtuous and not the other way round.
(b) Nor can it be the product of our concern for our **private interests or reputation**, since this concern does not always lead men to honest actions.
(c) On the other hand, the reason for such honest actions cannot be concern for **the public interest.** On the one hand, because the relationship between justice and the public good is not natural, but the product of convention. Secondly, because the duty or obligation of a just act does not depend on whether the act is public or private (or even secret). Finally, because ordinary men in their daily lives are not so concerned with the public interest. In conclusion, Hume considers that there is no such thing as a general 'love of humanity' that motivates respect for the rules of justice. Sympathy allows us to feel concern for other people, but especially for those who are close to us, but this does not represent a 'universal affection for humanity'.
(d) Respect for the rules of justice cannot be derived from **private benevolence or consideration** for the interests of the other party. Men do not, as a rule, have as a motivation for their actions a special regard for the interests of the other party, who might even be their enemy.

In this way, Hume rules out every possible natural virtue that could act as a motivation for respecting the rules of justice and finally comes to the conclusion that the rules of justice are the product of human artifice.

We have already referred to Humean's view of human nature, its objective aspect—scarcity—and its subjective aspects—self-interest and limited generosity—and to the difficulties that individuals must face in the state of nature: limitation of strength, impossibility of attaining perfection in any art and lack of security. We also show how, through sympathy and the ability to put oneself in the place of others, individuals begin to relate 'sentimentally' (today we would say emotionally) and to form judgements of approval and disapproval of the acts of others and of their own, through the gaze of the other. Finally, we saw how, for Hume, communities and common moral judgements arise.

Thus, the problem Hume faces is the possibility of establishing certain common rules among individuals who do not belong to the closest or most intimate circles of each individual (family, neighbourhood, etc.). That is to say, given this description of human nature, how is it possible that justice could arise as a social convention?

Therefore, Hume proposes a solution based on a **classification of the goods** that a person can enjoy, dividing them into three types (Hume, 2000, p. 313):

(a) The internal satisfaction of our mind.
(b) The external advantages of our body.
(c) The enjoyment of the possessions we have acquired by our industry and good fortune.

Hume considers that, while the possession or enjoyment of the first two kinds of goods are generally not in danger, the possession of the third kind of good—those material goods which we have obtained by our industry or fortune—is the one which might be most exposed to the violence of others and could be taken by others without alteration or loss. It also reaffirms the idea that nature does not provide men with enough of these goods to satisfy every want and need.

In this sense, Hume thinks that "As the improvement, therefore, of these goods is the chief advantage of society, so that the *instability* of their possession, along with their *scarcity*, is the chief impediment" (Hume, 2000, p. 313, parr 7). And so, it is the scarcity and insecurity of the possession of these goods which, for Hume, are the foundation not only of markets but also of what he calls the **three fundamental laws of justice: (a) the stability of possession, (b) its transference by consent and (c) the performance of promises.**

One might object that this view is mistaken, since the goods of mind and body can also be a source of conflict between men. We consider, however, that the main feature of Hume's analysis of justice relates to the objective and material aspect of human nature, namely the issue that individuals have infinite wants and needs, and that external possessions—acquired through industry or good fortune—are the means of satisfying these needs. These material goods are scarce, a characteristic not shared by the other goods 'of mind and body'.

On the other hand, we should bear in mind that when Hume refers to these goods of mind and body, he is not referring to the concrete body or mind, but to immaterial or abstract goods, such as the 'internal satisfactions of our mind' and the 'external advantages of our body', so the problem of 'scarcity' may not apply to these abstract goods. Hume may also be thinking of other ways of resolving the conflicts raised by the possession of goods of the soul or body, perhaps by way of natural virtues or via other artificial virtues.

Again, we believe that Hume tries to explain the origin of justice as a way of offering a solution to the problem of the relationship with other human beings, given a certain description of human nature. If, as he himself says, one of these characteristics were to change (for example, if the scarcity of goods did not apply in this case), it is possible that the rules of justice would no longer be needed as a means of resolving conflict.

Finally, we consider that, although conflicts over the possession of external goods might seem sophisticated, they are in fact the most basic ones. If individuals cannot guarantee each other a minimum of respect for each other's possessions and the enjoyment of some stability in those possessions, it would be much more difficult to reach agreement on other, more complex issues. Let's imagine the following extreme example: A guarantees B that he will fully respect B's freedom of conscience, religion, expression, opinion, etc., and all his physical rights, but—A being bigger than B—he takes without restrictions (since there is no principle or rule that establishes this) all the goods that B acquires by work or luck at the moment B acquires them, so that B dies of starvation. At this point, Spector (Spector, 2014, p. 56) agrees that the stability of possession is here posited as a *sine qua non condition* for the very existence of society.

The idea of justice, then, appears as a solution that can be provided by artifice and convention. This convention would establish the stability of the possession of external goods by all members of society and allow the peaceful enjoyment of what each individual has acquired by fortune or industry. In Hume's terms, this convention is not a promise, but a mutual and general 'sense of common interest' (Hume, 2000, p. 315) mutually expressed by the members of society. This agreement also consists of certain expectations that people have of each other's behaviour.

This view of the convention that gives rise to justice is related more to an evolutionary explanation of the phenomenon than to a contractarian view. In Hume's view, "Nor is the rule concerning the stability of possession the less deriv'd from human conventions, that it arises gradually, and acquires force by a slow progression, and by our repeated experience of the inconveniences of transgressing it. On the contrary, this experience assures us still more, that the sense of interest has become common to all our fellows, and gives us a confidence of the future regularity of their conduct: And 'tis only on the expectation of this, that our moderation and abstinence are founded" (Hume, 2000, p. 315).

"After this convention, concerning abstinence from the possessions of other, is enter'd into, and every one has acquir'd a stability in his possessions, there immediately arise the ideas of justice and injustice; as also those of property, right, and obligation. The latter are altogether unintelligible without the first understanding the former" (Hume, 2000, p. 315). Thus, the ideas of property, of right and of obligation are intrinsically connected with the idea of justice, since they are the product of the rules of justice. In Hume's view, the relationship between a person and his property is based on these rules of justice. Moreover, the establishment of these rules, which prescribe the distinction of property and the stability of ownership, are fundamental to the establishment of society.

In this way, the natural tendency to self-interest is offset by consideration for the preservation of society. "Thus self-interest is the original motive to the establishment of justice: But a sympathy with public interest is the source of the moral approbation, which attends that virtue" (Hume, 2000, pp. 320–321). In this way, we can also relate the ideas of justice and injustice to those of virtue and vice, justice and virtue producing pleasure and injustice and vice producing uneasiness or discomfort.

We agree here with Spector that this proposal of Hume's is not intended to offer a justification of justice as a creation but to offer an explanation of the emergence and consolidation of justice (Spector, 2014, p. 59).

Finally, we believe that Hume's explanation of the genesis of the rules of justice is very valuable and has inspired many contemporary views of human institutions, such as those of F. A. Hayek in "Law, Legislation and Liberty" or Douglass North in "Institutions, Institutional Change and Economic Performance", to which we will refer afterwards. The spontaneous, not deliberate, view of the origin of justice allows us to revisit the idea of convention. In Hume's terms, it does not refer to a covenant or contract that we can deliberately create or modify or that can be artificially produced by the desire of a group (for example, politicians). Justice is a spontaneous creation of individuals, responding to certain human needs and sustained by certain cultivated dispositions. In this sense, we agree with his view of the origin of justice and with the idea that it can be artificial, in the Humean sense, i.e. that it does not arise naturally from the nature of the individual alone but from the relations between men in society, but that it does not consist in a deliberate or arbitrary creation by an individual or a group.

On the other hand, this view of the emergence of universal principles of justice and their origins has, in our opinion, some limitations: (a) it does not allow us to explain clearly how these principles emerge and stabilise in larger and more complex societies, where the anonymity among members of the society might weigh, a task that Adam Smith somehow proposes; (b) this view does not provide us with a detailed or rigorous explanation of the process of emergence, stabilisation and change of each rule or institution. Today, on the other hand, there are several explanatory models that address this task. Evolutionary game theory, among others, seems to offer greater precision for this type of explanation. We do not agree with Spector (Spector, 2014, p. 59) that game theory does not allow us to model these Humean ideas. At least in its evolutionary version, this theory seems to show us how the processes of emergence of normative systems take place.

1.4 The Notion of Justice for Adam Smith

We will now analyse Adam Smith's conception of Justice. As is well known, Smith and Hume were contemporaries and, although they had important differences, they shared a naturalistic view of moral and political phenomena. As we did with Hume, we propose a brief introduction to Adam Smith's moral philosophy, which will later lead to the emergence of the notion of justice. Then, we will specifically analyse how Adam Smith studied the different stages of the evolution of justice as a juridical-political institution.

1.4.1 Adam Smith's Moral Philosophy

In the Theory of Moral Sentiments (Smith, 1982), Adam Smith analyses the origin of moral judgements both with respect to our own actions and with respect to the actions of others. Understanding his conception of moral philosophy, sympathy, virtues and moral rules will help us to grasp his vision of justice.

The role that sympathy plays in Smith's analysis of morality is well known. Sympathy enables individuals to 'put themselves in the shoes' of another person, allowing them to judge that person's actions and even their own. As in Hume's work, Smith's also conceptualises the individual as a complex subject, with various edges, including self-interest or selfish action, but also a very strong bond of sympathy with others, which allows the individual to speculate about the morality of their own and others' actions. Since this is a universal characteristic of individuals, these judgements are mutual and interspersed, creating a network of uses and rules that allow the emergence of a common morality.

In this sense, we are encouraged to propose a reading of the "Theory of Moral Sentiments" in which the analysis seems to move slowly by steps from a totally subjective perspective of sympathy and moral judgements to an almost entirely objective one. This 'shift' occurs first from the subjective gaze to a more intersubjective perspective, sustained by feelings such as gratitude and resentment. Cross-subjective judgements are then introduced, creating a strong network of intersubjective judgements that give rise to general principles, allowing the emergence of the view of the 'impartial spectator'. Thus, a more 'objective' or realistic view of values and moral judgements is introduced, first through the figure of the impartial spectator—which we will analyse below—and then even through the figure of a deity at the end of the book. We will briefly analyse each analytical step:

I. In the first part of the Theory of Moral Sentiments (Smith, 1982, p. 16), Smith states that to 'approve or disapprove' of another's passions is to observe whether we 'sympathise' with them. At this point, he seems to be establishing a wholly subjective criterion for understanding how individuals morally value or appreciate the passions and reactions of others. In this sense, using more modern terminology, we could say that, for Smith, we recognise ourselves in the actions, perceptions or reactions of others, providing a psychological basis for moral judgement.

   A little later (Smith, 1982, pp. 71–73), he introduces the idea that approving an action or passion implies 'adopting' the opinion, feeling or passion of another person. In this case, it is no longer a direct, sentimental or intuitive relation with the other person's situation, but rather a reflection on whether we share the motives that inspire their actions. To achieve this, he considers how an ordinary person judges actions and passions in their daily life.

   We consider that, in these cases, the approval or disapproval of an action or feeling can be conveyed through an opinion or attitude about an event that has been held implicitly for a considerable time (which we may not have been aware of before) and which, in a specific situation, is made explicit and applied to the concrete case.

II. The second step is the adoption of a criterion that we consider to be intersubjective. Smith, thus, introduces the treatment of gratitude and resentment as the appropriate feelings that inspire reward or punishment (Smith, 1982, p. 69). Consequently, our moral evaluation is no longer based solely on our sympathy for the actor, but rather on more elaborate feelings regarding how that action would appear from a certain distance, how things ought to be, and so on.

It thus incorporates a third actor who is neither the agent nor the spectator who is making the moral judgement, but a third party, an impartial spectator, an 'indifferent third party' and his or her view of the action, feeling or passion to be evaluated.

Much has been discussed about the figure of the 'impartial spectator' in Adam Smith's moral philosophy. Consider, for example, Amartya Sen's view in his "The Idea of Justice" (Sen, 2009). Here Sen identifies this notion, introduced by Smith in his Theory of Moral Sentiments (Smith, 1982, p. 70), with a position equidistant from both the contractarian conception—of the Kantian tradition, represented by Rawls—and the utilitarian conception that would demand the maximisation of the 'sum total' of utilities.

In this sense, Sen acknowledges the capacity of this 'impartial spectator' figure to provide a more comprehensive perspective on the issue of justice than that suggested by contractarianism (at least in its Rawlsian form).

Among other 'advantages', the impartial spectator's view of justice would enable us—with respect to justice—to work with comparative assessments rather than transcendent solutions and to allow for incompleteness in social evaluation, while providing a guide to solving problems of manifest injustice or to take into account voices beyond the members of the contracting group, whether to take note of their interests or to avoid being trapped in a localist parochialism.

Later, referring again to the figure of the 'impartial spectator', and comparing it to contractarianism, he considers that this view allows for a 'more open impartiality' that seeks to broaden our understanding and scope of ethical enquiry (Sen, 2009, pp. 124–125). Sen says: "Smith invoked the reflective device of the impartial spectator to go beyond reasoning that may—perhaps imperceptibly—be constrained by local conventions of thought, and to examine deliberately, as a procedure, what the accepted conventions would look like from the perspective of a 'spectator' at a distance" (Sen, 2009, p. 125). Sen considers that Smith's justification of such a procedure of open impartiality is exposed in this paragraph: *"We can never survey our own sentiments and motives, we can never form any judgment concerning them; unless we remove ourselves, as it were, from our own natural station, and endeavour to view them as at a certain distance from us. But we can do this in no other way than by endeavouring to view them with the eyes of other people, or as other people are likely to view them*" (Smith cited by Sen, 2009, p. 125).

In Sen's opinion, this conception of the impartial spectator even allows—unlike other exercises of objectification such as the 'veil of ignorance'—plurality of lines of reasoning that can pass the test of impartiality and, therefore, does not set out to seek unanimity or a single possible social contract.

III. Finally, Adam Smith raises the issue of injustice in judgement arising from social intersubjectivity or from the perspective of the 'impartial spectator'. What could happen when a wise man is judged unjustly, when he receives the applause or the blame that he considers he does not deserve?

It is here that Smith introduces the notion of the 'principles established by nature' (Smith, 1982, pp. 128–130 footnote), that should govern our judgements concerning the conduct of those with whom we live. Smith refers here to a 'superior tribunal' which he locates 'within our own breast', and which represents the judgement of an abstract man—representative of humanity—who will give us insight into what is deserving of praise or blame. It also refers to this inner court as a substitute for divinity. The weak or vain man, who is merely satisfied with the approval of his fellows, will never appeal to this higher court, for he is a 'slave of the world'. But, in the case of the wise man, this 'supreme arbiter' is the omniscient judge of the world, this 'demigod' (Smith, 1982, p. 131) within our own breast will appear.

1.4.2 The Evolution of Justice for Adam Smith

In addition to his theory of how moral sentiments and judgements arise and stabilise, Adam Smith also proposes an evolutionary explanation of the institution of justice in his "Wealth of Nations" (Smith, 1981, pp. 689–723). In Book V of this book, "Of the Revenue of the Sovereign or Commonwealth", which deals specifically with the revenue of the

Sovereign, Smith offers an initial chapter on Defence expenditure and a second chapter devoted to the expenditure on Justice that the sovereign must face.

When first addressing Defence expenditure (Smith, 1981, pp. 689–708), Smith proposes an evolutionary reading of the development of the militias or defensive forces of the communities. He, thus, **distinguishes several 'stages':**

(1) **Hunter nations**—the roughest and lowest stage of societies—where all are hunters and warriors at the same time, either to defend their society or to avenge some harm done to it. At this stage of evolution, hunters/warriors are self-supporting both when they are 'at home' and when they are warring, there being no other source of support or higher state/government structure. He gives as an example of such communities the native tribes of North America.

(2) **The nations of shepherds**: a 'more advanced' stage of societies in which individuals—often nomads—all become warriors in the face of external attack. Not only men participate in this scheme, but also elders, women and children who cannot be left alone in the territory while the men advance. In this case, he exemplifies this type of community with the Tartars and Arabs.

(3) He then distinguishes a **more advanced stage of society, mainly farmers, whom he calls 'husbandmen'**, who have little trade with foreign countries and little manufacturing. These individuals, who work in agriculture and spend most of their time outdoors, are equally prepared to go to war, quickly becoming warriors in the face of necessity. In this case, the elders, women and children are left 'behind', guarding the land or property and bearing the costs of maintaining the warriors.At an even more advanced stage of society, two factors emerge that alter the situation regarding the costs of warriors or militias: (a) the cost of manufacturing and (b) improvement in the art of war.

(4) Unlike farmers, manufactures are not produced 'on their own' by nature but depend directly on the labour of each individual. Here Smith propounds another stage where **craftsmen or manufacturers** must leave their activities to go to war. In this case, if the carpenter

stops working, no one will do the work for him. Therefore, when he goes to the battlefield, in defence of 'the public' and he has no other income to support himself, he must necessarily be supported by the public while he is employed in this task of 'warfare'.

(5) Ultimately, as 'the art of war' became increasingly sophisticated and those engaged in it required specialised skills and devoted a large part of the year to those activities, then the public was obligated to support those who served, even if only for the duration of their enlistment. Likewise, the number of men engaged in war as a proportion of the total number of individuals needs to be much smaller in a civilised society than in a 'rough' society. He thus introduces **a final stage where 'warriors or soldiers' become professionalised and receive an income for their specialised work.**

Smith, then, uses the same type of argument when discussing the "Expenditure on Justice" in the next chapter (Smith, 1981, pp. 708–723). He asserts that the second duty of the sovereign is to protect every member of society from the injustice or oppression of any other member or, in other words, "the duty of establishing an exact administration of justice". This, in his view, "*requires, too, very different degrees of expence in the different periods of society*" (Smith, 1981, pp. 708–709). (a) So, he enumerates, in this sense, different 'evolutionary stages'.

(1) In the **hunting nations**, where there was only some property and if so, the property scarcely exceeded the value of two- or three-days' labour, there was no established magistrate or regular administration of justice. In this sense, Smith considers that in the absence of greater property and although subject to passions such as envy, malice or resentment, men could live in society with a tolerable degree of security without the need for a civil magistrate to protect them. But then he considers that the rich man's avarice and the poor man's aversion to labour, and his preference for ease and present enjoyment, are the passions which tend to invade property. And here is Smith's understanding that situations of inequity can arise such that the rich man's wealth can excite the indignation of the poor man and that

his passions such as envy or desire lead him to invade those possessions. So, it is only under the protection of a civil magistrate that the owner of that valuable property, which may have been acquired by the labour of many years or of many generations, will be able to sleep a single night in safety.

"The acquisition of valuable and extensive property, therefore, necessarily requires the establishment of civil government. Where there is no property, or at least none that exceeds the value of 2 or 3 days labour, civil government is not so necessary" (Smith, 1981, p. 710). At this point, the idea that property of material goods and the conflicts that may arise from them are the reason for the necessity of the emergence of rules of justice (or of a magistrate to dispense justice in this case) coincides, to a large extent, with David Hume's approach. For the latter, the main reasons for the emergence of universal principles of justice and the establishment of civil magistrates can be attributed to the same fundamental factors.

(2) In this sense, Smith understands **the age of the shepherds** as a second 'period of society' in which inequality of fortune takes place and this introduces among men a degree of authority and subordination which could not exist before. This entails, in his view, a necessity for some level of civil government indispensable to its preservation, and he adds that "and this seems to have been done naturally, and even independently of the consideration of such a necessity" (Smith, 1981, p. 715, the highlighting is ours).

Furthermore, this description of the origin of institutions under scrutiny here is remarkably similar to the one posited by Adam Ferguson (which we will see later in this chapter), emphasising that the emergence of institutions is not a deliberate act of creation but may have occurred almost by chance to resolve a particular situation. These institutions then survive by adapting themselves to other situations or contexts not originally foreseen by those who originally proposed the solution.

In this sense, civil government, instituted for the security of property, represents a defence of those who have some property against those who have none. According to Smith's perspective, judicial authority does not constitute a cost to the sovereign but is sustained by an income (which could be considered taxation in contemporary terms) since individuals who seek for justice through this authority will always be willing to pay for this service.

(3) He then proceeds to offer a long disquisition **on the evolution of the judiciary**—first as 'envoys' of the king or sovereign, and then as an independent power—always referring to the ways in which it was financed. He concludes this section by stating that when the judiciary is linked to the executive, it is scarcely possible that justice is not often sacrificed to what is commonly known as politics.

Smith considers that persons who are entrusted with the great interests of the state may, even without any degree of corruption, sometimes imagine it necessary to sacrifice the rights of private men to those interests of the state. However, it is crucial to recognise that the fundamental right to feel secure in the enjoyment of all one's rights is contingent upon the impartial administration of justice. Consequently, it is not only necessary for the judiciary to be separate from the executive branch, but it must also be as independent from that branch as possible. In this sense, he advances the argument that judges should not be subject to removal from office at the discretion of the executive branch and that the regular payment of their salaries should not be contingent upon the goodwill or sound financial management of that branch.

1.5 Some Differences Between Hume's and Smith's Views

In this work, we explore the seminal contributions of David Hume and Adam Smith, renowned exponents of the evolutionary view on rules and institutions, in the light of the 'resurgence' of evolutionary ideas in recent decades. And, although we do not engage here in a detailed exegesis of both works, we can observe, despite some similarities between the two works, interesting differences between these two thinkers.

We highlight, together with Fleischacker (Fleischacker, 2015), some divergent perspectives between their moral and political conceptions, which significantly influence their views on justice. Among the main differences, the following stands out:

1. The different views on sympathy of these authors: While Hume's view is more 'contagious' and is related to the ability to 'feel what the other feels' effectively, Smith's view is more 'projective'. For the latter, individuals do not have the capacity to feel exactly the same as our fellow human beings, but our capacity to imagine ourselves in the other's place will always lack the intensity that the protagonist experiences when living through that circumstance.

   Fleischacker stresses that for Smith, we individuals make constant efforts to adjust our feelings, as spectators, to those of the individuals 'primarily concerned' in a specific circumstance. In other words, we try to harmonise our feelings with those of 'the main protagonists' in the situation. He even remarks that, for Smith, sharing the feelings of others as much as possible is one of our greatest drives or 'motivators' in life.
2. Another important difference, connected to the aforementioned one, is in the conception of moral motivation held by each of the authors, which also connects to their divergent conceptions of justice. While for Hume moral motivation is predominantly founded on the virtues—which he classifies into natural and artificial, as previously discussed—for Smith moral motivation is sustained by two 'normative guides': rules and virtues. According to Fleischacker (Fleischacker, 2015), Smith believed that moral rules constitute the basis of our reactions to specific instances (we say to ourselves: 'I will never do that!') and prohibit certain types of particularly outrageous behaviour, such as killing, raping or stealing, and provide a framework of shared societal expectations. They also allow people who are not entirely virtuous to behave with a minimum of decorum and decency and help us all to break through the veil of self-deception that causes us to misrepresent our situation to ourselves.

   But, for Smith, virtue requires more than respecting or following moral rules. Our emotional dispositions need to be reconfigured, for which we not only 'affect' the feelings of the impartial spectator, but we also 'adopt' those feelings: we identify with them, we 'become' the impartial spectator as far as that is possible. In this framework, we deal without rules; instead we cultivate dispositions of appropriate gratitude, kindness, courage, patience and endurance.

3. If we take this question of individual motivation to the level of the foundation of ethics, the difference remains. Faced with the question of whether ethics is virtue based or rule based, Hume would seem to hold more to the former view. Hume considers that we can act morally simply motivated by our virtues without the need for further rational reflection on the action or its motivations. Whereas Smith's view would seem to be closer to Kant's or the utilitarians' view of rules. In reality, Smith's vision is mixed and refers, as we have already analysed, to rules and virtue.

   Smith even refers, in many passages of the Theory of Moral Sentiments, to learning processes in relation to which feelings we should have in certain situations. In this work, he outlines the various ways in which we learn to evaluate our feelings and how this also enables us to express them properly and even to change them.

4. This prompts the assertion of a distinction between Hume and Smith with regard to a more utilitarian or consequentialist perspective on morality and justice, as held by Hume. In contrast, Smith incorporates a viewpoint in which what is morally 'appropriate' is not necessarily commensurate with the happiness it may ultimately engender. In contrast to Hume, Smith conceptualises happiness as the possession of morally appropriate dispositions and does not evaluate it solely by its effects. Nevertheless, his analysis of the question seems rather 'mixed'.

   On the one hand, he would seem to anticipate Kant in the need to subsume ourselves, in some cases, to general rules—since relying on feelings alone might feed our 'self-deception'. On the other hand, he insists in many passages that we judge actions by their effects and by their intentions. Thus the 'merit' of actions depends on their consequences, even if their 'property' is independent of their consequences. Thus, he conceives of two different elements of moral judgement: consequences and intentions.

5. If we relate these reflections to the more libertarian readings of Adam Smith, we will then see that a significant element of the evolutionary

view of rules and institutions appears: the unintended consequences of individual actions. It would seem here that these consequences would appear to be even more important than the agent's intended consequences (intention or proper motivation).

Fleischacker (Fleischacker, 2015) sees Smith's version of sentimentalism as having some advantages over that of his contemporaries. For one thing, his approach to moral judgement is closer to what we normally do in our everyday lives (it would be, in our words, a better description). Also, according to this author, Smith seems to make more sense of the complexity and richness of both virtue and the judgement of virtue and is equidistant from Hutcheson's view—which would reduce virtue to benevolence—and from Hume's—which places great emphasis on utility.

Finally, he stresses Smith's 'social conception of the self' whereby the process of socialisation becomes important in the analysis. He thus reconciles self-interest and benevolence; the social view of the self with the respect for each individual and his capacity to choose. Even in the view of the impartial spectator, Fleischacker sees a product and expression of the social, which is then internalised and the source of the moral evaluation that enables the individual to distance himself, to stand alone and criticise his society.

1.6 The Notion of Institutions for Adam Ferguson

In this section, we will provide a conceptual introduction to the notion of institution proposed by Adam Ferguson in his work "An Essay on the History of Civil Society" (Ferguson, 1767). A detailed analysis of his entire work is beyond the scope of this study; however, the notion of institution that he proposes will be the primary focus. It is imperative to incorporate this notion into the history of our evolutionary view, as it is pivotal to comprehending authors contemporary to Ferguson, as well as subsequent authors such as F. A. Hayek and even several contemporary authors who appear to adopt this notion.

In particular, in Section Two of the aforementioned work, entitled "The History of political Establishments" (Ferguson, 1767, pp. 205–206), Ferguson refers—like Hume or Smith—to what could be the genesis of political institutions as we know them today. He noted that the origins of institutions are contingent upon the prevailing needs and contextual factors that characterise the moment of their emergence. They then follow their course, often unnoticed by the very individuals who make use of the institution, and fulfil other objectives or functions, not necessarily identical to those they fulfilled at the time of their birth. In this manner, he introduces the notion, as do Mandeville, Hume and Smith, that social, moral, political and legal institutions can be the unintended outcome of the behaviour of individuals.

Thus, he says: "Mankind, in following the present sense of their minds, in striving to remove inconveniencies, or to gain apparent and contiguous advantages, arrive at ends which even their imagination could not anticipate; and pass on, like other animals, in the tract of their nature, without perceiving its end. He who first said, "I will appropriate this field; I will leave it to my heirs;" did not perceive, that he was laying the foundation of civil laws and political establishments. He who first ranged himself under a leader, did not perceive, that he was setting the example of a permanent subordination, under the pretence of which, the rapacious were to seize his possessions, and the arrogant to lay claim to his service" (Ferguson, 1767, p. 210).

In this manner, he illustrates how the emergence of political and legal institutions is gradual, arising from the interaction of individuals who each pursue their own distinct plan. We understand that, while concurring with the positions of Hume and Smith, Ferguson elucidates the emergence of such institutions as unintended consequences of individual interactions, synthesising this idea in a concise manner.

It is not that individuals act blindly or just following instincts or exogenous forces; each person has a life plan and diverse projects with clear objectives. What they cannot master, however, are the medium- and long-term consequences (even some short-term ones) that arise from the intersection between the results of their plans and projects and those of others. This is where certain social regularities allow for the emergence of certain rules or institutions, which are not the creation of any legislator or 'planner', as Ferguson puts it.

"Men, in general, are sufficiently disposed to occupy themselves in forming projects and schemes: But he who would scheme and project for others, will find an opponent in every person who is disposed to scheme for himself. Like the winds that come we know not whence, and blow whithersoever they list, the forms of society are derived from an obscure and distant origin; they arise, long before the date of philosophy, from the instincts, not from the speculations of men. The crowd of mankind, are directed in their establishments and measures, by the circumstances in which they are placed; and seldom are turned from their way, to follow the plan of any single projector" (Ferguson, 1767, p. 210).

And here Ferguson introduces the words that would later become the 'battle cry' of authors such as Hayek and others who would incorporate the evolutionary view of rules and institutions. A paragraph whose words could be taken as the ultimate explanation of the origin of institutions for this vision. Ferguson says:

"Every step and every movement of the multitude, even in what are termed enlightened ages, are made with equal blindness to the future; and nations stumble upon establishments, which are indeed the result of human action, but not the execution of any human design"*. If Cromwell said, "That a man never mounts higher, than when he knows not whither he is going; it may with more reason be affirmed of communities, that they admit of the greatest revolutions where no change is intended, and that the most refined politicians do not always know whither they are leading the state by their projects" *(he includes here a footnote that says: de Retz Memoirs) (Ferguson, 1767, p. 210, the highlighting is ours).

As will be discussed in Chapter 2, these ideas have had a significant influence on twentieth-century authors, including Friedrich Hayek and Douglass North. Today, these ideas are experiencing a renewed academic interest and are reflected in numerous studies on 'self-generated', 'emergent', 'pluri-centric' and related orders. The conclusion of this first chapter highlights the seminal contributions of the eighteenth-century Scottish School to the evolutionary perspective on social phenomena—particularly rules and institutions—preceding the advancements in evolutionary biology and its subsequent influence on the social sciences in recent decades.

References

Binmore, K. (2005). *Natural justice*. Oxford University Press.

Darwin, C. (2004). *The descent of man, and selection in relation to sex*. Penguin Books. Original work published 1871.

Ferguson, A. (1767). *An essay on the history of civil society*. T. Cadell.

Fleischacker, S. (2015). Adam Smith's Moral and Political Philosophy. In E. N. Zalta (Ed.), *Stanford encyclopedia of philosophy, Philosophy* (Winter 2015 ed.) http://plato.stanford.edu/archives/win2015/entries/smith-moral-political/

Gallo, E. (2008). *Vida, Libertad, Propiedad. Reflexiones sobre el liberalismo clásico y la historia*. Editorial de la Universidad Nacional de Tres de Febrero.

Hayek, F. A. (1983). *Law, legislation and liberty* (Vol. I). University of Chicago Press. Original work published 1973.

Hayek, F. A. (1978). *New studies in philosophy, politics, economics, and the history of ideas*. University of Chicago Press.

Hume, D. (2000). *A treatise of human nature*. Oxford University Press. Original work published 1739–40.

Mandeville, B. (1732). *The fable of the bees or private vices, publick benefits*. Liberty Fund.

Sen, A. (2009). *The idea of justice*. Harvard University Press.

Shaftesbury, A. (2001). *Characteristics of men, manners, opinions, times*. Liberty Fund. Original work published 1737.

Smith, A. (1981). *An inquiry into the nature and causes of the wealth of nations* (Vol. II). Liberty Fund Press. Reproduction of the edition published by Oxford University Press in 1976; Original work published 1723–1790).

Smith, A. (1982). *The theory of moral sentiments*. Liberty Fund Press. Reproduction of the edition published by Oxford University Press in 1976; Original work published 1723–1790.

Spector, H. (2014, May). Hume's theory of justice. *Rationality, Markets and Morals (RMM), 5*, 47–63.

2

Law for Friedrich A. Hayek

2.1 Introduction

In this chapter, a detailed examination of Friedrich A. von Hayek's theoretical approach to law will be presented. This subject has been previously explored in our earlier works, some of which have already been published, and to which we will refer in their relevant parts.[1] Hayek produced an extensive body of work in various areas, such as economics (for which he was awarded the Nobel Prize in 1974), political philosophy and even the philosophy of social sciences. And, in several of his essays and especially in his work "Law, Legislation and Liberty"(Hayek, 1983), he addressed the notion of law from an evolutionary perspective.

[1] These previously published works are: "The Legal Theory of Friedrich A. von Hayek. Its background and epistemological contributions to legal theory" (in Spanish), Revista de Análisis Institucional No 2, Friedrich A. von Hayek Foundation, Argentina, March 2008, pp. 113–187; "Hayek's influence on current evolutionary thinking", paper presented at the Second International Congress "La Escuela Austríaca en el S XXI", Fundación Bases, UNR, 7–9 August 2008 and together with Federico G. M. Sosa Valle, "Selected Texts by Friedrich A. von Hayek", in Revista Estudios Públicos No 120, Santiago de Chile, Spring 2010.

E. M. Santanatoglia, *An Evolutionary Account of Law*, Palgrave Studies in Classical Liberalism, https://doi.org/10.1007/978-3-032-12162-2_2

This evolutionary view of law was informed by the Scottish tradition that was examined in Chapter 1, with Hayek referencing this tradition, its primary exponents and its fundamental notions throughout his work. In the opening chapter of the inaugural volume of the aforementioned "Law, Legislation and Liberty", he articulates the evolutionary perspective, distinguishing it from constructivist interpretations of society.

Hayek's work is situated within the domain of the philosophy of law that took place in the mid-twentieth century, a period during which schools of thought such as legal positivism, iusnaturalism or legal realism (in its American and Scandinavian forms) were subjects of debate. As will be examined in this chapter and Chapter 3, in the face of this panorama, he adopts a position on several of these theories and the most prominent authors, citing some, rejecting others, approaching or differentiating himself from each of them.

Hayek thus presents a 'fourth position', proposing an evolutionary view of law, different from the positivist, iusnaturalist and realist views. From this evolutionary perspective, current legal systems are regarded as the continuous result of an evolutionary cultural process of emergence, stabilisation and change of different types of rules that constitute law as an order. Consequently, law is not only composed by legislation or judicial decisions; rather it is regarded as a complex system formed also by other principles, habits and self-generated rules from the interaction of individuals.

At this stage, we propose that the tradition of Scottish thought, as discussed in the preceding chapter, in conjunction with the contributions of Hayek and other twentieth-century authors who have continued this line of thought—such as Douglass North—can be designated as 'classic evolutionism' (CE). In this work, we will claim possible conceptual connections between this tradition (CE) and the new currents of evolutionary explanation of social phenomena such as 'evolutionary game theory (EGT) and other similar ones. We believe that this intersection of theories could provide greater precision to the explanation of the evolution of legal norms and law as an order.

Just as we did with the main notions proposed by the authors of the Scottish Enlightenment, we will present in the following sections a comprehensive examination of Friedrich Hayek's theoretical proposal for understanding law through an evolutionary lens.

2.2 Law as a Spontaneous Order

In contrast to the Scottish thinkers, Hayek's work is situated within the context of the twentieth century, a period that, from his perspective, was characterised by constructivist perspectives on society. In this sense, Hayek notes that, despite their ideological diversity, the views of the twentieth century conceive social, political, moral, legal and economic orders as arbitrary social constructions. These constructions, it is presumed, are capable of being modified by legislators or citizens who are assumed to be rational. Most of the juridical-political conceptions of the era are regarded as advocating social changes that are brought about—according to them—by the decision, volition or endeavours of benevolent social engineers/reformers.

This constructivist view is grounded, according to Hayek(Hayek, 1983), Ch. 1. pp. 8–34), upon a great confidence in reason. Instrumental and reality-building reason is also indebted to Cartesian dualism, which allows us to think of the rational mind and the extended world as profoundly distinct and separate instances. A viewpoint which is clearly at odds with the evolutionary perspective of social orders proposed by Hayek.

Furthermore, he considers that a large part of the horrors experienced by humanity during the twentieth century is attributable to these attempts to transform reality through 'deliberate constructions', such as political revolutions or untimely legislative changes. For Hayek, these endeavours have not only been unsuccessful—in the sense that reality was not transformed as intended by the constructivist legislator/revolutionary—but also detrimental to the evolution of institutions that could have been gradually incorporated with less bloodshed. The question therefore arises as to what the law consists of if we analyse it from the evolutionary perspective. The following discussion will examine the primary tenets of his programme.

Hayek's initial proposition, which was influenced, as we have seen, by the thought of the Scottish authors—particularly Ferguson on this point—is that law is generally understood as an order (a similar viewpoint exposed in Skoble, 2006, p. 171). However, in this case, the positions are divided between those who regard it as a natural order and those who regard it as an artificial order. For the advocates of law as a natural order— among them various versions of iusnaturalism—law is an order which can be discovered, recognised and respected or disregarded—but cannot be modified or eliminated by individuals. This kind of order is presented to men as 'given'—by God, nature, human nature, etc. Thus, individuals cannot 'transform' these orders, but can only respect them or not: this is the case in several versions of Natural Law theory. On the other hand, we find those views of law as an 'arbitrary order' or one created or designed by men, a prevalent view among positivists. That is, law is regarded as a system of rules established by deliberate human agency, subject to specific formal criteria. In this sense, social orders, and particularly law, are thus seen as a malleable order that can be altered by the mere will of citizens or legislators, without the slightest difficulty (beyond the formal requirements).

Hayek opposes conceiving law within the limits of this dichotomy and proposes to look at law as an order of a third kind, based on Ferguson's definition of order—already discussed—as a product of human action but not of human design. This third type of order, which Hayek will call 'spontaneous orders', falls within the notion of 'complex phenomena', that he has already introduced earlier in his work (Hayek, 1967a). This type of phenomena, for Hayek, cannot be studied using a simple model or formula composed of two or three variables. That is to say, it is a type of phenomenon that cannot be easily reduced to a small number of variables in order to be understood and to formulate predictions about its particular instances. This is why he understands that in this type of phenomena—among which we find, in his opinion, the human mind and social phenomena—what can be observed are certain regularities or patterns of behaviour. Consequently, predictions can only be made based on patterns or predictions of principles, rather than on specific cases.

Hayek, thus, proposes that among complex phenomena we can find what he calls 'spontaneous orders', i.e. those orders already studied by

Ferguson as the product of individual actions and interactions, but not of the design or creation of any individual or group or of individuals in particular. Indeed, he considers the notion of order to be indispensable to the discussion of complex phenomena. Among the 'classical' examples of these spontaneous orders referred to by Hayek are language, the price system, currency, and even moral orders or social rules. In "Law, Legislation and Liberty"he extends this notion to legal orders.

Prior to the analysis of the various aspects of law as a spontaneous order from the Hayekian perspective, it is pertinent to introduce the notion of 'order' that this author propounds at the beginning of Chapter 2 of the first volume of "Law, Legislation and Liberty"(Hayek, 1983, p. 36), in which he incorporates, in our opinion, the main ingredients of his perspective on spontaneous orders, which can subsequently be applied to the analysis of law. He also clarifies that the use of the term 'order'—much discussed at that time—can be understood as 'system', 'structure' or 'pattern'.

So, it is fundamental to ask: what characteristics of a social situation would enable us to conclude that we are dealing with an 'order'? Hayek establishes that by order he shall describe "a state of affairs in which a multiplicity of elements of various kinds are so related to each other that we may learn from our acquaintance with some spatial or temporal part of the whole to form correct expectations concerning the rest, or at least expectations which hence have a good chance of proving correct. It is clear that every society must, in this sense possess an order and that such an order will often exist without having been deliberately created" (Hayek, 1983, p. 36).

It is, thus, clear that the role of expectations is fundamental in identifying the existence of a social order. To be more precise, the formulation of correct or highly probable expectations enables individuals to execute their life plans within the order of which each one can only know a limited part, both spatially and temporally (on partial knowledge held by each individual see Hayek, 1980).

With the notion of order already in place, Hayek then introduces the distinction between those orders that arise without deliberation from the interactions of individuals and those that are deliberately created by individuals. He will refer to the former as 'Cosmos' orders and the latter as 'Taxis' orders.

The notion of 'spontaneous order' becomes relevant here. As we have already said in another work: "(…) throughout his work he provides an account of an order of events to which he successively names market, big society, spontaneous order, abstract order or complex phenomenon. He thus presents those emergent orders that arise from the interactions between individuals and that allow a better coordination between the plans of each one, reaching increasing degrees of complexity in the processing of the information dispersed between them" (Santanatoglia & Sosa Valle, 2010, p. 247).

As Sosa Valle explains: "Spontaneous will mean non-deliberate because it is not susceptible of complete knowledge by any observer, given that every observer is inserted in the social order and there is no way of observing this social order if one does not introduce oneself into it. As a corollary, any social order will have a complexity greater than that of the minds of the individuals within it. Consequently, every social order will be 'uncreated', since it is unsusceptible of being designed by an intelligence that rests on that same order" (Sosa Valle, 2008, p. 190).

Hayek comments that, although the study of these orders appears to be the task of economics, biology has been concerned with studying these spontaneous orders called 'organisms' since its beginning. And in physics, cybernetics had already emerged as a discipline dedicated to the study of systems.

In this regard, Hayek refers to the spontaneous orders in nature (Hayek, 1983, p. 40), referring to them as 'abstract orders' which are, in short, the order resulting from the regularities in the behaviour of the elements. However, these regularities will only determine the general character of the resulting order, but not its particular manifestations. He continues: "The particular manner in which the resulting abstract order will manifest itself will depend, in addition to the rules which govern the actions of the elements, on their initial position and on all the particular circumstances of the immediate environment to which each of them will react in the course of the formation of that order. The order, in other words, will always be an adaptation to a large number of particular facts which will not be known in their totality to anyone" (Hayek, 1983, p. 40).

What follows from applying these notions to the study of law? Hayek proposes to think of law as a spontaneous order, like language, currency or the price system.

2.3 Types of Orders and Types of Rules

Hayek introduces here a distinction between two types of orders: *cosmos* orders and *taxis* orders. We will see here the main characteristics of each of these types of orders and then try to understand how, for Hayek, law as a spontaneous order results from the interaction between these two internal orders (Hayek, 1983, Ch. 2 "Cosmos & Taxis", Hayek, 1978, Ch. 5):

The 'cosmos' order: This order is composed of principles and rules that are, in Ferguson's words, "the result of human action but not of human design" (Ferguson cited by Hayek, 1983, p. 20). That is, certain behavioural patterns develop from the interrelationship between individuals in a society, without them being sought, giving rise to rules of behaviour. These rules evolve from mere regularities to normative or prescriptive rules. In the latter sense, rules of behaviour generate expectations about the specific consequences of certain behaviours.

Hayek focuses his attention on the unintended consequences of human action. In the field of law, the unintended consequences of social regularities are translated into principles and rules of behaviour. These rules and principles that comprise the *cosmos* order have their own particular characteristics:

(a) They **have no determined or determinable origin**. The 'lack of origin' of these rules refers not only to the difficulty of establishing their historical origins, but also to the impossibility of determining the creators or 'legislators' behind them, given that they are the unintended consequences of the actions of a multiplicity of diverse individuals who may not know each other. But, in addition, this absence of origin refers to the inability to establish their distinctive principle in metaphysical or logical terms. In conclusion, these orders are not 'motivated' by a general principle that provides them with foundation, meaning or coherence in general terms. This is evidenced by the assertion that there is no 'legislator' in these cases that refers not only to the fact that they are not orders created voluntarily by a man or group of men, but also to the fact that there is no single rationality or principle that sustains them or gives them ultimate meaning.

(b) They **have no specific purpose.** A *cosmos* order does not serve any particular objective, purpose or goal. The rules that appear as it evolves serve as constraints on human action, but in an abstract form. That is, these rules do not imply orders or prohibitions to satisfy a pre-established objective but can be adopted (consciously or unconsciously) by any individual with his or her own plans, values and goals.

Consequently, in the *cosmos* orders we cannot determine a single principle of origin or purpose. This is why it is so difficult to grasp them conceptually and understand them from the notions that are usually employed to study 'created orders'. Thus, Hayek argues: "The preservation of an enduring system of abstract relationships, or of the order of a cosmos with constantly changing content, did not fit into what men ordinarily understood by a purpose, goal or end of deliberate action" (Hayek, 1983, p. 112). We will return to this point when we analyse the relation of the *cosmos* order to the *taxis* order.

(c) Finally, cosmos orders **are general, i.e. they are not addressed to any particular group.** The norms that emerge in such orders are not intended to issue prescriptions to be observed by a particular group or influence specific populations within society, but rather, these norms apply to all those individuals who interact within that order.

On the other hand, we find **the '*taxis*' order***:* this order comprises rules and principles that consist of prescriptions, mandates or orders that are the product of conscious and deliberate human acts of will. Among them, we could name as the most obvious example legislation emanating from a legislative power, but we can also think of rules between private subjects, such as contracts between parties.

In Hayek's view, these rules possess, in turn, distinct characteristics that differ from those observed in the rules of the *cosmos* order:

(a) These rules have **a determined or determinable origin**, since they are, for the most part, deliberate acts of creation by certain individuals in certain circumstances. In this sense, it is possible to identify not only the historical principle, the 'creator(s)' of these rules and principles, but also the logic that drives them.
(b) They are intended for a **specific purpose**. Although not explicitly stated in the wording of the rules, they are intended to fulfil a purpose envisaged by the rule-maker. The purpose of such a rule may be broad or narrow, but in general there is a more or less identifiable 'reason' behind the rule.
(c) Finally, they **are particular** in the sense that they aim to regulate the actions of a specific group within society. This regulation may be pernicious or beneficial to that group, but it is evident that these rules lack the abstraction and generality characteristic of those belonging to the *cosmos* order.

We could exemplify these two orders—*cosmos* and *taxis*—and their rules. The first case we could bring up is that of the **principle of 'good faith'**, which regulates the whole field of private legal relations of men, and we could also extend it to the field of public law relations—as has been discussed lately-. A contract signed by two or more individuals would become invalid if it were proven that one of the parties did not act in good faith. Now, this is a good example of a rule of the *cosmos* order since this principle is both abstract and general. **Abstract** because it does not determine what the subject matter of the contract should be (buy/sell/let/lease, etc.) nor its terms or time limits. **General** because it applies to any individual who contracts, regardless of the group they belong to or their activity. That is, it limits human action by determining that any contractual interaction must be made in good faith; otherwise its validity could be questioned; but it does not do so by establishing concrete restrictions for the individuals or the objectives sought by them.

Finally, we may also conclude that this type of principle has **not had a determined or determinable origin.** Although today this principle may have been 'positivised' by legislative or judicial means in most of the legal systems today, it was not 'invented' by a 'rational legislator' but rather came about as the result of the evolution of hundreds of years of contracts between private parties.

As an example of a typical **rule of the *taxis* order,** we could speak not only of state legislation or judicial decisions but also of rules deliberately created by private individuals, as we have already said. One example would be the co-ownership rules of a condominium building. These rules are usually created through the conscious decision of a group of individuals living in the same building, with the aim of establishing the rights and obligations of the co-owners, as well as the sanctions for non-compliance.

Thus, these are **concrete rules**, as they have been created to fulfil certain defined objectives, such as establishing the powers of the board of directors and the permitted use of communal areas. Furthermore, these rules are concrete because they only apply to owners of functional units in the building, as well as its managers and employees. They do not apply to any other person outside this relationship.

In this sense, it should be clarified that the rules of the *cosmos* order are not necessarily rules of the public order, as we have already seen with the example of the principle of 'good faith', which is typical of the sphere of private relations. The rules of the *taxis* order are not necessarily of the private order either, nor vice versa. Both orders can contain rules from the public or private spheres.

As the positivisation processes of both spheres do not always occur simultaneously, parallel positivisation processes can be found in different legal systems. For instance, in countries with positive, written constitutional systems (such as Argentina and the United States), many rules of 'spontaneous origin' can still be found in the private sphere (e.g. commercial law). Other systems, such as the British system, maintain many constitutional rules originating in custom and common law, while 'codes' are created to regulate certain private legal relations.

Again, what would result from thinking about law from this classification? Clearly for Hayek law cannot be reduced to a *taxis* order, that is to say, it cannot merely be observed as the deliberate creation of an individual or a group. However, it must be acknowledged that contemporary legal systems, particularly those derived from the European continental tradition, are replete with 'legislated' norms which, as we shall see, can also be interpreted within a *cosmos* order, despite their positive codification, as illustrated by the Constitution. Law, then, can be defined as a 'spontaneous order', comprising the rules arising from these two sub-orders, *cosmos* and *taxis*—which Hayek will call *Nomos* and *Thesis*, respectively, as we shall see in the next section

It is worth making several clarifications that are fundamental to understanding these two orders and the spontaneous order 'law' resulting from them. First, these two sets of principles, norms or rules—*cosmos* and *taxis*—do not exist separately and the resulting order—*law*—is not the mere sum of both but it is the result of a complex web of interactions between them. It is possible to posit that, at some point, the two orders interdefine each other and adapt and readapt in the light of changes in the other order.

Following the above examples, the principle of good faith would have no value if we do not apply it to a concrete case. It is expressed and produces significant legal consequences if there are individuals who want to contract and, for example, establish rules, rights and obligations to carry out a purchase, sale, etc. In other words, the concrete case actualises the meaning of the general principle. On the other hand, it would be impossible to think of a co-ownership regulation that does not presuppose various principles and rules of the *cosmos* order, from the right to private property to the principle of good faith, which governs the relations between co-owners and between owners and administrators, employees, etc.

Hayek places law within the spontaneous orders, as those orders that are comprised of heterogeneous elements, which renders them incapable of identifying a singular feature that distinguishes them from one another. This idea is one of the main elements that place Hayek within a tradition of evolutionary thought which, today, could be considered as part of a broader 'research programme'. This tradition, which Hayek inherited from the Scottish School of the eighteenth century, understands social orders not as the result of the conscious construction of one or more subjects, but rather as the result of the interactions between them. Accordingly, individuals within this tradition—introduced in Chapter 1—characterised in broad terms as imperfect (composed of virtues and vices) and motivated by self-interest, interact with one another, giving rise—without being conscious—to certain regularities in their actions. These regularities can be described as rules of behaviour and institutions.

These regularities do not arise, then, with a specific goal, but they serve as a regulatory framework for these interactions. As propounded by Ferguson and elaborated by Hayek, these rules or principles arise, in many cases, to address a specific situation and subsequently prove useful or efficient in other contexts, not initially anticipated by their original proponents. This enables them to survive within the system over time, demonstrating stability and predictability as solutions or strategies for the interacting individuals.

As a result of this evolution, societies have developed various 'spontaneous orders' such as the market, language, morality and law. In Hayek's terms "We have already seen that in the usual sense of purpose, namely the anticipation of a particular, foreseeable event, the law indeed does not serve any purpose but countless different purposes of different individuals." (…) "In the ordinary sense of purpose law is therefore not a means to any purpose, but merely a condition for the successful pursuit of most purposes. Of all multi-purpose instruments, it is probably the one after language which assist the greatest variety of human purposes" (Hayek, 1983, pp. 112–113).

2.4 Law is Older than Legislation

In Chapter 4 of 'Law, Legislation and Liberty' (Hayek, 1983, p. 72), Hayek proposes the idea that law is older than legislation. This proposal is directly aimed at discussing the 'constructivist' views of social orders, and particularly of legal orders, as previously mentioned. Constructivist perspectives regard social orders as the result of deliberate acts of creation by individuals. In this sense, in the domain of legal-philosophical thought, it is observed that several theories conceive law as the set of rules explicitly elaborated, positivised and enforced by certain political or technical bodies within a community. These theories can be identified as constituting the school of Legal Positivism. This issue will be discussed in the next chapter.

When Hayek affirms that law is older to legislation, he is responding to those views that tend to identify law with a system of positive norms, understood as prescriptions conceived consciously and voluntarily by individuals to limit their own actions and which have been established by certain formal processes. In this sense, it is worth introducing Hayek's distinction between *nomos* and *thesis*. The term *nomos* corresponds to those rules that emerge spontaneously from the interactions of individuals in a bottom-up process, while the term *thesis* refers to legislation established by the sovereign, in a top-down process (Skoble, 2006, p. 171).

Discussing the role of the judge—analysed in the next section—Hayek argues that "(…) it is necessary to free ourselves wholly from the erroneous conception that there can be first a society which then gives itself laws" (Hayek, 1983, p. 95). For Hayek, this 'erroneous conception' is foundational to the constructivist view and has been held by the most diverse authors, from Descartes to Hobbes or from Rousseau to Bentham, up to contemporary legal positivism. And he adds "It is only as a result of individuals observing certain common rules that a group of men can live together in those orderly relations which we call a society" (Hayek, 1983, p. 95). And he goes on "Not all law can therefore be the product of legislation; but power to legislate presupposes the recognition of some common rules; and such rules which underlie the power to legislate may also limit that power" (Hayek, 1983, p. 95).

In Hayek's opinion, the development of articulated and codified rules was contingent on the presence of a shared common ground among members of a given group. These commonalities of opinion, then, precede explicit agreement or positive rules of conduct, even in the absence of consensus on specific ends of actions. He then goes on to comment that we may find groups that have stayed together because of common rules, but without the deliberate creation of an organisation to enforce those rules, although he clarifies that we will not find such examples in cases where a state territory is recognised.

2.5 The Heterogeneous Elements of Law

Hayek, thus, understands that law is not only composed of rules and principles of the *thesis* type (or of *taxis* orders) but also of principles and rules of the *nomos* type (or of *cosmos* orders). Furthermore, from this standpoint, the codified legal rules—*thesis*—could not be conceived without an underlying abstract order that encompasses them and confers on them meaning—*nomos* or *cosmos* order. Law cannot be reduced to legislation alone, as it would become incomprehensible and would have no practical validity unless the principles that underpin them, whether explicitly or implicitly, are deeply internalised by the individuals that make up that society.

By this last idea, we do not mean that individuals are constantly aware of the principles of the *cosmos* order; rather it suggests that their actions, worldview and interpersonal relations are influenced by these principles. Individuals assume and apply a set of principles or rules in their legal relations which have not been deliberately created or consciously incorporated, and which are subject to modification.

In this sense, law is regarded as the outcome of the interplay between heterogeneous elements, including sets and subsets of values, habits, unintentional rules and created rules, among others. These elements, within the framework of a complex and not entirely apprehensible system of selection, gradually evolve to shape specific modes of conflict resolution as the legal order of a specific community.

Most legal theories, whether explicit or implicit, attempt to establish identification criteria that facilitate the clear determination of which elements fall within the legal system, and which do not.[2] These theories propose a common character to the elements of law, identifiable through some scientific method, whether by the procedure for the creation of its rules, by the particularities of its legislative organs or by the specific characteristics of its elements (norms). Some do so by extensional means, listing all the elements that belong to the whole of what is called law.

[2] Among others, Hart's 'rule of recognition' should be mentioned here. A secondary rule that Hart considers indispensable in any evolved legal system (Hart, 1961, Ch 5).

Others provide intentional criteria that allow for the identification of current and future legal production.

The abstract and general principles of the *cosmos* order without a determined origin must not be conceived only as the historical antecedents of the rules of the *taxis* order. That is, as habits of the community which are articulated in legal custom which, recognised as a privileged source of law, is then positivised by legislation or judicial decisions. Adopting such an approach would result in the confusion of the Hayekian conception of law with a mere description of the common law system or with an empiricist vision, in the style of legal realism. Legal realism, while exhibiting some points of coincidence with Hayek‘s vision, imposes a form of empirical 'visibility' on the principles that govern legal conduct that Hayek does not demand. In summary, Hayek‘s conception does not reduce the legal phenomenon to an empirical-sociological description of conduct considered as legal. If this were the case, his vision of law would not correspond to his epistemological conceptions, which are less (scientifically) positivist and more Popperian.

Finally, he adds that "For our present purposes we are interested in any rules which are honoured in action and not only in rules enforced by an organization created for that purpose" (Hayek, 1983, p. 96 and quotes Hart on this point). In this sense, it is possible to observe, throughout Hayek‘s work and especially in "Law, Legislation and Liberty" (Hayek, 1983), that the author proposes a distinction between different types of rules. Therefore, among these principles, rules and values emerge involuntarily from the interaction between individuals—*cosmos* order—three distinct groups can be identified:

(a) **Explicitly articulated rules**, such as legislation and contracts, or any other deliberately created or positivised norm.
(b) **Articulable but unarticulated rules**: those that can be articulated or made explicit but have not yet been articulated or made explicit.
(c) **Non-articulable rules**: those that correspond to values and conceptions that are not capable of such a conscious articulation and that function as presuppositions of thought (Hayek, 1967b), p. 3 "Degrees of Explanation" & Hayek, 1978, p. 35 "The Primacy of the Abstract"). The abstract principles that are assumed when acting

> 'legally' in a community have a significant influence in the creation, interpretation and application of 'positive' rules of the *thesis* type. This also allows us to understand why certain codified legal instruments, despite their similar appearance in various legal systems, have such different interpretations, applications and consequences in different societies.

In conclusion, Hayek, in asserting that law is prior to legislation, seems to be arguing on several fronts simultaneously. On the one hand, he clearly confronts the positivist and constructivist conceptions of law which regard law as the set of rules created deliberately through specific formal procedures and are distinctly differentiated from other normative systems. On the other hand, his vision cannot be merely assimilated to that of the authors of legal realism, who proposed an external view of law as a set of habits that motivate human conduct and whose effects can be 'verified' empirically, as we shall see in the following paragraphs.

Hayek challenges most legal theories on the point of the origin and selection of norms by not providing a single specific criterion for determining the legal status of a rule, beyond the fact that they are honoured or respected in practice. The possibility to clearly identify the procedure, origin or creator of a rule becomes increasingly uncertain. This issue demands the integration of contributions from various disciplines including politics, morality, sociology and economics, to facilitate a comprehensive understanding of the emergence of the legal phenomenon. To illustrate this point, we bring here a remark made by Hayek regarding the relationship between facts and values:

"The understanding of the role which values play here is often prevented by substituting for 'values' factual terms like 'habits' or 'practices'. It is, however, not possible in the account of the formation of an overall order to replace adequately the conception of values which guide individual action with a statement of observed regularities in the behaviour of individuals, because we are not in fact able to reduce exhaustively the values that guide action to a list of observable actions. Conduct guided by a value is recognizable by us only because we are acquainted with that value" (...) "The complex relationship between values and facts creates certain familiar difficulties for the social scientist who studies complex social structures that exist only because the individuals composing them hold certain values. In so far as he takes for granted the overall structure which he studies, he also implicitly presupposes that the values on which it is based will continue to be held" (Hayek, 1983, pp. 111–112).

With respect to the aforementioned paragraphs, the following observations are in order. First, we can see a clear illustration of Hayek's understanding of law as a complex order, comprising different kinds of elements and his recognition that the theoretical reduction of one element to another can result in that part of the phenomenon remaining unexplained.

Regarding the relationship between values and facts, it is crucial to understand this in order to comprehend a legal order, not only to consider what happens, but also why it happens. That is to say, it is necessary to observe the basis for the actions of individuals in society. While it may not always be possible to fully comprehend and articulate the complete system of values underlying each individual action, it is crucial to approach the component of values that, in combination with the acts and the rules, constitute the legal order.

Furthermore, Hayek's analysis in these paragraphs challenges the prevailing stance within the school of Legal Realism, which reduces the study of law to the description of regularities in the actions of individuals. He considers this to be an aspect for observation but asserts that a comprehensive understanding of individual actions and the order they unintentionally produce can only be achieved if the values behind these actions are understood.

Some of the most renowned exponents of legal realism, for instance Karl Olivecrona of Scandinavian realism, allude to the 'motivations' behind individual actions (Olivecrona, 1947). He describes the legal norm as a psychological representation of the consequences of a certain action that 'motivates behaviour'. This can be inferred by observing the actions of the individual. However, this author distinguishes between the psychological instance, which is empirically observable through conduct, and the 'magical' component, which is the belief underlying this representation. This belief is qualified as 'magical' due to its lack of empirical or logical support, and as such, it falls outside the realm of rational explanation that theory can provide.

As we can see, Hayek moves away from this strict empiricism of the school of legal realism. The latter claims that the law can only be known though the discovery and description of certain regularities in the actions of judges, lawyers or citizens. However, Hayek emphasises that a deep understanding of these actions can only be achieved if one approaches the values that give them meaning and impetus. In summary, there will be an area for the study of values within legal theory that should not be confused or reduced to the study of the rules and facts that are also part of the legal order. The challenge he proposes then is to elaborate a theory that does not fall into the danger of reducing all the elements of different natures to the nature of only one of them.

2.6 The Role of the Judge

Finally, it is worth mentioning the role that Hayek proposes for judges (Hayek, 1983, Ch 5, p. 94). In Hayek's opinion, judges occupy a very particular place in the evolution of legal orders. In contrast to a strict legal positivist conception, Hayek does not consider judges to 'apply' the codified rules (from *taxis* order) in a deductive or quasi-automatic way. Nor does he subscribe to the legal realist position that judges 'create' the law (Holmes Jr., 1897). The role of the judge for Hayek is to resolve disputes between individuals who consider their expectations and claims to be legitimate. The judge must resolve the dispute by determining which of these expectations is legitimate and which is not, which requires a deep understanding of the legal order within which these expectations and claims are embedded.

As we have seen, individuals create their expectations based on a set of beliefs, principles, habits, etc., that have not all been consciously assimilated. As with many elements of the *cosmos* order, many of these principles have never been explicitly articulated either by them or by others. The judge must then attempt to identify the rules or principles—whether articulated or not—upon which individuals have relied to create the conflicting expectations. The judge must then consider how these principles and expectations relate to the other principles that exist within that legal order and make a decision that takes into account the consequences for both the individuals who are litigating, and the legal order as a whole. If, for example, the judge decides to grant the legitimacy of the claim to one of the parties, it is the judge's responsibility to consider the repercussions of this solution on the entire legal order, including the potential for frustrating or incentivising divergent expectations that may arise from this ruling.

In deciding the case, the judge may consider explicit (articulated) principles that have been recognised by legislation or by other judges in previous cases. In certain circumstances, he will also be required to make explicit some hitherto unarticulated principle. In other words, the relevant legal principle must be 'discovered' and 'made explicit' within the context of the existing legal order. However, should the judge be confronted with a 'new' case, which has not been legislated or ruled upon, and for which the judge is unable to find, articulate and apply an implicit or explicit principle, then it falls to the judge to formulate a 'new' rule. In this particular instance, Hayek considers that he should not be responsible for establishing a 'new order' but rather for 'filling a gap' within the general order. "But in neither case will the judge be free to pronounce any rule he likes. The rules which he pronounces will have to fill a definite gap in the body of already recognized rules in a manner that will serve to maintain and improve that order of actions which the already existing rules make possible" (Hayek, 1983, p. 100).

Hayek's conception of the role of the judge is closely linked to his view of law as a spontaneous order, consisting not only of common rules but also of shared values and opinions that give rise to those rules. Consequently, he criticises those views that conceive law as a phenomenon purely 'constructed' by human will and reason and identify its rules only with legislation. The significance of the judge's role is, therefore, rooted in his function as 'spokesman' of the spontaneous order of law, embodying the nexus between the *cosmos* and taxis orders and articulating it in the principles to be applied in each case under consideration.

As a conclusion to this chapter, it is our opinion that this proposal to conceive law as an evolutionary phenomenon is a very fruitful basis for a 'progressive research programme', in Imre Lakatos' terms. We consider that Hayek's work offers a framework of epistemological proposals that support his theory and allow it to advance in the face of new contributions from current evolutionary theories. In the following chapter, we will attempt to delineate his principal contributions to legal theory, whilst offering a concise comparison with other theories and perspectives on law.

References

Hart, H. L. A. (1961). *The concept of law*. Oxford University Press.

Hayek, F. A. (1967a). The theory of complex phenomena. In *Studies in philosophy, politics and economics* (pp. 22–42). The University of Chicago Press.

Hayek, F. A. (1967b). Degrees of explanations. In *Studies in philosophy, politics and economics* (pp. 3–21). The University of Chicago Press.

Hayek, F. A. (1978). *New studies in philosophy, politics, economics, and the history of ideas*. The University of Chicago Press.

Hayek, F. A. (1980). The use of knowledge in society. In *Individualism and economics order* (pp. 77–91). The University of Chicago Press. Original work published 1948.

Hayek, F. A. (1983). *Law, legislation and liberty* (Vol. I). The University of Chicago Press. Original work published 1973.

Holmes, O. W., Jr. (1897). The path of the law. *Harvard Law Review, 10*, 457.

Olivecrona, K. (1947). Law as fact. In *Interpretations of modern legal philosophies. Essay in honor of Roscoe Pound* (pp. 542–557). Oxford University Press.

Santanatoglia, E., & Sosa Valle, F. (2010). Selección de Textos de F. A. von Hayek. *Estudios Públicos, 120*(dic. 2010), 245–332.

Skoble, A. J. (2006). Hayek the philosopher of law. In E. Feser (Ed.), *The Cambridge companion to Hayek* (pp. 171–181). Cambridge University Press.

Sosa Valle F. (2008, October). "*El Concepto Hayekiano de Orden Espontáneo*". Revista de Instituciones, Ideas y Mercados (Special Issue: ESEADE-Thirtieth Anniversary), 49, p. 190.

3

Main Contributions of Classic Evolutionism to the Study of Law

3.1 Epistemological and Anthropological Assumptions of the Hayekian View of Law

Hayek proposed theories and ideas within the scope of discussion of various social sciences. His contributions to economics and political theory have survived the debates that originated them. Many of these ideas—such as the notion of disperse knowledge—have been extensively studied and discussed, earning him several awards, including the Nobel Prize in Economic Sciences in 1974.

Moreover, Hayek's contributions to the field of what is today referred to as the 'philosophy of the social sciences', have been significant, in terms of both content and methodology. In this sense, some of Hayek's works, such as the essays published in *Individualism & Economic Order* (Hayek, 1980), *Studies in Philosophy, Politics and Economics* (Hayek, 1967) and *New Studies in Philosophy, Politics, Economics, and the History of Ideas* (Hayek, 1978b) and many of his ideas on social orders expressed in *Law, Legislation and Liberty* (Hayek (1983)) constitute a legacy on

E. M. Santanatoglia, *An Evolutionary Account of Law*, Palgrave Studies in Classical Liberalism, https://doi.org/10.1007/978-3-032-12162-2_3

how to approach the study of the social sciences, that has yet to be thoroughly explored.

In this sense, Hayek propounds his theory of law within the framework of a more general view of the cognitive capacities of individuals, the way in which information is produced in society and the capacity of the social sciences to account for these phenomena.

In the domain of the philosophy of the social sciences, with regard to the epistemological assumptions of his theories, Hayek made several significant contributions. These contributions relate to his conceptions of dispersed knowledge, the various types of knowledge, the transmission of each of these types of knowledge and the limited human capacities to account for all the information that is socially produced at every point in history.

In this section, an overview of the main notions proposed by Hayek will be offered, followed by an analysis of their impact on his conception of law. In addition, the main differences of this conception of law with other legal theories will be examined. Finally, the impact of some of Hayek´s ideas on current views of normative orders.

Hayek´s theoretical contributions to the realm of rationality and knowledge in society are numerous. In addition to the 'moral' limitations already proposed by the Scottish School´s authors, such as self-interest and limited generosity, Hayek's perspective on human nature—if the term can be applied—adds cognitive limitations. In this sense, in his essays "*The use of knowledge in society*"and "*Economics and Knowledge*"(Hayek, 1980) Hayek puts forward a number of ideas related to rationality and knowledge in society. The following four points could be considered as a summary of his main contributions in this respect.

A. Knowledge is dispersed in society Hayek postulates the absence of a complete and coherent "core of knowledge" available to each and every individual (Hayek, 1980, p. 77). Individuals possess fragments of knowledge that enable them to act and make decisions. The dissemination of knowledge applies not only to scientific knowledge but also to the practical knowledge or know-how of certain activities. Ultimately, it is the interactions between individuals in possession of fragmentary and dissimilar knowledge that ldefines the prevailing social order.

To provide an illustration, each individual within a social order is acquainted with a number of other individuals in that order. Even if an individual were to be highly 'popular', they would likely have knowledge of a few hundred or a few thousand people, out of perhaps millions, who constitute that social order. This phenomenon is not exclusive to individuals, but is also observed in institutions and organisations. The assertion is made that each individual's relations will only be with a 'slice' of the social order, the result of individual interactions. As discussed in the preceding chapter, despite the 'limited' nature of this knowledge, the individual is capable of formulating relatively accurate expectations regarding the remaining components of the social order.

B. Knowledge of specific circumstances of time and place In the context of everyday life, individuals make decisions based on fragmented information and knowledge that are dependent on specific situations. This specific knowledge is as important (or perhaps more so) than any theoretical knowledge that the agent possesses when determining their course of action. In fact, Hayek contends that this knowledge of specific circumstances of time and place is fundamental to the decision-making process, yet it is generally not considered in scientific reconstructions of this process, which seek to explain the rationality behind human interactions.

In order to illustrate this notion, we can imagine the scenario of an individual considering the purchase of a property in their current city. In addition to the theoretical knowledge he may possess, such as the market prices of real estate in each area of the city, the legal form of the purchase contract and even the 'customs' for negotiating such a contract, there will be many other particular and specific 'facts' that he will take into account when making the decision. There are various factors to consider, including the desired proximity to family members, friends, place of work, children's school, transportation options and access to green spaces. Similarly, the individual is aware of the precise amount of money available to them, their preferences in terms of architecture and other essential data that are crucial for their decision-making process in that specific instance. However, this information may be irrelevant to another individual who may find themselves in the same situation (or even for another decision of that same individual in a different past or future scenario). In this sense, Hayek stresses that this specific information, which each individual considers when making his or her particular decision, is not usually considered by theories of decision-making. This subjective and, in many cases, not even conscious knowledge is not transferable from the agent to other people. In this sense, it is not possible for it to be transmitted to and concentrated in a central decision-making agent or body. This leads us to the subsequent point.

C. Transmission of knowledge 'Practical knowledge' cannot be transmitted from one person to another, which is a fundamental difference from scientific knowledge. Here, Hayek is thinking not only of the knowledge of specific circumstances of time and place previously mentioned, but also of what we might call practical knowledge or *know-how*: the practical skills and abilities acquired through experience that cannot be learned through theoretical study but are usually acquired through imitation or repeated practice.

This knowledge is not transmissible in the same manner as theoretical knowledge is communicated and consequently cannot simply be articulated and concentrated in a scientific theory. However, it can be incorporated, albeit inadvertently, within the mechanisms of knowledge transmission that communities spontaneously generate. In this sense, there are some social mechanisms, such as the market price coordination mechanism, or abstract rules, that concentrate on dispersed knowledge and provide a guide for human actions and decisions.

D. The human capacity for knowledge is limited According to Hayek, no single mind can contain all the knowledge that a social order can produce. In this sense, each individual makes decisions based on fragments of such knowledge. Meanwhile, the aforementioned mechanisms of knowledge transmission and coordination have spontaneously developed within the social order to help individuals make decisions. These mechanisms include language, prices and normative orders. Each individual makes decisions and interprets the information provided by these mechanisms under specific circumstances of time and place, based on their own values and skills. This indicates that it is not possible to concentrate this information and replace these decentralised decisions by a central decision-making body or a single decision-making mechanism.

The following section will show how these notions, presupposed by Hayekian legal theory, allow us to place this theory outside the traditional schools of legal-philosophical thought, i.e. iusnaturalism, legal positivism and legal realism.

Moreover, we consider that these points represent merely the proverbial tip of the iceberg, denoting a comprehensive conceptualisation of the relationship between the rationality of agents, the study of decision-making processes, the non-deliberated shaping of emergent orders and numerous other issues that have been subjects of debate for a long time. In this sense, Hayek—often inspired by Scottish thinkers—had already anticipated many of the current approaches within the debate in the philosophy of social sciences. In the third section of this chapter, an attempt will be made to outline some points of contact between these Hayekian proposals and current theoretical approaches.

3.2 Comparison with Other Schools of Legal Theory

In this section, we will not attempt an exhaustive exegesis of each school of ius-philosophical thought, nor will we make detailed comparisons between Hayek's notions and those proposed by other contemporary authors. Instead, we will highlight the features of his theory that differentiate it from the 'classic' schools of general legal theory, namely iusnaturalism, legal positivism and legal realism. Despite the fact that legal realism is not a current school today, Hayek refers to its ideas and authors on several occasions and even postulates notions similar to those proposed by realist authors. Conversely, the possible 'heir' theories of legal realism—'law and economics' and critical theory—were not yet so relevant, nor were they within Hayek's area of discussion, although the ideas of American and Scandinavian realist thinkers were.

Hayek, an heir to the Scottish tradition, found himself, at the time of formulating his legal theory, in a significantly different context from that of his teachers. Confronted with the questions of the origin of or the nature of law, in the middle of the twentieth century, he found—to use Lakatos' terms—various 'scientific research programmes' in the field of legal thought. Each of these programmes developed its own problems and solutions in parallel.

Firstly, the school of iusnaturalism refers here especially to the theories of the Natural Law tradition, and views law as being intimately related to morality, adopting a normative rather than a merely descriptive perspective (see Nino, 1988, p. 16 and Freeman, 2008, pp. 88–90 for general description of the school). However, although Hayek acknowledges that legal and moral norms may have the same kind of origin in terms of cultural evolution, and that values can inform our understanding of law, he does not establish a moral criterion for evaluating legal rules nor imposes any teleological purpose on the system of rules. In this sense, Hayek's view differs from approaches that focus on the substantive analysis of legal rules and their conformity to moral principles.

Likewise, Hayek's vision differs from those that regard justice as central to the conception of law, as well as from those that seek the ultimate and transcendent foundation of law. We consider that the fundamental element for distinguishing the Hayekian theory of law from the differing varieties of iusnaturalism is that it does not propose any substantive criterion in relation to the content of the norms, whether these are of a transcendent, metaphysical, moral or merely external order to the legal order. In other words, it does not establish any benchmark of delimitation of the legal order that implies a necessary content, nor the satisfaction of a substantive criterion exogenously established.

In this sense, the spontaneous orders identified as law, which comprise a variety of rules and are in constant evolution, are considered 'endogenous' products of the interpersonal relations of individuals. It has also been observed that, in some of his other significant works, such as "The Constitution of Liberty" (Hayek, 1978a), he defends legal-political orders that, through their general rules, especially protect the liberties of individuals. However, he does not deny the juridical nature of those other legal orders that do not do so, although he does not prefer them.

In this regard, as previously discussed, Hayek distinguishes between spontaneous orders and those that are deliberately created or 'given' by external forces, categorising the former as distinct from both natural orders and deliberate orders. Despite the efforts of certain scholars to draw parallels between Hayek's concept of spontaneous order and the natural order of iusnaturalism (thus proposing a clearly conservative reading of Hayek's ideas), Hayek himself made several clarifications regarding the central role of change in his conception of order ((Hayek, 1978a, Proscript: Why I Am Not a Conservative, p. 397.), and about the co-evolution of mind and society (Hayek, 1983, Ch1, p. 17). In these insights, the author shows that there is not any pre-fixed outline for this evolutionary path nor any ultimate finality to it. This point, in which the author incorporates the idea that there is no clear separation between the evolution of the minds that 'think' and the world and the evolution of the institutional environment in which they develop—in a strongly anti-Cartesian gesture—also implies a pioneering position, which can be observed in many current theories and thinkers (these points will be discussed in the next section).

Alternatively, the doctrine of legal positivism, as expounded by such theorists as Hans Kelsen (Kelsen, 1979) or H. L. Hart (Hart, 1961), emphasises the conception of law as a system of norms or rules. These theories are closely related to the emergence of national states and the study of 'positive norms' identified, in most cases, with the law of the state. These theories propose precise methods for the identification, classification and systematisation of rules. Thus, law is identified with positive norms deliberately created by authoritative entities with prescriptive powers and by different means such as legislation or judicial decisions. Consequently, the source of the norm or other formal characteristics—such as the inclusion or not of the punitive element in its formulation—become criteria for identifying legal norms and distinguishing them from other types of norms, such as moral or social norms. Law is thus conceived as a system of such rules organised in a particular manner—often hierarchically. This enables the analysis of the validity of rules based on their conformity to specific formal requirements in their formulation (procedure, competent authority, etc.) established by their superior or secondary rules or meta-rules of the system.

Finally, from a legal positivist perspective, this system of positive rules can be studied by deploying a logical-analytical apparatus. In certain cases, the application of traditional logic is proposed, while in others, a special logic—such as deontic logic—is proposed to study this specific type of proposition.

Furthermore, despite the fact that some of the most eminent exponents of legal positivism are of Anglo-American origin—such as H. L. Hart—it is evident that the positivist conception of law, mostly in its Kelsenian or post-Kelsenian versions, has been profoundly integrated within civil law tradition communities. In countries that are rooted in either the continental or civil law tradition, this positivist conception of law is not merely a theoretical position; rather, it is a perspective that has been internalised by individuals through their common sense. Most of the actors involved in the legal world—from ordinary citizens, law students, lawyers and even judges—almost automatically associate the concept of law with positive law, particularly with legislation, codified legal statutes and codes and treaties. This influence manifests in two key areas: firstly, it shapes the manner in which individuals formulate expectations regarding their own actions and those of others; secondly, it impacts the formulation of public policy proposals that are grounded in this conception of law. Taking this into account, Hayek's proposal to study law as an evolutionary and dynamic phenomenon, in continuous change and adaptation to the environment, appears to align more closely with the Anglo-Saxon Common Law tradition. However, as we shall see, we consider that his vision of law can be equally applied to the analysis of legal systems of continental origin.

Now, in considering the classic distinction proposed by Norberto Bobbio (Bobbio, 2012, Ch. 2) of legal positivism as a) a way of approaching the study of law (methodological legal positivism), b) as a theory of law (theoretical legal positivism) and c) as an ideology of justice (ideological legal positivism), it becomes evident that Hayek's proposal does not coincide with practically any of these points. Moreover, given that each of the 'stages' described here by Bobbio presupposes the previous one, the demonstration that Hayek's theory does not align with the initial stage of legal positivism, namely its 'approach to the study', enables the supposition of its incompatibility with subsequent stages. Consequently, it can be concluded that a definitive separation exists between positivist views and the evolutionary vision.

Regarding this first aspect, legal positivism as 'the way of approaching the study of law', Bobbio clarifies that this is not to be understood as merely a methodological requirement or as a stipulation for the techniques used for research, but rather as a distinct manner of defining the object of study. In this sense, Bobbio asserts that positivists hold an ethically neutral position, establishing a clear distinction between real law and ideal law or, in other words, the law as it is and the law as it ought to be, incorporating a 'scientific' perspective.

It can be posited, up to this point, that Hayek's position concurs with the methodological legal positivist position, given the absence of any 'normative' intention in his legal theory, at least in the work he dedicates especially to legal theory: "Law, Legislation and Liberty" (Hayek, 1983). However, some divergences emerge when attempting to define precisely what positivists understand as 'the law that is' and what the 'scientific' aspect of the view consists of.

In addressing the former, Bobbio delineates the object of legal theory for positivists, characterising it as positive law. In this sense, positivists conceptualised positive law (Bobbio, 2012, Ch 2) as the law in force in a given society comprising the complex of rules emanating from established procedures, usually obeyed by citizens and applied by judges. While there may be some general coincidence in this definition, Hayek's perspective is evidently divergent from the one outlined by Bobbio. In this section, we will attempt to delineate the distinguishing points of the two perspectives:

(A) As analysed in Chapter 2, Hayek places particular emphasis on the idea that law is prior to legislation and that the legal order is comprised of different types of rules—*nomos* and *thesis*—incorporating rules that have an indeterminate origin and do not necessarily meet a specific requirement or criterion. Therefore, identifying the law in force with only one type of norm or one specific procedure for its production would clearly restrict or limit the evolutionary view of law, as proposed by Hayek.

(B) On the other hand, the question of what constitutes 'scientific' in each view becomes relevant in order to differentiate between the 'way of approaching the object' of positivism and evolutionism. Of course, this varies between Continental and Anglo-Saxon Positivism and between authors. However, it can be observed that positivism tends to rely on the most relevant scientific methods of its time, whether through formal-logical reconstruction or through empirical observation. Meanwhile, following his friend Karl Popper, Hayek tends to hold more sceptical views on what science can and cannot do. In this sense, the hypothetical and transitory nature of knowledge would apply not only to the individual expectations considered when making decisions, but also to scientific knowledge, which would also be shown to be the result of the trial-and-error processes inherent in all knowledge acquisition.

(C) As we have already seen in previous sections, Hayek's conceptions of both reason and the knowledge capacity of individuals within social orders are limited and partial. All agents—not only 'citizens' but also legislators, judges, policymakers, etc.—face situations with only a 'portion' of the available societal knowledge and with various expectations of how the rest of the order works.

Positivist theories, on the other hand, seem to assume that human reason can fully comprehend the legal phenomena. According to this view, human reason and its logic enable us to create, organise, understand and systematise law. Kelsen (and to a certain extent Hart) believes that he can show the logical structure of law, without conceiving that this can only be a partial view of the complex phenomenon in question, as Hayek puts it. Hayek, on the other hand, believes that human rationality and understanding are limited and cannot control all the various elements that interact in the social order.

(D) For legal positivism, law is an independent object of study that is not necessarily related to other social phenomena such as morality or politics. There is an attempt to distinguish law from other influence or social suborder. This attempt to distinguish the disciplines sharply is not only characteristic of legal positivism, but also of scientific positivism, which was very influential in the twentieth century. Nevertheless, it does not have much influence on Hayek's later work.

Although Hayek in some of his early works (Hayek, 1952) proposes a clear separation between the social and the natural sciences, distinguishing their different methods (a distinction he relaxes in his later work), he never proposes such a strict division between the different theories within the social sciences. Each type of rule emanating from spontaneous processes (moral, social, legal, etc.) will surely take diverse forms and incorporate different content, and may even incorporate different forms of 'enforcement'. However, this is neither a characteristic nor an ex ante identification or classification criterion.

(A) On the basis of the foregoing points and what has already been discussed in Chapter 2, we shall revisit the issue of identifying the elements that constitute law. Unlike Hayek, both Kelsen and Hart conceptualised the legal phenomenon as consisting of homogeneous elements—namely, statements of a specific kind that constitute legal rules. Hayek, on the other hand, believes that the legal order comprises two distinct types of rules (*nomos* and *thesis*), as well as other elements such as values and customs and that it is not appropriate to reduce one type of element to another, given their different natures. The most accurate understanding of the phenomenon would be achieved through a vision that does not attempt to homogenise the complexity of its constituent elements.

(B) The position of both Kelsen and Hart is that the legal phenomenon can be defined as having a fixed identity. This is achieved by describing the characteristics of law itself and its differences from other social phenomena, and it is not believed that this identity can change or vanish. On the other hand, for Hayek, law can be

> defined as a spontaneous order in which unintended consequences of human action cannot be predicted or controlled, and which are likely to produce a change in the order itself. We shall now consider some of the practical consequences of the various assumptions of legal theories.

For instance, in the face of a political or institutional crisis, many social actors (including legislators, politicians and representatives from academia and the third sector) propose legal reforms to resolve the crisis. Specifically, the reform, sanction or repeal of a piece of legislation is proposed. And, once such a reform has been carried out, they do not understand why the situation does not improve.

Furthermore, there are instances where individuals have 'imported' a formal institution from another legal system into their own, yet find themselves unable to comprehend why it does not work as it does in their country of origin. In these cases, it is evident that these individuals hold a positivist view of law, believing it can be reduced to written laws, failing to grasp the complexities of the social order in which that legal order emerges and changes. The evolutionary and complex vision of law proposed by Hayek, on the other hand, considers these elements of the context and offers us a vision of the legal order as an order interconnected with the rest of the phenomena that make up the social order, such as politics or morality. From this vision, although we must take a more humble view of our capacity to change reality from one moment to the next, we will be able to have a better understanding of the circumstances in which a rule emerges, changes or dies. And, in any case, we will be able to embrace the circumstances and 'cultivate' the more positive tendencies even if we cannot 'construct' reality according to our conscious plans.

Finally, Hayek also encounters the perspective of legal realism. Specifically, American legal realism, represented by some prominent thinkers including Oliver Wendell Holmes, Benjamin Cardozo and Jerome Frank, who propose a view that relates law to facts and actions. Despite the differences between each thinker, legal realism identifies law with the actions of concrete individuals, such as judges or lawyers, and with the actual consequences of those actions, as in the case of judicial decisions, emphasising 'existing law' over formally valid law. In this manner, they employ and advocate an empirical methodology for the study of law. As will be shown in the following pages, the capacity to predict decisions is discussed in the context of this school.

American legal realists believe that to understand the current law in force in a community—that is, the law that is truly respected and enforced—one must observe what is happening in the courts. Oliver Wendell Holmes (Holmes, 1897) claims that "What I mean by the law" are "the prophecies of what the courts will do in fact". Others, such as Jerome Frank (Frank, 1948), propose observing how judges work in court. Frank recommends paying particular attention to how judges shape the 'facts of the case' in actual court proceedings by interpreting the parties' accounts of the facts. He considers this aspect much more important for understanding the law than the judges' work interpreting the law.

Other authors, such as Roscoe Pound (cited by Russo, 1995, p. 135), also focus on the 'functions' of law, or how the judicial system itself creates 'reality' through the decisions of individual judges. Based on the idea of having a 'realist' view of law, many of these authors will even invoke a 'law-creating power' in the hands of judges.

Finally, we can also refer to the Scandinavian school of legal realism, which incorporates a sociological vision that observes how 'ordinary citizens', rather than lawyers or judges, act with respect to the 'law as a fact' (Olivecrona, 1947). They coined the notion of 'popular legal consciousness' in an attempt to reconstruct the law on the basis of individual's actions and beliefs. This is all based on an empirical methodology of observation and the use of surveys and other similar sociological methods.

Here, then, we find many points of contact with the Hayekian view of law. In fact, Hayek includes multiple references to the authors and ideas of legal realism, in particular some ideas of Oliver W. Holmes and Roscoe Pound. For example, when Hayek treats law as 'Nomos' (Hayek, 1983, Ch 5, p. 105), he refers to the relationship between the system of rules of conduct and the factual order of actions. In this sense, he argues that it is inconceivable to create a science of law that is purely a science of rules and does not take the factual order into account. In this sense, he asserts "This is the reason why the Cartesian or 'geometric' treatment of law as a pure 'science of norms', where all rules of law are deduced from explicit premises, is so misleading" (Hayek, 1983, Ch 5, p. 106) In fact, he quotes a sentence by Holmes in his *"Common Law"* which reads: "The life of law has not been logic, it has been experience. The felt necessities of the time, the prevalent moral and political theories, intuitions of public policy, avowed or unconscious, even the prejudices which judges share with their fellow-men, have a good deal more to do than syllogisms in determining the rules by which men should be governed. The law embodies the story of a nation's development through many centuries, and it cannot be dealt with as if it contained only the axioms and corollaries of a book of mathematical" (Holmes, 1963, cited by Hayek, 1983, p. 106 and note 14 p. 170).

In the same vein, he quotes Roscoe Pound, who exhibits a 'functionalist' view of law, whereby it serves a very clear purpose—we believe, coincides with a possible reading of Hayek's theory. Roscoe Pound, in the quote, says the following: "The problem of law is to keep conscious free-willing from interference with each other. It is so to order them that each shall exercise his freedom in a way consistent with the freedom of all others, since all others are to be regarded equally as ends in themselves" (Roscoe Pound, 1926, p. 97 cited by Hayek 1983 note 14 p. 171).

Consequently, it can be observed that Hayek and legal realists undoubtedly share their dynamic and empirical view of law. The concept of examining "rules that are observed in practice" by citizens, as well as by judges and lawyers (sometimes consciously, and sometimes unconsciously) is of fundamental importance. These rules clearly exhibit social regularities with legal pretensions.

There is only one important point which, we believe, divides the waters between Hayek and the legal realists. The latter explicitly refer to scientific positivism, which postulates the formulation theories of empirical content, with a high degree of 'verifiability'. For instance, the work of authors such as Felix S. Cohen who, in his work "The Functional Method in Law" (Cohen, 1962, Ch 2), explicitly states the need to redirect the science of law exclusively to the elaboration of notions containing empirical and verifiable content, excluding any kind of concept of 'transcendental meaninglessness'. While Hayek's vision of law can concur, in general terms, with the conception of law as clearly informed by empirical observation and the rules that citizens, judges and lawyers actually adhere to, he does not subscribe to the 'verification' perspective held by Cohen and other authors of legal realism.

In contrast, Hayek propounds a divergent perspective on science, one that is informed by the seminal contributions of his friend Karl Popper. In this theoretical framework, scientific hypotheses are inherently open to future refutation, and the validation of knowledge concerning the 'truth' of observed regularities is contingent on provisional approaches, a process that is incessantly shaped by trial and error. In other words, it is likely that the realists and Hayek agree on numerous aspects of legal phenomena, although they may diverge on how to unravel them empirically or how to provide an explanation for them. In this sense, it would be worth bringing in the whole Hayekian conception on prediction by principle and pattern prediction (see "Degrees of Explanation" and "The Theory of Complex Phenomena"in Hayek, 1967).

Moreover, another point of differentiation—and here the difference is more applicable to American realism—is Hayek's explicit acknowledgement of the role he assigns to the judge in the formation of law. In the works of numerous realist authors, the judge is depicted as having an active, even 'creative', role, exercising a broad capacity to respond to social requirements. In contrast, as discussed in Chapter 2, Hayek's approach limits this capacity to responding to the expectations already formulated by the parties involved in a specific case, and to the application of the law based on a systematic interpretation of the law.

In conclusion, it can be argued that the characteristics of Hayekian legal theory position it equidistant from the most notable expressions of the most recognised twentieth-century theories, i.e. natural law theory, legal positivism and legal realism. Hayek's theory posits law as comprising heterogeneous elements that do not adhere to a unified criterion of common recognition or identification; elements that do not constitute a rigorous, formal order. This perspective marks a notable departure from the most prominent expressions of legal positivism. However, it does not establish a moral, substantive, external or metaphysical criterion to determine when law exists or is legitimate. While values and other normative and social 'regularities' play a role, they are not the ultimate determinant of the legal order. This clearly distances the theory from iusnaturalism. Finally, although he agrees with many of the legal realist proposals of his time, in their North American and Scandinavian versions, he assigns a less decisive role to the judge. He also considers the process of acquiring legal knowledge to be one of trial and error, rather than one that can produce verifiable empirical knowledge, as consistent realists would claim.

This is why we argue that this evolutionary view is unique and should not be confused with different versions of the above-mentioned schools. We also believe that the key aspects of this proposal align with many of the current social science theories and debates on normative orders. We will explore these similarities with the current debate in the following section.

3.3 Contributions of the Classic Evolutionism to Current Evolutionary Theories

Hayek's theory of law offers a compelling starting point for understanding the legal order from a more complex and dynamic perspective. Moreover, it makes assumptions that are still relevant today, such as the existence of dispersed knowledge, limited rationality, individual learning and the adaptation of social and legal systems to circumstances. These ideas are currently being explored and developed by various schools of thought and theories, forming new hypotheses about change and learning. Consequently, we believe that Hayek's legal theory, which considers the problem of knowledge and is based on the evolutionary conception of social change, represents a fundamental tool for improving our understanding of the social order (law, politics and economics) at both the theoretical and practical levels.

We note that many of Hayek's ideas, whether fully developed or merely outlined, are of great interest today in various disciplines and theories that cut across all social sciences. Many of these ideas will be analysed in detail in the following parts of this book. As a bridge between this first part and the one that follows, we will briefly discuss some of Hayek's ideas that currently occupy a pre-eminent place in new approaches to explaining social phenomena, which could be applied to the analysis of law. Among Hayek's most inspiring and influential conceptual proposals are some that bear a striking resemblance to the most widely recognised current theories.

3.3.1 Bounded Rationality

We have already outlined here the main proposals of this author on dispersed knowledge, the impossibility of theoretical transmission of practical knowledge and knowledge of specific circumstances of time and place, which he already outlined in his work *Individualism and Economic Order* in 1948.

These notions are quite similar to the notion of 'bounded rationality', which was later proposed by authors such as Herbert Simon (Simon, 2000). Simon explores how the human mind's capacity to formulate and solve complex problems is very limited compared to those required by objectively rational behaviour in the real world. Furthermore, when making a decision, agents consider the possible future actions of other individuals. In other words, they face interdependent choice problems and formulate expectations relating to the actions of others (problems that will be examined in depth in game theory).

This notion of bounded rationality has been the subject of extensive research and refinement through the development of numerous new theories in recent years. On the one hand, it has been incorporated into evolutionary theories such as evolutionary game theory, which we will see in the next part of this work.

In addition, a range of psychological theories—including those propounded by several recent Nobel Prize winners in Economics, such as Daniel Kahneman (Kahneman, 2013) or Richard Thaler, in conjunction with Cass Sunstein (Thaler & Sustein, 2008)—put forward innovative conceptions of the cognitive processes underlying decision-making in various contexts. Consequently, numerous scholars have proposed the idea of a dichotomy between a primary cognitive function, termed 'Brain 1', and a secondary one, termed 'Brain 2'. The former is characterised by traditional logical and rational thought processes, which were historically prevalent in twentieth-century theoretical frameworks. In contrast, the latter encompasses automatic mechanisms, such as heuristics and procedural routines.

As we will explore in more detail in chapters 4 to 7 of this book, the work of the authors of Classic Evolutionism—not only Hayek but also the authors of the Scottish Enlightenment—already contained latent explanations of the functioning of the brain and the intervention of reason in the decision-making of agents.

There is another illustration of the tacit influence of Hayekian thinking in contemporary social sciences. It is a book by Dan Ariely, a professor of Behavioural Economics at MIT, entitled "*Predictably Irrational. The Hidden Forces That Shape Our Decisions*" (Ariely, 2008, p. 46). The title itself reminds us of Hayek, bounded rationality, abstract rules and the potential for identifying recurring patterns in our seemingly 'irrational' decisions.

To illustrate the point, I would like to highlight one example of what can be found in this book. In a chapter devoted to what he calls 'the fallacy of supply and demand', Ariely postulates the notion of 'arbitrary coherent preferences'. This notion would allow us to provide explanations for a wide range of decisions—from the most insignificant to the most substantial—by observing that they do not respond to the expression of our desires or values (what we might refer to as rational or instrumental action), but rather, are based on previous decisions. In doing so, we unconsciously assume that these prior decisions were wisely made. We often make choices that involve compromising on money, time or other resources in order to maintain internal consistency. According to Ariely (2008, p. 46), within the framework of 'arbitrary coherence', market relationships between demand and supply would not be based on our preferences, but on our memory.

In this way, the author demonstrates, based on a series of experiments, how individuals make consumption decisions based on expectations formed from previous actions that act as 'anchors' in our daily behaviour. Thus, we can see that this theory could provide empirical support for many of Hayek's proposals, such as the importance of specific knowledge of time and place in decision-making, and the influence of certain 'abstract rules' on our perception and interpretation of daily situations, such as the desire to be consistent with our own line of conduct.

3.3.2 Complex Phenomena and Spontaneous Orders

In his essay "The Theory of Complex Phenomena"published in *Studies* (Hayek, 1967, p. 22), Hayek introduces the notion of such phenomena. To this end, he establishes that the minimum number of elements or variables that an instance—formula or model—of the pattern must comprise in order to exhibit all its characteristic attributes determines the degree of complexity of that pattern.

In this sense, most of the phenomena studied by the social sciences are complex in nature, given the considerable number of interdependent variables that must be represented in their models, of which only a fraction can be observed. Consequently, it is unfeasible to test all possible combinations of factors and thus make predictions with complete information. As a result, it will not be possible to predict individual events; rather, knowledge of the conditions under which a certain type of regularity may appear can be produced.

In addition to this vision of complex phenomena, there is the concept of spontaneous orders, which has already been analysed. As previously discussed, the concept of 'spontaneous order', a notion derived from eighteenth-century Scottish School thought, pertains to those orders that, as Ferguson elucidates, emerge from human action yet are not the consequence of human design. In analysing this idea, Hayek introduces the concept of order as that state of affairs in which a multiplicity of elements of various kinds is so related to each other that, on the basis of knowledge of one spatial or temporal part of the whole, we can form correct expectations about the rest, or at least expectations with a good chance of being correct (Hayek, 1983, p.36).

This relates to previous points about knowledge. As we have already seen, the individual is aware of the social order to which they belong, albeit in a fragmented way. From the signals provided by the order, they can create expectations about its regularities. Incorporating the possibility of error in understanding and in the formulation of expectations, as well as the impossibility of affirming the continuity of the given order up to the present moment, introduces a greater degree of uncertainty than is usually considered in other social theories.

This suggests a view of human understanding of social orders that is both optimistic and pessimistic. The optimistic view is that individuals can form expectations with a high degree of accuracy based on their own knowledge. It is pessimistic because humans will only ever understand aspects of the social order in which they live and will never grasp the totality of the knowledge produced by that order. The rules he adopts to motivate his behaviour are based on fallible expectations.

Consequently, spontaneous orders can be described as 'self-generated', 'endogenous' or 'evolutionary' orders. Spontaneous orders are distinguished from 'created' or 'artificial' orders in three ways, since the latter are: firstly, simple or confined to a moderate degree of complexity; secondly, they are concrete, in the sense that their existence can be intuitively perceived by inspection; and thirdly, as having been made deliberately, they do (or at one time did) serve a purpose of the creator. On the other hand, spontaneous orders are firstly, not necessarily complex, but can attain any degree of complexity; secondly, they are abstract in nature, consisting of systems of abstract relations between elements that are also defined in terms of abstract properties; and thirdly, they cannot be directly perceived by the senses and recognised except through a theory that accounts for them. Spontaneous orders do not serve any particular purpose, although their existence may be useful for many individual purposes (Hayek, 1983, pp.38–39).

These notions of complex phenomena and spontaneous orders are related to what is currently being studied by various authors and schools as 'complex systems'. These systems, in conjunction with the methodologies presently referred to as 'agent-based models', appear to exhibit significant parallels with those postulated by Hayek.

For instance, in his essay entitled "Was Hayek an Ace?" (referring to agent-based computational economists), Vriend (Vriend, 2002) argues that the notion of a complex system proposed by Tesfatsion (a renowned academic devoted to the study of agent-based models) and other founders of the theory of complex systems is closely related to the notions proposed precisely by Hayek.

Tesfatsion (1998) quoted by Vriend (2002) says: "Agent-based computational economics (ACE) is roughly characterized as the computational study of economies modelled as evolving decentralized systems of autonomous interacting agents. A central concern of ACE researchers is to understand the apparent spontaneous formation of global regularities in economic processes, such as the unplanned coordination of trade in decentralized market economies that economists associate with Adam Smith's invisible hand. The challenge is to explain how these global regularities arise from the bottom up, through the repeated local interactions of autonomous agents channelled through socio-economic institutions, rather than from fictitious top-down coordination mechanisms such as imposed market clearing constraints or an assumption of single representative agents. ACE is thus a specialization to economics of the basic complex adaptive systems (CAS) paradigm".

In this sense, it can be observed that the definition of the economics of agent-based models (which are currently at the centre of the discussion in the social sciences) is very similar to that proposed by Hayek in his work on complex phenomena, pattern prediction, knowledge limitations and other ideas which have previously been discussed. Vriend (2002, p. 811) highlights these similarities with Hayek's bottom-up view of the economy and emphasises his vision of the market economy as a truly decentralised system of interactions between individual agents, thus proposing true individualism, since it is the only theory that would make the formation of spontaneous social products intelligible.

Finally, given these similarities between what Hayek proposed and the theory of complex systems and ACE, Vriend (2002, p. 811) notes that many experts on Hayek are interested today in the recent literature on these systems, although not all complexity theorists and ACE are thoroughly familiar with Hayek's work. Here he considers the idea that Hayek may have been an ACE *avant-la lettre*. Some of these ideas will be examined in the following sections, but it is worth presenting first this conceptual and theoretical relationship between them.

3.3.3 Abstract Rules and Cultural Evolutionism

The notion of 'abstract rules' is a pivotal element in fully understanding Hayek's conception of the evolution of knowledge within the individual and his interaction with the environment. In his essay "The Primacy of the Abstract" published in *New Studies* (Hayek, 1978b, p. 35), Hayek proposes that reason and perception are articulated by a system of rules belonging to a more abstract plane. Thus, the perception and interpretation of reality by the cognising subject are conditioned by abstract and supra-conscious rules. These rules prescribe a certain range of events and allow the formulation of specific expectations. As we have analysed in Chapter 2, these abstract rules encompass a series of proscriptions and permissions concerning human thought and behaviour. But, although these rules are not conscious, they are in continuous adaptation to the environment. When faced with an anomaly or counterexample (for example, that a person does something that does not coincide with our expectations), the abstract scheme of perception and intelligibility itself is obliged to readjust. Facts will come to be perceived or interpreted according to the new abstract schema.

The spontaneous social order is produced by individual actions yet it also acts as a framework of expectations and rules for these individuals, thereby feeding back into that order. This does not necessarily imply a determinism engendered by the social framework, as there is also room for freedom since the individual actor can deviate from the expectations and thus promote a rearrangement of these rules and expectations.

Furthermore, in the initial pages of his seminal work *Law, Legislation and Liberty*, Hayek reveals the evolutionary nature of spontaneous orders, delineating the process of emergence of the institutions and practices that constitute such orders. These practices are initially adopted for a specific purpose, whether intentionally or inadvertently, and then maintained due to their capacity to enable the group in which they are born, to emerge over competing groups (Hayek, 1983, p. 9). Concurrently, these rules that individuals follow (as rule-following and end-seeking animals) are not always articulable for individuals. In conclusion, the thinking and action of individuals are governed by abstract rules that, by a process of selection, have evolved in the society in which they live, a product of the experience of generations (Hayek, 1983, p. 11).

The idea of the evolution of rules and institutions within the theoretical framework of 'cultural evolutionism' has been the focus of extensive research in recent years. From the perspective of evolutionary game theory to those who consider the potential co-influences between biological and cultural evolutionary processes, such as the authors of co-evolutionism Richerson and Boyd (2006). Hayek's conceptualisations concerning the genesis of regular societal practices, their internalisation as expectations and rules, and their transformation in the face of frustrated expectations are noteworthy for their advanced state of development.

References

Ariely, D. (2008). *Predictably irrational. The Hidden forces that shape our decisions*. HarperCollins Publishers.

Bobbio, N.,(2012), *El problema del positivismo jurídico* (p. 2). Distribuciones Fontamara.

Cohen, Félix S., (1962), El método Funcional en el derecho, Ed. Abeledo-Perrot. (Original work published 1935)

Frank, J. N. (1948). Say it with music. *Harvard Law Review, LXI* (6), 921–957.

Freeman, M. D. A. (2008). *Introduction to jurisprudence* (8th ed.). Sweet & Maxwell.

Hart, H. L. A. (1961). *The concept of law*. Oxford University Press.

Hayek, F. A. (1952). *The counter-revolution of science*. The Free Press Glencoe.

Hayek, F. A. (1967). *Studies in philosophy, politics and economics*. The University of Chicago Press.

Hayek, Friedrich A., (1978a), The constitution of liberty, The University of Chicago Press. (Original work published 1960).

Hayek, F. A. (1978b). *New studies in philosophy, politics, economics, and the history of ideas*. The University of Chicago Press.

Hayek, Friedrich A., (1980), Individualism and economics order, The University of Chicago Press. (Original work published 1948).

Hayek, Friedrich A., (1983) Law, legislation and liberty, *Volume* I, The University of Chicago Press. (Original work published 1973).

Holmes, O. W. (1897). The path of the law. *Harvard law review, 10*, 457.
Holmes, O. W., (1963), "The common law".
Kahneman, D. (2013). *Thinking, fast and slow*. Farrar, Straus and Giroux.
Kelsen, H. (1979). *Teoría pura del derecho*. Universidad Autónoma de México.
Nino, C. S. (1988). *Introducción al análisis del derecho*. Editorial Astrea.
Olivecrona, K. (1947). "*Law as fact*", in interpretations of modern legal philosophies. In *Essay in honor of roscoe pound* (pp. 542–557). Oxford University Press.
Pound, R. (1926). *Law and morals* (p. 97). The University of North Carolina Press.
Richerson, P. J., and Boyd, R. (2006). *Not by genes alone - how culture transformed human evolution*. The University of Chicago Press.
Russo, Eduardo A., (1995), Teoría general del derecho, Ed. Abeledo Perrot,. Chapter 5 'Normas como Manzanas'.
Simon, H. A. (2000). Bounded rationality in social sciences: Today and tomorrow. *Mind & Society, 1*, 25–39.
Tesfatsion, L. (1998). *Agent-based computational economics*. www.restate.edu/tesfatsi/ace-htm
Thaler, R., & Sustein, C. R. (2008). *Nudge: Improving decisions about health, wealth, and happiness*. Yale University Press.
Vriend, N. J. (2002). Was hayek an ace? *Southern Economic Journal, 68*(4), 811–840. https://doi.org/10.2307/1061494

Part II

New Evolutionary Perspectives in Social Sciences

4

Panorama of New Evolutionary Perspectives in Social Sciences

4.1 New Evolutionary Perspectives in Social Sciences

The purpose of this second part of the book is to introduce a repertoire of schools of thought and theories, nowadays widely debated in the social sciences, that share an evolutionary perspective of social phenomena. This approach is sometimes applied to the study of individual human behaviour and, at other times, to the rules or institutions that emerge from the interrelation of these behaviours. Presently, there are many different theoretical currents, and we can only provide an overview of the various proposals and explore some of them in more depth. Specifically, we will focus on those that we believe can provide the necessary elements to 'construct' our legal theory from an evolutionary point of view. As we will see in the following chapters, we believe that many of these new theories not only build on, but also refine and add precision to, the proposals offered by the evolutionary view in previous centuries.

In this sense, we propose a relationship, and even complementarity or continuity, between the notions put forward by what we refer to as 'classic evolutionism' (CE) in the social sciences, and some of the current evolutionary thought schools presented here.

E. M. Santanatoglia, *An Evolutionary Account of Law*, Palgrave Studies in Classical Liberalism, https://doi.org/10.1007/978-3-032-12162-2_4

As we saw in the first part of this book, evolutionary thought in the social sciences has its roots in the Scottish Enlightenment of the eighteenth century. In this sense, we could speak of a pre-Darwinian evolutionary tradition within social thought, which is now reinterpreted in the light of Charles Darwin‘s work and the current debate within the social sciences, which analyses social reality based on Darwinian notions.

We have already reviewed the work of the main exponents of the Scottish Enlightenment in brief. It is worth quoting Hayek here on Mandeville's work, as he draws bridges between this line of thought and Darwin's evolutionary theory (and even post-Darwinian theory). He states (Hayek, 1967, p. 253):

> "But the tradition which Mandeville started includes also Edmund Burke, and, largely through Burke, all those 'historical schools' which, chiefly on the Continent, and through men like Herder and Savigny, made the idea of evolution a commonplace in the social sciences of the nineteenth century long before Darwin. And it was in this atmosphere of evolutionary thought in the study of society, where 'Darwinians before Darwin' had long thought in terms of the prevailing of more effective habits and practices, that Charles Darwin at last applied the idea systematically to biological organisms. I do not, of course, mean to suggest that Mandeville had any direct influence on Darwin (though David Hume probably had). But it seems to me that in many respects Darwin is the culmination of a development which Mandeville more than any other single man had started."

As we have seen, Hayek built on ideas proposed by Scots in the twentieth century, continuing a tradition of thought that recognises the gradual emergence of social orders and institutions from the interaction of individuals. These individuals have the capacity to adapt to new environments and learn from past experiences. We have proposed calling this evolutionary view, which combines the ideas of the Scottish Enlightenment with Hayek's work, 'classic evolutionism'(CE).

Classic evolutionism precedes Darwin's work, and therefore biological evolutionism, which in turn has inspired many evolutionary theories in the twentieth and twenty-first centuries. As discussed in Chapter 3, there are several points of contact between CE and new evolutionary theories, which we will highlight as they arise (before providing a comprehensive synthesis in the third part of this work). In this sense, it is interesting to analyse how new schools studying human phenomena from an evolutionary perspective have emerged. We will see that the imprint of Darwinian thought on the social sciences is currently omnipresent.

4.2 Classification of the New Evolutionary Perspectives in Social Sciences

The new evolutionary theories combine two compatible traditions: the naturalistic and sentimentalist philosophy of the Scottish Enlightenment of the eighteenth century, and evolutionary biology, mainly represented, though not exclusively, by the work of Charles Darwin. Some of these theoretical proposals directly connect the biological aspects of evolution with explanations of social institutions, rules and practices.

Others use the vocabulary and processes described by biological evolutionism to explain social phenomena, albeit metaphorically. In other words, they adopt the terminology of biological evolutionism (e.g. genotype/phenotype, selection, mutation) but apply it to social phenomena. In this case, the application of a social rule arises from a social process described in terms of cultural evolutionism, not a biological selection process.

Finally, there are theories that explain different social phenomena, such as the emergence of a social rule, as the result of the interaction between biological and cultural aspects, leaving aside the dichotomy between nature and culture (nature/nurture).

In the light of this, we hereby propose the following classification of the broad spectrum of theories that currently address the study of human behaviour and social institutions from various evolutionary perspectives. The criterion suggested herein essentially consists of establishing the fundamental nature of these phenomena. It is evident that while there is consensus among theorists regarding the provision of explanations of behavioural and social phenomena as 'adaptations' or as the consequence of a process of 'natural selection', the crux of the disagreement lies in the determination of whether these processes are in response to biological or social survival needs, or both. In this sense, a distinction is made between theories that propose a purely biological foundation, those that propose a purely social foundation and thirdly, those that propose a mixed foundation, taking elements of biological evolution and elements of cultural evolution in a plane of co-evolution. In each case, we will propose some of the most important exponents:

(a) **Biologically based evolutionary theories:** Those that explain different phenomena, such as social, moral or legal rules, on the basis of biological evolution, i.e. as sophisticated biological survival strategies. Among these approaches, 'sociobiology' has emerged as a seminal theory, evolving today into a more sophisticated 'evolutionary psychology' (i.e. Leda Cosmides & John Tooby).
(b) **Culturally based evolutionary theories**: Other approaches to behaviour, rules and institutions provide explanations based on different cultural or social survival mechanisms. This 'cultural evolutionism' has many representatives, some of the most recognised being 'Richard Dawkins"memes theory' or the 'evolutionary game theory' (i.e. Skyrms, Alexander).
(c) **Co-evolutionary theories:** These theories take into account elements of both biological and cultural evolution to explain social behaviours or regularities. Thus, for example, rules and institutions are seen as the result of the interaction between both interrelated and or co-determined evolutionary processes (i.e. Boyds & Richardson).

Based on this classification, the following chapters will provide a brief analysis of some of the key figures in these schools of thought, alongside the criticisms and debates surrounding them. In this chapter, we will begin with an overview of the key concepts in Richard Dawkins'work, particularly his influential book The Selfish Gene, which we believe represented a pivotal moment in the development of new evolutionary thought in biology and the social sciences.

In the following chapters, we will present the main ideas of evolutionary psychology, evolutionary game theory and finally co-evolutionism. In each case, we will present the theoretical proposals of some of the field's most influential thinkers.

4.3 Dawkins and 'the Biological Turn'

We would like to introduce the work of an author whom we consider to be one of the main figures responsible for the resurgence of evolutionary theories in the social sciences at the turn of the twenty-first century. His first work, "The Selfish Gene", had a significant impact on both the scientific community and the general public. This work of 'popular science' effectively presents biological evolution from the perspective of the gene. The first edition was published in 1976, followed by a corrected and enlarged second edition in 1989.

This work is regarded as a dissemination of a gene-based view of biological evolution, which had already begun to be proposed by other well-known scientists such as George C. Williams, William D. Hamilton and John Maynard Smith. In the 1960s, they all launched a strong critique of the group selection view, proposing that the gene was the unit of selection in biological evolution. Later, we will see how some of these authors were highly innovative in their respective fields of study. For instance, Maynard Smith was one of the first to apply game theory to biological evolution and to propose ideas that were later applied to the evolution of human institutions, such as the notion of an 'evolutionarily stable strategy' or the idea of the 'hawk-dove' game.

In this sense, Dawkins can be regarded as a key disseminator of these ideas. The merits of the work extend beyond its gentle prose, which at times evokes the feel of a novel more than a popular science book. Indeed, it is in this first book that the author introduces several highly original themes that were previously unheard of. For example, evolutionary game theory, which involves the 'competition' of strategies to identify the most stable in evolutionary terms. Dawkins also introduces his original 'meme theory', which seeks to explain cultural evolution as a process parallel to biological evolution (paradoxically, Dawkins is not a 'biologicist' in terms of the foundation of cultural institutions). This 'meme theory' gave rise to the whole memetic movement, which then spread during the decades following the first publication of his work.

Before proceeding to a detailed analysis of the main notions, it is important to note that in this work, Dawkins accomplishes several objectives simultaneously. Firstly, he has achieved a phenomenal diffusion of evolutionary biology among the general public, disregarding those versions of the process of biological evolution that emphasised race, group or even the individual, effectively leaving it without a biological foundation. Furthermore, it has been successful in incorporating the entire lexicon of evolutionary theory into the scientific vocabulary, extending beyond the natural sciences to encompass the social sciences. This work, along with several contemporary works in the same vein, has been successful in establishing terms such as 'adaptation', 'mutation', 'natural selection' and 'genotype/phenotype', within everyday scientific vocabulary, even in the most current lines of analytical and experimental philosophy.

In this sense, we believe that a sort of 'biologic turn' takes place in the discourse of the different scientific disciplines, especially in the philosophical debate and in the social sciences. Evolutionary biology is thus elevated to the status of 'standard' within the scientific disciplines, with its explanations of processes becoming the model for numerous new theories. This is not only the case for behaviour that has been explained on biological grounds, but also for theories that provide culturalist explanations but incorporate biological vocabulary as a metaphor for social processes.

It is therefore necessary to introduce some fundamental concepts of evolutionary biology and the main notions of Dawkins' work "The Selfish Gene"in order to understand his main contributions, which are taken for granted by other theorists and finally the main ideas of his theory of memes, which has been the subject of debate for a considerable time.

4.3.1 Some Concepts of Evolutionary Biology

It is widely acknowledged that the foundational figure in the field of evolutionary biology is Charles Darwin. Consequently, all authors who offer evolutionary explanations of social phenomena tend to reference Darwin's concepts, even to challenge them. It is evident that Darwin's seminal work, "The Origin of Species" (Darwin, 1998), has had a profound impact on the field of evolutionary biology. However, for the purposes of this discussion, it is imperative to acknowledge "The Origin of Man" (Darwin, 1871) which applies evolutionary theory especially to human evolution and which includes noteworthy observations on evolutionary psychology, evolutionary ethics and even the development of institutions.

In this case, we will also refer to the main notion presented in his first work, namely the notion of 'natural selection'. This notion remains a central component in contemporary debate on evolution, both biological and cultural. We will review the concept here and then provide a brief analysis.

Darwin, in chapter 4 of his "Origin of Species" (Darwin, 1998, pp. 63-64), says: "Let it be borne in mind how infinitely complex and close-fitting are the mutual relations of all organic beings to each other and to their physical conditions of life. Can it, then, be thought improbable, seeing that variations useful to man have undoubtedly occurred, that other variations useful in some way to each being in the great and complex battle of life, should sometimes occur in the course of thousands of generations? If such do occur, can we doubt (remembering that many more individuals are born than can possibly survive) that individuals having any advantage, however slight, over others, would have the best chance of surviving and of procreating their kind? On the other hand, we may feel sure that any variation in the least degree injurious would be rigidly destroyed. This preservation of favourable variations and the rejection of injurious variations, I call Natural Selection. Variations neither useful nor injurious would not be affected by natural selection, and would be left a fluctuating element, as perhaps we see in the species called polymorphic".

There are several aspects of this definition that, when applied to the analysis of social institutions, may be of interest. Firstly, there is the observation of the enormous variety of traits that an organism can develop, representing the possibility of different variations showing diverse performance in various environments. Thus, we find that the same type of organism can exhibit diverse characteristics, and that the variations best adapted to their environment 'survive'. Consequently, a trait that exhibits high degrees of adaptability in one context may be 'maladapted' in another environment and, over time, disappear.

Another interesting aspect to note is that—although it may seem a truism—organisms with different variations do not necessarily compete with each other in a conflictual sense but can coexist peacefully for extended periods of time. Natural selection, as described by Darwin, operates over time and successive generations. Organisms exhibiting variations that show greater superior adaptability to the specific environment will have a greater propensity for survival and reproduction, consequently ensuring their survival over time. It is so common to see the misleading image of different species or groups, with different variations, 'fighting' for survival, as if it were an open fight to kill or be killed, that we consider it necessary to emphasise this aspect of natural selection.

Likewise, if we were to attempt, as several authors have previously endeavoured to do, to employ the notion of 'natural selection' for the analysis of human behaviour, habits, rules or institutions, we could begin to advance some reflections. This approach would demonstrate that it is not unusual to find a wide range of social behaviours which, although sometimes similar, exhibit numerous 'variations' in different groups (even within each social group). This could assist in elucidating the reasons why certain variations are more resilient in certain contexts (i.e. physical and cultural) than in others, and why specific institutional arrangements appear to demonstrate greater stability than others.

Finally, a remark on the "unit of evolution"is in order. In Darwin's work, the individual—or even groups—is presented as the unit of evolution. In the next section, it will be shown how modern biology places the gene as the ultimate unit of evolution. This paradigm shift in perspective has profound implications for the conceptualisation of the 'protagonists' of the evolutionary process, effectively displacing the individual from a central role in the narrative. Similarly, the application of these concepts to the realm of cultural evolution gives rise to the question of what constitutes the ultimate unit of evolution at this level. As will be explored in this study, there are divergent theoretical propositions in this regard (for instance, Dawkins' 'memes' as a unit of cultural evolution). However, the question remains unresolved and will be a crucial element to be examined in our theoretical proposal.

On the other hand, we consider it essential to include here two notions widely used, or even assumed, by many current evolutionary theories. These notions are also relevant to the debate on the importance of genetic inheritance and cultural inheritance in shaping the profile of behaviours and institutions, the traditional 'nature/nurture' or 'nature and culture' discussion. These are the concepts of genotype and phenotype (we consider here Taylor & Lewontin, 2017).

The concept of **genotype** generally refers to the genetic content (specific genome) of an organism. This genetic content is found in the DNA and is inherited from the parents. Therefore, when we refer to the genotype of an individual, we are indicating the class to which it belongs with reference to its specific physical matter. In the context of this genotype in relation to a specific environment, the phenotype emerges.

In this context, the term **phenotype** refers to the traits, appearance or behaviours of an organism or individual. In this sense, it is defined as "the class to which this organism belongs as determined by the description of the physical and behavioural characteristics of the organism, e.g. its size or shape, its metabolic activities and its pattern of movement" (Taylor & Lewontin, 2017).

In order to determine an individual's genotype, we examine their DNA; to identify their phenotype, we observe their external manifestations. Additionally, genotype and phenotype are not directly correlated. It should be noted that the manifestation of a phenotype is also contingent on environmental conditions. Consequently, a genome may exhibit a specific phenotype in a particular environment but not in other environments. Conversely, the same phenotype may be attributable to different genotypes.

This distinction is made between the particular 'genetic inheritance' that an organism (even a human organism) may possess, such as an inclination to suffer from a certain disease or a specific natural talent, and how these traits develop in a specific physical and cultural environment. Therefore, the specific product of the relationship between that genotype and the particular environment is known as the phenotype. As we continue with the example, we have to consider whether the disease will manifest itself, or whether the natural talent will develop or remain latent.

4.3.2 The Selfish Gene

As previously mentioned, Richard Dawkins published the first edition of "The Selfish Gene"in 1976 (a second, enlarged edition was published in 1989), in which he synthesised the findings of evolutionary biology up to that time. In this section, we aim to present the main lines of his theory, which will allow us to understand not only his contributions, but also the foundations of those theories based on evolutionary biology that explain behaviour and social regularities and even those that, using the vocabulary of biology, offer explanations from cultural evolutionism.

A. The first question Dawkins asks himself is: Why are there people? (Dawkins, 1989 Ch 1, p.1) He goes on to reflect that intelligent life on the planet has reached an age where, for the first time, it is working out the reason for its own existence. He also contends that it was Darwin who first proposed a coherent and sustainable theory of why we exist. It is at this point that we observe a confrontation between Dawkins and the philosophy and humanities of his era, as we will subsequently see in other theories, such as evolutionary psychology. Dawkins, thus, argues that these disciplines were still being studied (in 1976/1989) as if Darwin had never existed. In other words, philosophy and the humanities have historically approached their subject matter as if humans were not part of the evolutionary process, as if biological explanations did not apply to us and so on.

In this sense, Dawkins sets out to examine the biology of selfishness and altruism in this work. However, it is not the individuals that are of interest here, but rather the genes, since, as previously mentioned, they are the leading actors in the process of biological evolution that is explained by the author. Dawkins highlights that the fundamental trait of genes is their rude self-interest. And that this tendency towards selfishness in our genes could lead to selfishness at an individual level, but this is not always the case. There exist specific circumstances under which the gene may promote a limited form of altruism at the level of individual behaviour, in order to achieve its objectives.

It is now worth introducing some thoughts on Dawkins' proposal (Dawkins, 1989, pp. 2-3). Firstly, this author does not pretend to present a morality based on evolution, but to show how things have evolved. He also argues that "(...) it is a fallacy -incidentally a very common one- to suppose that genetically inherited traits are fixed and unmodifiable". In his opinion, education has the capacity to teach us generosity and altruism (as we shall see, he propounds a theory of cultural evolution that runs parallel to biological evolution).

On the other hand, he clearly does not want to take a firm position on the nature/nurture debate, i.e. on whether it is nature or culture that ultimately determines the behavioural profile of 'human' individuals. In this sense, he even advances the idea that genes appear, in many cases, to be irrelevant in determining modern human behaviour. Humans would be, in this respect, an exception to the rest of the animals, and Dawkins considers that it is interesting to understand the rule to which we are the exception, if that is the case. Moreover, he doesn't pretend to present a detailed description of human behaviour or of a particular animal species.

B. Later, he introduces a series of definitions that will allow us to understand his description of biological evolution These definitions are behavioural and non-subjective; they do not consider the motives of individuals carrying out an act, but only observe its effects.

He therefore proposes that an entity is **altruistic** when it behaves in a way that increases the welfare of another entity at its own expense. **Selfish behaviour,** then, has the exact opposite effect. An entity's **well-being** translates to its chances of survival, even if the effect on its actual chances of life or death are negligible. Taking all these notions into account, he outlines what he considers to be the **fundamental law: 'the selfishness of the gene'.** This law explains both altruism and individual selfishness.

He also introduces what he considers to be a 'false step' in evolutionary explanations, namely the deduction that 'perpetuation of the species' is the function of reproduction, when in fact it is a consequence of it.

C. Dawkins then asks himself If **natural selection** occurs—that is, if Darwin's theory of survival of the fittest is true—**at what level does it occur?** At the level of the individual? Or the race? Or the species? Dawkins answers without hesitation: at the level of the genes. In other words, it is the genes that are selected. The debate then moves from biology to the social realm. The idea of 'group selection' seems to align with our moral and political ideals, such as the belief that members of one's own species deserve special moral consideration. It is also noted that in-group altruism occurs alongside inter-group selfishness. So, at what level is group selection important: within species, between species, between genus, between class…? Dawkins concludes that the best way to study evolution is in terms of **selection occurring at the lowest possible level, and that the fundamental units of selection and measurement are genes.**

Now, in the process **of gene selection, the 'survival of the fittest' translates into the survival of the most stable** (Dawkins, 1989, p. 12). In this sense, a stable thing is a collection of atoms that is either sufficiently permanent or sufficiently common to deserve a name. When atoms meet, they can form molecules through chemical reactions. These molecules can be more or less stable and can be very large (e.g. diamond). The earliest form of natural selection was simply the selection of stable forms and the rejection of unstable ones.

D. The origin of life Dawkins believes that the existence of entities as complex as humans cannot be explained by the same principle of selection as the most stable forms. This, he says, is where Darwin's theory comes to the rescue. This is where the story of the origin of life begins: at the origin, there is a group of raw chemical materials (water, carbon dioxide, methane, etc.) and a source of energy (e.g. ultraviolet light). These produce a faint brown soup containing a large number of more complex molecules than were originally present, known as the 'primordial soup'.

E. The replicator and evolution (Dawkins, 1989, p. 15) Here the notion of the 'replicator' begins to play a major role. This is a molecule that may have formed by accident and possesses the ability to create copies of itself. This molecule may not be the most complex or largest, but it has this ability to act as a 'template' or 'mould'. An important property of any copying process is that it is not perfect. Errors occur, and when it comes to copies of copies, the errors accumulate and become significant. Even the erratic copying of biological replicators can represent an improvement, and the fact that some mistakes do happen is essential to the progressive evolution of life. According to Dawkins, the strength of replicators thus depends on three factors: a) longevity, b) fecundity and c) accuracy.

Evolution is 'blind'; there is nothing that wants to 'evolve'. It happens in spite of the replicator's efforts to prevent it. At the time of the 'primordial soup', there was competition between replicators, and as the soup could not support an infinite number of replicator molecules, they fought for survival amongst many varieties. Thus, those forms of copying that result in greater stability, or reduce the stability of rivals, survive. Dawkins' explanation is that there is a process of cumulative improvement, with stability increasing in a more elaborate and efficient way.

F. Survival machines In order to ensure their continued existence, the replicators began building containers, and only those that built survival machines survived. Through a cumulative and progressive process, they built larger and more complex colonies—giant robots—isolated from the outside world, communicating with them by tortuous indirect routes, manipulating them by remote control. And Dawkins says: "They are in you and in me; they created us, body and mind; and their preservation is the ultimate rationale for our existence. They have come a long way, those replicators. Now they go by the name of genes, and we are their survival machines" (Dawkins, 1989, p.20).

G. Cultural Evolution Dawkins (1989, pp. 189-190) argues that our species is unique because it possesses culture. He also claims that cultural transmission is analogous to genetic transmission in that it can give rise to a form of evolution, citing language, fashion and food as examples of 'cultural mutations'.

At this point, Dawkins distances himself from biologicist explanations of culture, arguing that Darwinism is too broad to be confined solely to the limited context of the gene (Dawkins, 1989, p. 191). To understand the evolution of modern humans, he argues, we must discard genes as the sole basis for our ideas about evolution, and consider the new 'primordial soup' to be the soup of human culture. Here, he introduces the notion of 'memes', which he identifies as the ultimate unit of cultural evolution. In the 'soup' of human culture, 'memes' are the replicators. Examples of memes include ideas, songs, fashionable clothes and catchphrases. Memes spread by jumping from brain to brain in a process that, broadly speaking, can be called 'imitation'.

According to Dawkins, memes should be viewed as living structures (Dawkins, 1989, p.192). "When you plant a fertile meme in my mind you literally parasitize my brain, turning it into a vehicle for the meme's propagation in just the way that a virus may parasitize the genetic mechanism of a host cell".

H. The theory of memes Some memes that are more successful than others in the 'meme pool' are analogous to natural selection. In the case of memes, it is not so much their longevity that counts, but their fecundity. Unlike genes, memes are not high-precision or high-fidelity replicators, and their transmission may be subject to continuous mutation and mixing. This is evident in the transmission of scientific ideas, for example.

It posits that the complexity of certain cultural productions, such as a symphony, is the result of a combination of memes. It also postulates the notion of the 'idea-meme' which is an entity that is capable of being transmitted from one brain to another. For example, in relation to a theory, the 'idea-meme' would be the essential basis of the shared concept held by all brains that grasp the theory. The differences in how people represent the theory are not part of the meme itself.

The 'computers' in which memes live are human brains, with time being a more significant limiting factor than storage capacity (we cannot do more than a few things at a time). Furthermore, memes can be organised and associated into stable, co-adapted sets that support each other. Dawkins uses the organised church as one of his favourite examples here, where memes of architecture, ritual, music, art, etc., are combined. He also conjectures that co-adapted meme complexes evolve in the same way as co-adapted gene complexes. Selection would favour those memes that exploit the cultural environment to their own advantage. This cultural environment consists of other memes that are also subject to selection. This 'meme pool', then, comes to have the attributes of an evolutionary stable set, which new memes find difficult to invade.

I. Genes and Memes Finally, Dawkins argues that, just as genes and memes can be mutually reinforcing, they can also be in opposition. Neither genes nor memes have foresight; they are both blind replicators. Indeed, memes can even outlive genes. In this sense, a philosophical or artistic work can survive much longer than its author's genetic information through the generations.

Dawkins concludes that, although we are gene machines and are cultured as meme machines, we have the power to turn against our creators. In his view, this is a unique human ability: the capacity to consciously prevent and 'rebel against the tyranny of the selfish replicators' (Dawkins, 1989, p. 201).

4.4 Hume's Revival

It is relevant here to acknowledge a phenomenon that has occurred alongside the entire process of the 'biological turn' we are analysing, which consists in the reconsideration and revaluation of David Hume′s work. His naturalistic philosophical perspective is now widely adopted, and he is recognised as one of the most important figures in the history of philosophy in this line of thinking. This has sparked several debates and analyses that we will only briefly touch upon here, but which help us to better understand the place of the ideas of the Scottish Enlightenment in contemporary philosophy and the pivotal role of the evolutionary view in many philosophical and social-scientific disciplines today.

On the one hand, the influence of David Hume's work, and that of the Scottish Enlightenment authors in general, on Charles Darwin's work is discussed in various forums and specialised literature. Many contemporary authors, who apply evolutionary ideas to social phenomena, refer to Darwin's theory of natural selection that we have already analysed in this chapter. They find that there was already a precedent for applying the evolutionary view to social phenomena in general, and to political, legal and moral institutions in particular, which can be found in authors such as Hume, Smith and Ferguson. As Hayek referred to it in his work, they discovered 'pre-Darwinian' evolutionism and began exploring its influence on Darwin's work.

Some professors have tried to determine the extent to which Hume's works influenced Darwin's research. Some have even found a list of Hume's works that Darwin intended to read, or tried to identify which of Hume's—or even Smith's—works were on Darwin's desk at the time of his death.[1] Others discuss what Hume's influence is, not on Darwin, but on contemporary authors who are Darwin's followers, i.e. Dawkins.[2]

Regarding this discussion, we would like to bring up here a reference by Darwin to Hume in his "The Descent of Man" (Darwin, 2004, p. 132) where he deals with the subject of 'Man a social animal'. Darwin makes here a detailed disquisition on man's predisposition to sociability. At this point, he refers to what could be observed as 'evolutionary stages' of the individual's sociability, as he expands his social circle beyond his nuclear family. It is here that he begins his detailed analysis of the notion of 'sympathy', incorporating explicit quotations from Hume's *An Enquiry Concerning the Principles of Morals.*

On the other hand, Hume is today recognised as a precursor to many contemporary theoretical explorations. Given his vast oeuvre, some contemporary authors cite him for certain aspects of his work, such as those in the fields of psychology and neuroscience who refer to him as a 'connectionist', while others rely more on his moral and political philosophy, focusing on his evolutionary view of institutions or his ideas about 'reciprocal altruism'.

To illustrate and conclude this chapter, we can say that Hume is one of today's great inspirations for authors of evolutionary game theory, which we will explore in Chapter 6. In his work 'Natural Justice' (2005), Ken Binmore recounts his experiences in seeking support for his attempts to

[1] For an example of this see Prof. Mark Pallen's blog, where he also refers to the relationships Pinker finds http://roughguidetoevolution.blogspot.com.ar/2009/06/david-humes-influence-on-charles-darwin.html.

[2] In this regard, and just as an example of these debates, see: https://evolutionnews.org/2015/01/what_darwins_da/

propose an 'evolutionary' response to John Rawls's 'Theory of Justice'. After reading extensively about the history of philosophy, especially Kant and his disciples, he discovered Hume's work, particularly his concept of 'reciprocal altruism', which he considered to be the 'key' to solving the mystery of cooperation. Binmore (2005, p. 8) says: "The invisible hand can only be counted on to take a population to an efficient outcome of a game in the exceptional case when all of its equilibria happen to be efficient. Perfectly competitive markets are one such case, but markets didn't exist when our species separated itself from the other apes. So how did our unique style of cooperation evolve?" He continues: "Because relatives share genes, it is easy to explain the evolution of cooperation within the family. For example, any of my genes has half the chance of being present in the body of my sister. If I were genetically programmed to maximise the average number of copies of my genes that are transmitted to the next generation, I would therefore count each of my sister's children as being worth half of one of my own. This is presumably why some birds help bring up their nephews and nieces when their own chances of raising a family are not very promising."

Up to this point it would seem that Binmore supports the evolutionary theories with a biological foundation for social phenomena, such as sociobiology or, more recently, evolutionary psychology, which we will see in the next chapter. However, he introduces a twist to this approach, for which Hume's figure is fundamental. He says: "But human cooperation is more complex. The fierce loyalties that sometimes develop in street gangs or army platoons can perhaps be explained in terms of the collective serving as a surrogate family, but we often manage to cooperate very successfully with total strangers, or with people whom we actively dislike or despise. What is the secret of this seeming contradiction to the doctrine of the selfish gene? In 1976, Robert Trivers offered 'reciprocal altruism' as the solution to the mystery, but David Hume was already on the ball in 1739" (Binmore, 2005, pp.8-9).

Finally, he refers to a quotation from Hume that he will use to support the idea of reciprocal altruism. Hume explains: "I learn to do service the another, without bearing him any real kindness, because I foresee, that he will return my service in expectation of another of the same kind, and in order to maintain the same correspondence of good offices with me and others. And accordingly, after I have serv'd him and he is in possession of the advantage arising from my action, he is induc'd to perform his part, as foreseeing the consequences of his refusal." Binmore then presents a lengthy example involving vampire bats to illustrate this notion, considering it to provide the foundation for his elaboration of his theory of justice from a game-theoretic point of view. He even considers Hume to be the greatest philosopher in the history of thought. Many other game theorists, such as Skyrms and Alexander, cite Hume as the inspiration for their work. We will examine these ideas in more depth in the following chapters.

References

Binmore, K. (2005). *Natural justice*. Oxford University Press.
Darwin, Charles, (1998), The origin of the species, Wordsworth Editors. (Original work published 1859)
Darwin, Charles, (2004), The descent of man, Penguin Books. (Original work published 1871)
Dawkins, R. (1989). *The selfish gene*. Oxford University Press.
Hayek, F. A. (1967). *Studies in philosophy, politics and economics*. The University of Chicago Press.
Taylor, P., & Lewontin, R. (2017). The genotype/phenotype distinction. In E. N. Zalta (Ed.), *The stanford encyclopedia of philosophy* (Summer 2017 ed.). https://plato.stanford.edu/archives/sum2017/entries/genotype-phenotype/

5

The Biological View

5.1 The Biological Views of Rules and Institutions: Sociobiology and Its Derivations

As was mentioned in previous chapters, and in the light of the 'irruption' of the biological point of view in the study of social phenomena at the end of the twentieth century and the beginning of the twenty-first century, numerous theories have emerged that explain human behaviour and social regularities, including norms and institutions, as sophisticated strategies of adaptation or biological survival. In the light of the re-evaluation of the naturalistic view and evolutionary biology based on the gene, several explanations of the behaviour of individuals as 'human animals' have been put forward and tested.

In parallel with the work of authors such as Dawkins, and in intertwining with it, we observe a series of authors that begin to suggest that the tools used to study and understand animal behaviour, based on biological evolution, would also be useful for studying human behaviour. This has resulted in the formulation of numerous theories

E. M. Santanatoglia, *An Evolutionary Account of Law*, Palgrave Studies in Classical Liberalism, https://doi.org/10.1007/978-3-032-12162-2_5

within the domain of sociobiology, behavioural theories (behaviourists) and behavioural ecology.

This perspective finds historical precedents in the work of Piotr Kropotkin, who, in the late nineteenth century, writes "Mutual Aid: A Factor of Evolution" (Kropotkin, 1915), in which the author proposed cooperation as a motor of social cohesion and evolution. Kropotkin, a proponent of anarchist communism, seeks to propose an alternative model to Darwin's 'competitive' perspective on natural selection. It is important to note that the author incorporates cooperation as an evolutionary force, thereby paving the path for later disquisitions on the role of altruism and reciprocity in the survival capacity of groups.

In this line of thought, we find the work of E. O. Wilson, the 'father' of sociobiology, a term coined in his work "Sociobiology: The New Synthesis" (Wilson, 1975). This work marked the official birth of the discipline, with its intention to study the biological basis of social behaviour. This work and the subsequent theories based on it approach animal behaviour from its biological foundations and human behaviour as being a part of it. These attempts were heavily criticised for several reasons, including their extreme adaptationism, determinism and inability to account for the effects of culture and learning processes. We will address many of these criticisms below from Dupré, but it is worth mentioning this theory here since it has been the one that has promoted many current schools of thought.

Driscoll says: "The 'descendants' of sociobiology include human behavioural ecology, evolutionary psychology (Cosmides and Tooby, 1987) and more recently, dual inheritance theory (Boyd and Richerson, 1985; Cavalli-Sforza and Feldman, 1981). These projects as a group are now sometimes referred to as the 'evolutionary social sciences' (Smith et al., 2001, 1]. Over time the different theoretical views and choices of methodology have become entrenched in each project, increasing their disparity; the divisions also partly fall along disciplinary lines, with human behavioural ecologists tending to be anthropologists; evolutionary psychologists tending to be cognitive psychologists; and individuals working in dual inheritance theory tending to have some background in population biology modelling. All three evolutionary social sciences retain some of the features of the project that Wilson originally described in his book, however; in particular they retain its methodologically adaptationist approach. Of these three, it is human behavioural ecology that is most often called 'sociobiology' due to its focus on the evolution of behaviour (evolutionary psychology focuses on the evolution of psychological mechanisms or modules such as those for cheater detection; dual inheritance theory studies the cultural evolution of traits that are socially learned)" (Driscoll, 2022).

In this sense, and beyond the criticisms that Wilson's work and some of his followers have received, it is interesting to consider the contributions of this point of view to the understanding of human behaviour and institutions. These theories have retained a high level of philosophical interest since they argue for the existence of a 'human nature', or at least a set of distinctive features of human animals, which would allow us to understand their behaviour and social regularities. There is currently a very intense debate about the extent to which genetic inheritance and cultural evolution influence an individual's or group's behaviour. In addition, there is a strong debate within the field about the use of 'adaptationist' models, and a comparison of these with 'rational choice' views of agents. These explorations into the biological nature of human behaviour have also touched on the realm of moral and social norms, among others.

Driscoll (2022) reminds us: "As Wilson hoped, scientists working in disciplines which are the modern descendants of sociobiology have contributed to our understanding of the way that norms, including moral norms, might have become established in human evolution (…)". However, he clarifies that there is still no agreement on how the evolution of moral psychology should be understood, especially for the acquisition of norms.

In terms of legal normativity, it is of great interest to us to incorporate these approaches into the discussion and to evaluate the contributions of these schools to the understanding of the formation and internalisation of legal norms, as far as possible. For this reason, we will analyse here one of the schools of thought that has developed most in recent years and contributed much work to the study of norms and institutions from a biological perspective: evolutionary psychology. In this analysis, we will examine its fundamental concepts, notable contributions and significant criticisms.

5.2 Evolutionary Psychology

The evolutionary psychology school is represented by the work of Leda Cosmides and John Tooby, among others. Together with a group of interdisciplinary researchers, they founded the 'Center for Evolutionary Psychology' at the University of California, Santa Barbara. Their work covers a wide range of topics, including different aspects of human behaviour and institutions. Here, we will attempt to summarise the main postulates of this school and address some possible criticisms.

5.2.1 Basic Notions

As previously mentioned, evolutionary psychology (EP) is rooted in evolutionary biology, cognitive psychology and neuroscience. According to Dupré (2001), EP is a continuation of sociobiology, a theory that was unable to respond to significant criticism and subsequently retreated, later re-emerging as evolutionary psychology with fewer assumptions and renewed strength.

For Cosmides and Tooby, the primary focus of the enquiry in evolutionary psychology is "to discover and understand the design of the human mind" (Cosmides & Tooby, 1993, p.1). It is here that they present one of their most important and controversial hypotheses. They argue that the human mind is "a set of information-processing machines that were designed by natural selection to solve the adaptive problems faced by our hunter-gatherer ancestors" (Cosmides & Tooby, 1993, p.1). In other words, as we shall see, our brains are not born 'blank', but with a set of specific mechanisms that are designed to solve particular tasks and challenges—from recognising faces to selecting non-toxic foods.

For this task, EP challenges what Cosmides and Tooby refer to as the Standard Social Science Model (SSSM) (Cosmides & Tooby, 1993, pp.3–4). EP theorists observe that this standard model conceives of the human mind as a blank canvas on which the social world shapes and organises content and meaning. This is as if the architecture of the human mind has no particular structure and is unable to organise or influence the social world with characteristic meanings, but can be 'shaped' by the social world as it wishes. In other words, the SSSM describes the mind as a set of multi-purpose mechanisms without specific content, i.e. the mechanisms of 'imitation', 'learning', 'rationality', etc.

For Cosmides and Tooby, this SSSM would say something like "the contents of human minds are primarily (or entirely) free social constructions, and the social sciences are autonomous and disconnected from any evolutionary or psychological foundation" (Cosmides & Tooby, 1993, p.4). For EP theorists, this is, of course, a big mistake, since we are natural (as well as cultural) beings, born with many specific mechanisms worth studying. Therefore, they present an alternative to the standard social science view. To achieve this, they view psychology as a branch of biology which seeks to understand the nature of the mind, how it processes information, and how these information-processing mechanisms generate human behaviour.

In contrast, EP proposes a model of the mind comprising a number of developed regulatory circuits and reasoning systems that are specialised in specific functions and domains. These systems organise the way individuals interpret experiences and provide conceptual and motivational frameworks that enable humans to understand their own and others' actions and interactions (Cosmides & Tooby, p. 4). To this end, EP enunciates five principles derived from biology, which we will discuss below.

5.2.2 Evolutionary Psychology—The Five Principles

Here, we will summarise the five fundamental principles of evolutionary psychology that underpin all its claims and subsequent research. As we shall see, some of these principles are quite irrefutable, while others are highly controversial.

First: The brain is a physical system made of organic matter that functions like a computer. Its circuits are designed to generate behaviours appropriate to the environment's circumstances. In this case, cells—particularly neurons—are responsible for transmitting information. These neurons are interconnected, and these connections are studied as circuits. Some neurons are connected to sensory receptors, while others are connected to motor neurons. The latter, in turn, are connected to muscles, causing them to move. This movement is called behaviour. In summary, the first principle refers to the way our mind is designed to generate appropriate behaviour in response to information from the environment.

Second: Our neural circuits have been shaped by natural selection to solve the problems faced by our ancestors throughout our species′ evolutionary history. The authors consider the scope of the notion of appropriate behaviour, which is not specified by the environment. Natural selection then comes into play, shaping the complexly ordered machines that are our neural circuits. The authors observe that natural selection does not work for the good of the species,[1] **but rather consists of a process by which a phenotypic design feature causes itself to spread through the population.**

This is where EP introduces the idea that many of our neural circuits are the result of our ancestors' attempts to solve adaptive information-processing problems. These circuits include those that enable us to recognise faces, acquire language and interpret situations of danger.

Cosmides and Tooby make two points about these brain mechanisms that are worth bringing up:

First, they argue that acknowledging the brain's role in processing information has enabled cognitive scientists to solve the brain/mind problem. "For cognitive scientists, brain and mind are terms that refer to the same system, which can be described in two complementary ways—either in terms of its physical properties (the brain), or in terms of its information-processing operation (the mind). The physical organization of the brain evolved because that physical organization brought about certain information-processing relationships—ones that were adaptive" (Cosmides & Tooby, 1993, p 8).

The second point to note is that these circuits were designed to solve adaptive problems, rather than just any problems. But, **what constitutes an adaptive problem?** According to Cosmides and Tooby, adaptive problems have two defining characteristics: a) they appear repeatedly throughout the evolutionary history of the species and b) they affect the

[1] Idem 139, p. 5.

reproduction of individual organisms, no matter how indirect the causal chain or how small the effect on reproduction. This is because the driver of natural selection is not survival *per se*, but differential reproduction. In terms of natural selection, therefore, it is not only those best adapted to their environment who survive (survival *per se*) but those best adapted also leave more offspring on average (differential reproduction).

Of course, we face many adaptive problems today that our ancestors did not have to solve, and we no longer face others that they solved. However, according to Cosmides and Tooby (Cosmides & Tooby, 1993, p. 9), our ability to solve certain problems is a by-product of neural circuits created to solve adaptive problems. For instance, the neural circuitry that our ancestors developed to enable them to escape from a dangerous animal is what we use today to escape from a potentially dangerous moving vehicle.

Third: Consciousness is just the tip of the iceberg; most of what happens in our minds remains hidden from us. Consequently, our conscious experience can deceive us, giving the impression that our 'circuits' are simpler than they really are. Many of the problems we think are simple to solve are actually very difficult and require highly complex neural circuits.

We cannot be aware of our brain activity; we only notice the high-level results, which are the product of thousands of specialised mechanisms at work (Cosmides & Tooby, 1993, p.10). This is an important point for scholars of the human mind to bear in mind. When trying to understand how the mind works, we believe that our conscious experience of the world and of ourselves could lead us to interesting hypotheses. However, this conscious experience can mislead us into thinking that our neural circuits and activities are simple when, in fact, they depend on complex mechanisms.

Fourth: The different neural circuits in our brains are specialised in solving different adaptive problems. Our minds consist of a set of function-specific circuits, and it is rare for any one circuit to be able to solve more than one adaptive problem. This is because each mechanism is guided by different quality standards. For instance, the circuits responsible for selecting nutritious food and choosing a good partner are clearly based on different quality criteria (Cosmides & Tooby, 1993, p. 12).

These authors propose thinking of each of these specialised circuits as a mini-computer dedicated to solving a problem, and they refer to each of these mini-computers as a 'module'. The brain would then be a set of functionally integrated modules that produce behaviour.

Unlike traditional psychology, these modules evolve in response to their environment. Moreover, they contain information about properties that have recurred stably in this environment for thousands of years—since the time of our ancestors. In this way, these modules approach the problem to be solved with a great deal of prior knowledge, like an 'instruction manual' for that particular problem. Therefore, they are 'activated' in certain domains and not others, since different problems require different mechanisms. Thus, "a brain equipped with a multiplicity of specialized inference engines will be able to generate sophisticated behaviour that is sensitively tuned to its environment" (Cosmides & Tooby, 1993, p. 14)". Several studies now show that we possess distinct circuits for behaviours such as reasoning about objects, physical causality, other individuals' beliefs, numbers and so on.

In relation to the concept of brain modules, the EP authors consider the role of instinct in mental activity. They highlight that instincts were traditionally considered incompatible with learning or reasoning processes. However, the reasoning and learning circuits discussed by EP exhibit the following five characteristics: "(1) they are complexly structured for solving a specific type of adaptive problem, (2) they reliably develop in all normal human beings, (3) they develop without any conscious effort and in the absence of any formal instruction, (4) they are applied without any conscious awareness of their underlying logic, and (5) they are distinct from more general abilities to process information or behave intelligently". In conclusion, the reasoning and learning circuits analysed show that they have the characteristics of what we usually call instinct. Cosmides and Tooby argue that these circuits could also be called 'reasoning instincts' and 'learning instincts' (Cosmides & Tooby, 1993, pp. 14–15).

Fifth: Our modern skulls house a stone age mind. Evolutionary psychology considers that the processes through which natural selection designed the complex circuits of our brains took a very long time. Over the course of some ten million years, natural selection has shaped human brains, favouring the circuits best able to solve everyday adaptive problems. However, these were the adaptive problems of our ancestors, the hunters and gatherers. The ancestors whose brains were best at solving these problems left more offspring, and we are part of that offspring.

The EP authors argue that, because natural selection is a slow process, there have not been enough years or generations for the circuits in our brains to adapt well to the problems of life in post-industrial societies. They therefore argue that our skulls contain Stone Age minds, as our minds are well equipped to solve the adaptive problems faced by our hunter-gatherer ancestors.

In this sense, they propose the concept of an Environment of Evolutionary Adaptedness (EEA), which does not refer to a specific time or place, but rather to a statistical composite of the natural selection pressures that led to the development of a particular adaptation. Consequently, the EEA of one adaptation may differ from that of another. This is why EP considers that cognitive mechanisms, which have solved adaptive problems well in the past, will not necessarily generate adaptive behaviours in the present.

Finally, EP considers the five principles explained here to be tools that allow us to think about psychology, which can be applied to any topic—for example, cooperation, rationality, sexuality and mental illness. In the face of any issue related to human behaviour, they propose asking these questions: a) where in the brain are the relevant circuits and how, physically, do they work?, b) what kind of information is being processed by these circuits?, c) what information-processing programmes do these circuits embody?, d) what were these circuits designed to accomplish (in a hunter-gatherer context)? (Cosmides & Tooby,1993, p. 17).

5.2.3 Theoretical Foundations of Evolutionary Psychology

Now that we have a clear understanding of the key concepts proposed by EP, we will consider its stance on some of the theoretical challenges we have posed. In other words, we will examine the theoretical foundations of the EP, as set out in the work of Cosmides and Tooby in particular.

Understanding their positions on current debates will also help us to grasp the potential theoretical implications of applying this theory to the study of behaviour and institutions.

1. Adaptive logic vs. phylogenetic view We have already seen, through Darwin and Dawkins, the main notions of biological evolution and natural selection, which will allow us to understand the discussion presented here. Evolutionary psychology adopts the so-called *adaptationist logic* as opposed to the phylogenetic view of Darwin's theory. How do these positions differ?

The aim of Darwin's theory is to explain phylogenetic design (Cosmides & Tooby, 1993, p. 17). To this end, he posits two principles to explain the characteristics of animals (including humans): a) common descent and b) adaptation driven by natural selection. Given that we are all related, as are species, we might expect to find similarities between humans and our closest primate relatives. Thus, the phylogenetic view looks for continuities in the inheritance of homologous characteristics from common ancestors between animals and humans. In contrast, EP's adaptive view seeks those mental abilities unique to a species, which are differentiated by fields. Thus, EP applies adaptive logic to the architecture of the human mind.

2. How structure reflects function EP brings together several complementary and mutually compatible levels of explanation. The brain's function is to generate behaviour in response to information received from the organism's environment. Therefore, it is an information-processing device. Neuroscience studies the physical structure of these devices. Cognitive psychology, on the other hand, studies the information-processing programmes within that structure. However, there is another level of explanation: the functional level.

In evolved systems, form follows function. In other words, the physical structure is such because it 'embodies' a set of programmes. These programmes exist because they solved a particular adaptive problem in the past. This functional level of explanation is therefore essential to understanding how natural selection has designed organisms. As we have already seen, EP sees the phenotypic structure of organisms as a collection of micro-machines that perform specific functions (e.g. eyes).

To distinguish between these levels of explanation and to understand causal relationships, biologists developed a theoretical vocabulary in which structure and function are distinguished (Cosmides & Tooby, 1993, p. 20). In evolutionary biology, explanations that appeal to the structure of a device are called '*proximate*' explanations. In the field of psychology, these 'proximate explanations' will be oriented towards the most immediate causes of behaviour, such as genetic, biochemical, physiological, cognitive and social. Explanations that point to the functional aspects of a device are called 'ultimate' or 'distal" explanations because they refer to the causes of behaviour that have operated over evolutionary time (set out in the fifth principle).

Understanding adaptive function is fundamental for understanding nature. However, EP distinguishes between three types of phenotype feature: a) adaptations, b) by-products and c) 'noise' (Cosmides & Tooby, 1993, p. 19). The former, as we have already explained, are those mechanisms that have been selected because they solved an adaptive problem in the past. The second, the by-products, are present because they were causally related to the adaptations. Finally, 'noise' incorporates the random or chance element into evolution. Therefore, not all aspects of organisms can be explained in functional terms or in terms of adaptive behaviour. Moreover, not every evolved mechanism is adaptive to the current environment, and in some cases, they were selected for functions other than those for which they are used today.

3. Evidence provided by design Adaptive mechanisms have complex functional designs. One can identify a phenotype as an adaptation if: a) its design has certain features that are complexly specialised to solve a specific adaptive problem, b) these phenotypic properties are unlikely to have arisen by chance alone, and c) these properties are not better explained by the hypothesis that they are by-products of another mechanism designed to solve a different adaptive problem. On this point, Cosmides and Tooby quote Williams as saying that "finding that an architectural element solves an adaptive problem with 'reliability, efficiency, and economy', is *prima facie* evidence that one has located an adaptation" (Cosmides & Tooby, 1993, p. 20). EP adopts this view of 'design evidence' to explain not only why a mechanism exists, but also to discover new mechanisms. EP also uses adaptive function theory heuristically, as a guide to phenotypic design research.

4. Nature vs. culture In the adaptationist perspective, the EP authors find the basis for their position on the '*nature/nurture*' debate (Cosmides & Tooby, 1993, pp. 21–24). They consider that this debate is poorly formulated and does not address to the real problem they have raised.

Basically, EP considers that the human species, like any other species in nature, has developed a typical architecture. This is true not only for the heart or the digestive system, but also for cognitive programmes. PE departs from the evolved architecture of the human species, considering it to be typical and universal to the species and its mechanisms. It considers this cognitive architecture to be the joint product of beings and environment, without assuming that genes or 'innate factors' play a more important role than the environment or 'learned factors', and rejects these dichotomies.

In this sense, they also explicitly distinguished themselves from other disciplines such as *behaviour genetics*. While the latter is concerned with the extent to which differences between individuals in a given environment may be due to differences in their genes, EP is interested in studying individual differences only to the extent that they are manifestations of an underlying architecture shared by all humans. In conclusion, EP considers an individual's phenotype to be the result of the interaction between genes and environment (Cosmides & Tooby, 1993, p. 23). They claim that genes are simply regulatory elements, molecules that transform the surrounding environment within an organism. However, no aspect of the phenotype can be unaffected by environmental influences.

There are many other debates in which these authors elaborate further and clarify their position, but we believe that we have introduced the most significant elements of this theory. We will now address some of the objections to it, particularly those of John Dupré. We will then examine some of his responses and consider the specific application of evolutionary psychology to the field of law.

5.3 John Dupré: Critiques to Evolutionary Psychology and His Developmental Systems Theory

In his book "Human Nature and the Limits of Science" (2001), John Dupré devotes several chapters to analysing the main proposals of evolutionary psychology (EP), offering a synthesis of the EP argument and a number of objections. As mentioned previously in Chapter 4, Dupré believes that EP attempts to differentiate itself from sociobiology as presented by E.O. Wilson. In his view, EP emerges in the light of the criticisms that its predecessor had received, the two most important being: a) that sociobiology was a totally *a priori* project and b) its extremely adaptationist position. Dupré explains that, for sociobiology, any characteristic of an organism must be an adaptation, i.e. there must be a function that explains the selection of that characteristic in the evolutionary process (Wilson cited by Dupré, 2001, p. 19).

The criticism of this idea is that, in an object as functionally integrated as an organism, the development of a particular characteristic is massively constrained by its overall structure and functioning. In this sense, these structural constraints may be much more important than natural selection′s optimising tendencies in explaining an organism's final structure. Thus, we note that, although EP also adopts the adaptationist view, it does not consider every characteristic of an organism to be an adaptation and it also takes into account the functional aspects of the organism and its component mechanisms, thus addressing the objections that had been raised against sociobiology.

For Dupré, EP—introduced in the mid-1980s—attempts to distinguish itself from sociobiology by paying closer attention to empirical data on human behaviour, and by offering a clearer overview of all the elements involved in the evolution of behaviour. Dupré also presents his own synthesis of the key proposals of EP. He believes that the key to understanding human behaviour lies in understanding the structure of the human brain. This can be achieved by considering the genes or genetic programmes that guide brain development. The concept of humans possessing specific genetic programmes must be viewed in the context of evolution through natural selection.

Dupré then reminds us that the EP introduces the concept of an environment of evolutionary adaptation (EEA). This is based on the idea that recent history is too short to produce significant changes in the human genome. Therefore, to understand genes, we must trace the evolutionary history of human genetic traits, particularly the characteristic hypertrophied brain cortex that distinguishes us from nearby species (Dupré, 2001, p. 21). The time period referred to in EP is the millions of years preceding recorded human history, i.e. the Stone Age or the Pleistocene epoch.

Dupré identifies several objections to the EP proposal. Some of these objections will be discussed here.

5.3.1 The Problem of Evidence

Dupré's first criticism appears in relation to the type of evidence that evolutionary psychology offers to support its hypotheses. He takes as an example the 'modules' that EP claims the human brain possesses through natural selection, and that were originally adopted to solve specific adaptive problems in the EEA. Dupré notes that the existence of these modules does not necessarily imply that organisms possessing them will produce the specific behaviour for which these mechanisms are designed. This is because there are specific circumstances that can affect the behaviour produced by these modules or because the modules interact with each other, suppressing certain outcomes (Dupré, 2001, p. 22). The EP argument does not require the observation of any specific behaviour and, therefore, Dupré considers that it is unclear what might actually constitute evidence in favour of or against those modules.

From the point of view of the philosophy of science, we could argue that Dupré criticises EP for failing to provide any instance or counterexample that could potentially falsify his theory. While we consider this criticism important as it touches on the theory's empirical content, it should be noted that it could be applied to most evolutionary concepts that use natural selection to explain the development of an organism's mechanisms while also accepting an environmental influence. If behaviour or any other phenotypic trait is not predictable as a result of the interaction between cognitive mechanisms and the environment, then we cannot provide a counterexample that could serve as a 'potential falsifier' of our theory.

In this case, we believe there is an answer to Dupré's objection. Many of the 'predictions' proposed by these authors do not refer to specific cases, but rather to trends in human behaviour in certain situations. In other words, they consider which psychological mechanisms come into play and how they function in most cases when faced with certain problems or evolutionary or adaptive pressures. Following this line of thought, we propose that these are 'class or pattern' predictions, similar to the pattern predictions proposed by Hayek, rather than 'case' predictions, i.e. how a specific agent will behave in a given situation.

On the other hand, when confronted with certain counterexamples, pattern predictions may well be falsified. In other words, if a theory about how a mechanism would work in a certain 'type of case' cannot explain a significant number of cases, it will likely be revised or another mechanism will be proposed to explain that regularity. We will return to this point in the next section when discussing the application of Evolutionary Psychology to Law. However, in principle, we believe that we can address Dupré's objection.

5.3.2 How Much Does the Evolutionary View Explain?

Of course, Dupré agrees with EP that everything we do is something for which we have evolved a capacity, but he notes that the existence of such a capacity does not necessarily provide information about when, or even if, it will be exercised. In other words, the fact that a certain type of human behaviour has an evolutionary explanation does not provide a complete explanation of why people act as they do (Dupré, 2001, pp. 23–25).

Dupré illustrates this point with an interesting example (Dupré, 2001, p. 23).· Imagine a party or cocktail party observed, on one hand, by an alien with an evolutionary perspective similar to EP's and, on the other hand, by a social scientist, a figure much criticised by EP (remember the criticisms of the standard social science model). If someone were to ask them why these people were there, the alien, armed with insights into the evolutionary development of the human species, could respond by saying that they were all there to consume ethanol, and that they would eventually all go home and metabolise it to varying degrees of success. Dupré acknowledges that this answer is accurate and that explanations based on the evolution of capacities are generally part of a comprehensive explanation of the phenomena in question. However, he believes that this is not the most illuminating explanation. A much more enlightening explanation would be the information provided by the social scientist that all these people are members of a Bridge Club and that this is their Annual General Meeting.

What Dupré is suggesting is that the social scientist could provide some insight into the meaning of these actions independently of the evolutionary development of all the capacities that allow us to perform them. Following this line of thought, from a social science point of view, it is not the same as people who are drinking alcohol in a certain place or people who are attending a wedding party, a wake, the club's annual party or the celebrations of a political party's victory in an election.

In relation to this point, although the objection seems pertinent and worthy of analysis, it should be clarified that the authors of various works and applications of evolutionary psychology to different fields make use of other 'complementary' theories to provide more complete explanations. In many cases, the authors of EP propose combinations involving evolutionary game theory, co-evolutionism and other schools to address the aspects that their theory does not seem to cover.

5.3.3 Atavism

Dupré also devotes several pages to a critique of the atavism proposed by evolutionary psychology (Dupré, 2001, pp-25-31). That is, the idea—developed in the fifth principle of EP, discussed above—that the mechanisms for acquiring adaptations through natural selection emerge via the gradual accumulation of favourable genes, resulting in the complex biological structure observed today. Humans developed in an environment that remained stable for over a million years, and our brains are cognitively adapted to this environment—the Stone Age.

Dupré raises several objections to this argument:

(a) On the one hand, he criticises the centrality of genes in these evolutionary and developmental explanations. He also considers that a proper appreciation of the role of genes in biology does not require the atavistic view of human cognitive adaptation that is central to the EP argument.
(b) On the other hand, Dupré explains that there are two notions of 'evolution' and that EP adopts one of these views while he adopts the second. The biological conception of evolution, taken by EP, understands evolution to be "change over time in the frequency of genes in a population" (Dupré, 2001, p. 26). Dupré proposes another notion, which understands evolution as "any change over time in the distribution of properties across a population". This leads us to assess how much of this evolution actually consists of the natural selection of genes. According to his own theory, the 'Developmental systems theory', Dupré proposes that in the development of an organism, genes are only one of the resources to be analysed; others include chemicals in the maternal cells, environmental resources and parental behavioural patterns.

Dupré believes that the alternative to evolutionary psychology (EP) is no longer the 'standard social science model' (SSSM), or the idea of the brain as a 'blank slate' with infinite plasticity in response to environmental stimuli, both of which were criticised by EP. Today, other theories exist, such as his 'Developmental Systems Theory', which proposes the idea of a brain comprised of a variety of more or less stable and reliable resources, including those reproduced by human cultures. This view allows for the possibility that the human brain evolves at the rate of cultural change rather than gene accumulation, rendering the atavism proposed by EP optional.

This is one of the most controversial points in EP, and we consider Dupré's critique to be relevant in this regard. As we will see in the following chapters, several evolutionary theories propose a central role for cultural evolution in analysing the brain, the mind, its capacities and mechanisms, and consequently, human behaviour. While Dupré strongly advocates his own model as a replacement for EP, we will also consider the interesting model of interaction and inter-determination between biological and cultural evolutionary processes proposed by co-evolutionism.

5.3.4 Do Brains Cause Behaviour?

Here, Dupré raises the issue of the distinction between the brain and the mind. According to *'folk psychology'*, beliefs and desires are identified with physical states of the brain, which are considered to be the real causes of bodily movements that constitute actions to be explained. But is this translation between the two so straightforward? He also expresses his criticism of a potential reductionism on the part of EP in this way.

According to Dupré, there are two ways in which we can distinguish the mind from the brain (Dupré, 2001,p. 33). Firstly, it is impossible to characterise the human mind without appealing to language. Secondly, language is not a property of an individual, but of a linguistic community. Based on these reasons, Dupré presents several arguments to highlight the dependence of the mind on social factors.

Among these arguments are:

(a) The idea that many features of the human mind do not exist without language; for example, certain types of thought, ranging from metaphysics to quantum physics;
(b) Humans are self-aware and represent themselves and their environment, and much of this representation is symbolic and linguistic. Therefore, self-consciousness is possible only for beings embedded in a linguistic community.
(c) Symbolic representation depends on language.

The notion of meaning, understood in Wittgenstein's terms as the norms in a community, is only possible for those imbued with a linguistic community.

In general, Dupré considers the ability of humans to function in modern societies to be more a problem of socially provided resources than of basic physical capacities. He concludes that human minds must be considered ontologically dependent on their social contexts (Dupré, 2001, p. 33). If we think of ourselves as possessing a set of basic capacities, this provides an inadequate explanation of what people can do. Physical abilities must be understood in relation to the social context that enables certain types of thinking.

5.3.5 Nature and Culture

Finally, Dupré highlights an important distinction between Wilson‘s position, as cited by the EP authors, and evolutionary psychology. While Wilson discussed genes responsible for specific behaviours, EP focuses on the genetic determination of mental mechanisms.

Dupré also criticises the notion of 'cultural universals' proposed by evolutionary psychology. Just as there are regularities in the physiological and psychological aspects of human architecture, there are also regularities in human life in different cultures. EP refers to these regularities as 'cultural universals', and examples include the fact that humans have a typical physical form, reproduce through sex and chains of descent, and express fear and try to avoid danger. However, Dupré considers these 'cultural universals' to be mostly mere banalities, with a few 'Trojan horses' among them.

This relates to EP's idea of 'mental modules‘. A large number of examples of these modules are also given: a module for recognising faces, a module for spatial relations, a module for tool use, a module for social exchange, a module for sexual attraction, a module for semantic inference, a module for friendship and so on. However, Dupré (2001, p. 41) considers that, while we have reasons to believe that innate structures in the brain are important for some of these tasks, it is wild speculation with regard to others (e.g. the effort allocation module).

With respect to cultural variability, Dupré (2001, pp. 41–42) writes that some EP authors believe that cultural variability exists, but that its logic cannot be understood until the general, transcultural human nature underlying it has been elucidated. For Dupré, the problem is that cultural variability makes it difficult or impossible to provide evidence for the 'mental modules'proposed by EP.

Once we move away from the theoretical discussion, the two most common lines of enquiry within EP are: a) reflecting on the problem in terms of our Pleistocene ancestors or b) statistically examining current human behaviour. However, if one accepts the EP idea that the existence of certain modules does not imply universal production of a specific type of behaviour designed by those modules, it is unclear how a significant preponderance of a certain behaviour according to the module's supposed design could provide consistent evidence for the existence of such modules.

As we have already referred to in a previous section, EP authors make conceptual connections with other theories—such as evolutionary game theory or experimental economics—to support their views and, consequently, do not rely only on their own evidence to support the existence of certain modules.

5.4 Evolutionary Psychology Applied to law

5.4.1 Introduction

What might be the contributions of evolutionary psychology to the understanding of law? Which specific notions could we apply to the behaviour of agents in the legal order? Here, we will consider a paper by Cosmides and Tooby, titled 'Evolutionary Psychology, Moral Heuristics, and the Law' (2006), in which they make specific reference to the application of evolutionary psychology to law.

In this work, the leading figures in evolutionary psychology review some of the fundamental concepts that they will apply to the analysis of law. First, they remind us that we live in a modern world of nation-states populated by millions of strangers, who have little in common with the social world in which humans evolved. This was basically a world of small bands of people with a few dozen friends, relatives and competitors. Evolution equipped the minds of individuals with certain heuristics that allowed them to negotiate in that 'intimate' social world. These were essentially a number of decision rules that generated intuitions about fairness, disapproval, approval, right and wrong.

Thus, these authors warn us that each heuristic was designed by natural selection to operate in a different ancestral social situation. Each heuristic is triggered by signals that indicated the specific situation occurring in the ancestral past. They add that "Political debate in the present is often a struggle over how to characterize events in terms of these ancestral situation-types, because alternative framings trigger different evolved moral heuristics" (Cosmides & Tooby, 2006, p. 181).

Cosmides and Tooby consider that, to grasp what moral intuitions are 'triggered' among lawmakers—including in this category all those involved in the formulation of law, such as legislators, policy analysts and lobbyists as well as among judges, juries, lawyers, jurists and voters, among others—one would need to understand several points: "Which situational cues activate a given program? What inferences, emotions, and motivations will that program produce? Is the program designed to trigger responses that are contingent on the behaviour of others? Most importantly, will the intuition about right and wrong it generates in the minds of lawmakers and citizens lead them to propose a policy that will have the consequences they are hoping for? In many cases, we suggest, the answer will be 'no'" (Cosmides & Tooby, 2006, p. 188).

5.4.2 Decision-Making Rules Among Hunter-Gatherers

Working with a concrete case, they then refer to the decision rules that govern sharing. Firstly, they examine the way sharing schemes took place in the hunter-gatherer sphere. Contrary to the idea that all resources were shared indiscriminately in that society, they present numerous studies and evidence showing that 'sharing' among hunter-gatherers was more varied and specific to the type of relationship, as well as more nuanced, than is traditionally presented.[2] They then argue that studies of evolutionary analysis from the last forty years show that selection would not favour the development of a single decision rule for sharing. "Different kinds of sharing rules carry selective advantages in different situations, and there is evidence that the human mind indeed contains several different programs that regulate sharing. Each produces different moral intuitions about when to provide help and to whom, and each is activated by different situational cues. Thus, based on limited information, different decision rules for sharing are activated: different moral heuristics" (Cosmides & Tooby, 2006, p. 189).

They introduce an interesting example here. They comment that the sharing rules in this group of hunter-gatherers differ greatly depending on whether they apply to meat or plants. The triggering of such different sharing rules is not influenced by the type of food itself, but by the following variable: whether variations in resource acquisition are high and mainly due to luck, or low and mainly due to effort. Thus, the contribution of chance versus effort differs depending on the resource to be shared, with important implications for the evolution of distribution rules. For some resources, such as collected food, variations in foraging success are low and, when they do exist, are more due to effort or skill than luck. Therefore, when the majority have access to the same goods, indiscriminate sharing is not beneficial but can be costly. When chance has little bearing on the final outcome, sharing food with the whole group would simply redistribute food from those who expend more effort or are more skilled to those who expend less effort or have less skill. Sharing under these circumstances offers few, if any, fitness benefits to those who have acquired more food (Cosmides & Tooby, 2006, p. 190).

In contrast, when it comes to resources such as meat or honey, where luck plays a significant role in varying foraging success, one individual may have something one day and nothing the next, and vice versa. Therefore, it would be much better for an individual to redistribute food from

[2] Specifically, they are dedicated to challenging the Marxist interpretation of history and its portrayal of hunter-gatherer societies. They present a substantial body of research demonstrating the various forms of organisation and resource allocation observed in different contexts (Cosmides & Tooby, 2006, pp. 188–189).

periods of feast to periods of famine. The authors explain that there are two ways to achieve this: through food storage or by pooling resources with others. "If two people average their returns, variance decreases—each buys fewer days of privation at the price of fewer periods of superabundance. By adding more individuals to the risk-pooling group, variance may continue to decrease. Through a system of band-limited generalized reciprocity, food can be stored in the form of social obligations" (Cosmides & Tooby, 2006, p. 191). Thus, as Cosmides and Tooby observe, when hunter-gatherers faced random changes in their fortunes, natural selection began to favour decision-making rules that encouraged the desire to compensate community members for suffering caused by bad luck rather than a lack of effort.

From this example, these authors conclude that sharing or distribution rules do not result from a 'monolithic culture', as different rules are applied within the same culture for resources with high or low variation in procurement, for example. Instead, they argue that each rule is 'activated' by alternative, domain-specific programmes. They also suggest that the same behavioural patterns can be observed in individuals from industrialised cultures. They connect this finding with the idea that different evolved moral heuristics are activated by the perception that negative outcomes are caused by bad luck rather than a lack of effort. This gives rise to a 'grammar' of moral reasoning. This grammar links unluckiness with an obligation to help others, and links slacking off and wanting to live off others with undeserving help (Cosmides & Tooby, 2006, pp. 191–192).

They conclude this section by saying: "The grammar structuring these moral intuitions was selected for because of the fitness effects it had ancestrally. However, if this grammar is a reliably developing feature of the human mind—if it is part of our evolved psychology—it should continue to shape our moral intuitions about sharing and redistribution now, in policy makers, lawmakers, and the citizens they must convince" (Cosmides & Tooby, 2006, p. 192).

5.4.3 Law and Social Welfare

Cosmides and Tooby argue that two decision rules arise from the grammar of moral institutions described above. These rules state the following: 1) if an individual is the victim of an unfortunate tragedy, we should help them; and 2) if an individual spends their time slacking off and living off others, they do not deserve our help. According to these authors, these two rules relating effort/reward to outcome have not been 'selected' because they promoted or maximised the overall social benefit of the hunter-gatherer tribe. Rather, these decision rules were selected because they promoted the self-reproduction of individuals with these rules, who therefore shared according to them.

Cosmides and Tooby consider that (2006, p. 193) "General welfare — which sometimes occurs — is a side effect of their design, a fortuitous accident that emerges when minds designed for a vanished world interact in a modern context". They claim that moral heuristics, like other decision rules, were designed to operate well in specific environments and cannot be expected to produce the same effects outside these conditions. "There is no such thing as an omniscient, omnipotent algorithm, one that can calculate the best course of action in any imaginable environment" (p. 193).

But, we might ask "What happens when these moral intuitions operate outside the environment for which they were designed, in a modern nation of strangers, numbering in the millions?" (Cosmides & Tooby, 2006, p. 194). On the other hand, these authors claim that the objective of law is, among other things, to establish 'rules of the game' to promote general social welfare, and they wonder whether the rules embodied in heuristics types 1) and 2) are good candidates for such rules (Cosmides & Tooby, 2006, p. 194, adopting the concept of 'rules of the game' from Douglass North, 1990). Alternatively, they ask whether these heuristics, because of their easy activation in the minds of 'rule-makers' and citizens, prevent better solutions with a desired consensual outcome from emerging in the modern world.

Here, they introduce the notion of unanticipated or unplanned outcomes or consequences of individual interactions, or 'unintended side effects', as they like to call them. This notion was already discussed in the first part of this work. They argue that interactions between millions of relatively anonymous individuals in the modern marketplace can produce counterintuitive and surprising outcomes.

They offer the effects of 'rent control' policies, which are very common in US legislation, as an example of this situation. In this case, this public policy produces the opposite effect to that intended: a reduced supply of properties for rent, especially the most accessible ones. They even suggest that studies on the effects of these policies indicate that if one is looking for a predictor of homelessness, one should consider rent control policies and climate rather than unemployment or poverty rates (Cosmides & Tooby, 2006, p. 194).

5.4.4 Collective Action, *Free Riders* and Punishment

Here, Cosmides and Tooby introduce the concept of 'coalitional cooperation', which they define as the coordination of behaviour by three or more individuals to achieve a common goal and share the resulting benefits (Cosmides & Tooby, 2006, p. 195). Among hunter-gatherers, coalitional cooperation between non-kin most commonly occurred in two situations: cooperative hunting or inter-group aggression (low-scale warfare).

As economists, game theorists and evolutionary psychologists have studied, these sophisticated forms of cooperation often involve incentives to free ride, bringing this type of cooperation to a point of instability that is difficult to sustain. In fact, the authors remind us that humans and chimpanzees are among the few species hardwired for such multi-person cooperative alliances, although these alliances often dynamically shift, dissolve, re-arrange, etc. How does evolutionary psychology allow for this?

Faced with the decision to participate in a cooperative enterprise, the two options are to participate or to be a *free rider*. From evolutionary biology, it is established that the outcome of a strategy is relevant only if it makes a difference in reproduction and, in this sense, collective action is very rare in the animal kingdom, *free riding* being the default choice.

Various models of the evolution of collective action highlight the role of punishment in solving the problem of free riders. Therefore, contributing to a common good can be an evolutionarily stable strategy as long as free riders are punished. These analyses propose that humans have evolved moral heuristics that lead to the intuition that free riders should be punished. Both evolutionary psychology and experimental economics offer evidence to support these predictions (Cosmides & Tooby, 2006, p. 196). Contrary to what 'rational choice theory' would predict, free rider sanctions are observed in 'one-shot' games. Players in games where they contribute to a common good are also found to be continuously attentive to the penalties applied to under-contributors, constantly adjusting their expectations and behaviour in response.

If we apply this approach to government and production, we find that many of these regularities hold true. In the case of governments, for example, we observe that government officials who believe they are working for the 'common good' adopt very tough positions towards those they consider to be under-contributing to the cause.

The authors, referring now to the realm of production, ask: given that factories, farms or restaurants are all enterprises that involve multi-individual cooperation and collective action, should we organise these projects as public goods (i.e. everyone benefits equally, regardless of the level of participation) or should the outcomes be organised in such a way that efforts are remunerated and 'stowaways' sanctioned? (Cosmides & Tooby, 2006, p. 201). And they answer by stating that: "The operation of our evolved psychology creates large scale dynamics in mass societies. We need to pay careful attention to these dynamics scientifically, rather than being deluded by the outputs of our moral heuristics—heuristics that evolved when the social world was radically smaller. A great deal is still unknown about the motivational systems deployed in collective actions. But so far, the evidence suggests that the human mind has motivational systems that:

1. lower one's level of contribution when this does not adversely affect the welfare of oneself, one's family, or one's small circle of cooperators;
2. lower the amount of effort one expends on a collective action as a function of whether others are free riding; and

3. increase punitive sentiments toward under-contributors by contributors (which, presumably, includes those in leadership and coercive military social roles)" (Cosmides & Tooby, 2006, p. 202).

5.4.5 Private Exchange as a Fast and Frugal Heuristic

Cosmides and Tooby argue that the human cognitive architecture contains a neurocognitive system that is well designed for reasoning about dyadic social exchange, that is, for the mutually beneficial cooperation of two social agents (Cosmides & Tooby, 2006, p. 202). By this they mean that there is a precise fit between the inference and decision rules that comprise the system and the specifications derived from the models of the evolution of reciprocation developed by evolutionary game theorists and behavioural ecologists. This system includes a cheater detection function, requiring very little information to do so.

It is here that the authors of EP make a detailed reference to the tradition of thought analysed in the first part of this paper. With a particular focus on the work of Adam Smith and then Friedrich Hayek, they analyse the benefits of voluntary exchange in detail, highlighting the significant social benefits it produces in the modern world. Like their predecessors, they also discuss how the system of free and voluntary exchange can operate when each agent has limited information about the values and preferences of others and can mainly make decisions based on their own preferences, situation and cost/benefit analysis for each alternative. They consequently acknowledge the advantages of the price system as a 'fast and frugal heuristic' for ascertaining the preferences of others, or the emergence of money as a means of communicating such a heuristic.

In conclusion, Cosmides and Tooby state that: "In short, voluntary exchange systematically propels net aggregated social welfare upwards in a hill-climbing process to the extent the opportunity to engage in it is distributed through the population" (2006, p. 205). They also state that, as it is driven by a consent-based feedback mechanism, the system enables the identification of increasingly beneficial interactions between groups of individuals. In this way, modern market interactions far exceed anything that could have been planned or discovered by any rationally constrained entity, such as a government. In contrast, 'by decree' processes adopted by representatives, even elected ones, lack a sensitive feedback element to adapt the law to individual circumstances (Cosmides & Tooby, 2006, pp. 205–206).

Thus, as far as law is concerned, these authors suggest that a set of short and simple rules that allow dyadic cooperation to function as a fast and frugal engine for social benefit would be best. Along this line of thinking, they propose political and legal institutions that limit the scope of state coercion, through which specific groups (such as businesspeople, coalitions of citizens or 'rule-makers') can attempt to further their special interests.

Finally, the authors draw attention to an interesting issue that they illuminate: when analysing ways to improve social welfare, the idea of removing restrictions on private exchanges is rarely considered by anyone other than economists. In fact, many consider this suggestion to be counterintuitive or outdated. They explain that this is because a neurocognitive system activated by the opportunity to trade produces intuitions about private gains rather than public goods. While we can intuitively recognise how we can benefit if others sacrifice for the common good, our minds do not seem to be designed to recognise how we benefit as part of the aggregate through the private exchanges of others.

5.4.6 Reflections on EP and Law

Cosmides and Tooby conclude by introducing the idea of a colleague, Richard Korobkin, who explains that law has two main functions: an intrinsic function and an instrumental function. The intrinsic function is fulfilled when law codifies a social conception of the good, of justice or of morality, while the instrumental function is fulfilled when law is used to shape the behaviour of the governed and refigure social practices according to these conceptions (Cosmides & Tooby, 2006, p. 207).

It would seem that, in many cases, there is tension between these two functions. Our moral heuristics, formed during the hunter-gatherer era, provide us with guidelines for judging behaviour and rules that we deem to be good, just or moral, but they may not produce the desired outcomes. In other words, laws that satisfy the intrinsic function of law may fail to satisfy the instrumental function. At the same time, in the modern environment, there may be consequences that seem paradoxical to our evolved programmes. For example, self-interested motives may drive beneficial or humanitarian social outcomes, while the best intentions may produce terrible results.

These authors therefore conclude that, to understand the intrinsic function of law, we should turn to evolutionary psychology (EP), which shows how our conceptions of right, of good and of morality evolved and were selected in an ancestral environment. These were selected because they enhanced the fitness of their own genetic base in that environment. The 'strange events' of ancestral DNA editing provide an 'exotic' foundation for modern moral principles and legal systems.

To better understand the instrumental function of law, the authors recommend economic analysis and agent-based models to observe how the choices made by many individual decision-makers aggregate into patterns at the societal level. While these theories are an advance on 'rational choice theory' and moral intuitions, the authors argue that they need to be based on precise scientific knowledge of how the human mind is designed, including social and moral heuristics.

5.5 Some Conclusions on Evolutionary Psychology

In the light of all these ideas, objections and debates, we can now offer some concluding remarks on evolutionary psychology and its contributions to our evolutionary account of law. Firstly, we are greatly interested in the introduction of evolutionary biology and experimental methodology to the study of human behaviour. Beyond the criticisms that can be levelled at the theory and methodology of EP, the idea of identifying an evolutionary substrate common to all individuals can provide an enlightening perspective for other social science disciplines (such as economics and sociology) and for various attempts at institutional and cultural analysis.

Understanding the evolution of certain cognitive mechanisms could help to explain how we humans tend to perceive and react to certain phenomena in our environment and even make general predictions about human behaviour in the style of Hayek's pattern predictions. We might, for example, gain a better understanding of why we can run away from danger or react to a cheater in a certain way, why we can perform certain activities—such as sports—or why we find it so difficult to change certain behaviours. EP, together with evolutionary biology, can provide a good explanation for the evolution of the mechanisms and capacities necessary to understand many of these behaviours.

On the other hand, although the authors of the EP are open to the idea that nature and culture are closely linked in relation to evolution, we, like Dupré, have reservations about the direct application of this theory to the analysis of institutions and social rules. While it is true that for any rule or institution to have arisen, individuals must have developed certain physical and cognitive mechanisms that make them possible, the analysis is not limited to observing the evolutionary development of such capacities.

Returning to the example of the cocktail party observed by the social scientist and the PE-educated alien provided by Dupré, it seems that to fully understand a social phenomenon, we need more than the level of evolved mechanisms capable of generating such behaviour. We require a level of analysis that focuses on the meaning of actions that PE does not offer, or only offers partially, leaving room for other theories. We consider it very healthy on the part of the authors of this theory to continuously refer to theories that offer good analyses of the cultural environment and of individual motivations within those environments, as we will see with theories such as those of social rules or evolutionary game theory. The authors themselves offer studies from these other disciplines to provide complementary elements for the analysis of EP.

Finally, regarding the possibility of establishing a relationship between evolutionary psychology (EP) and classical evolutionism, it can be said that, like many other contemporary evolutionary schools, EP shares many points of convergence with the ideas of authors such as David

Hume, Adam Smith and Friedrich Hayek. As we have seen in Cosmides and Tooby's analysis of the phenomenon of law, the possibility of reconciling the two schools is clearly considered by their own representatives.

On the one hand, we note that EP's contributions regarding the mental mechanisms that humans developed, which define the way they react to certain environments to some extent, would allow us to 'feed' the assumptions about human nature in classic evolutionism (self-interest, limited generosity and limited knowledge, for example). This is important given EP's experimental work, as it provides more empirical support for the claims of classic evolutionary authors.

On the other hand, Cosmides and Tooby argue that EP's work should be complemented by studying those orders that occur as unintended consequences or unplanned 'side effects', such as the order of the market and social welfare, as proposed by classic evolutionary theorists such as the Scottish School and Hayek, and up to current evolutionary game theories and agent-based models. We will analyse some of these schools in detail in the following chapters.

Finally, it is worth introducing an idea that will be discussed in greater depth in the third part of this book: the notion that legal rules and institutions are the outcome of three parallel evolutionary processes: biological, social and individual. In previous chapters, we have considered the process of social evolution with the help of the Scottish School and Hayek. In this chapter, we have seen how the process of biological evolution can influence human behaviour. In the next chapter, we will use evolutionary game theory to see how evolutionary processes can occur at an individual level, starting with learning processes. We believe that this evolution on three mutually influencing levels is the key to understanding complex phenomena such as law.

References

Cosmides, L., & Tooby, J. (1993). '*Evolutionary psychology: A primer*', https://www.cep.ucsb.edu/wp-content/uploads/2023/06/Evolutionary-Psychology-A-Primer-CosmidesTooby1993.pdf

Cosmides, L., & Tooby, J. (2006). Evolutionary psychology, moral heuristics, and the law. In G. Gigerenzer & C. Engel (Eds.), *Heuristics and the Law*. The MIT Press.

Driscoll, C. (2022). Sociobiology. In E. N. Zalta (Ed.), *The Stanford encyclopedia of philosophy* (Summer 2022 ed.). https://plato.stanford.edu/archives/sum2022/entries/sociobiology/

Dupré, J. (2001). *Human nature and the limits of science*. Oxford University Press.

Kropotkin, Piotr Alekséyevich, (1915). *Mutual aid: A factor of evolution*, William Heinemann. (Original work published 1894–1896)

North, Douglass North's. (1990). *Institutions, institutional change and economic performance*. Cambridge University Press.

Wilson, E. O. (1975). *Sociobiology: the new synthesis*. Harvard University Press.

6

Cultural Evolutionism—Evolutionary Game Theory

6.1 Cultural Evolutionism and Game Theory

6.1.1 Introduction

As discussed in previous chapters, various evolutionary perspectives propose understanding rules and institutions as evolutionarily stable strategies. Notably, these strategies are not understood within the context of biological evolution, but rather within the framework of cultural evolution, which exhibits its own distinctive characteristics. Among these 'culturalist' perspectives on institutional evolution, we have previously examined the tradition of 'classic evolutionism' as exemplified by the Scottish Enlightenment and Hayek, as well as the 'meme theory' proposed by Dawkins. Despite being a biologist, he considers that the units of cultural evolution—the memes—reproduce and survive in a given cultural environment and, specifically, in the minds of the individuals who carry them, and that they are 'infected' with their contents.

Within this group of theories that insist on the 'cultural' character of the evolutionary environment of institutions, it is necessary to incorporate and analyse 'game theory' and especially 'evolutionary game theory'.

E. M. Santanatoglia, *An Evolutionary Account of Law*, Palgrave Studies in Classical Liberalism, https://doi.org/10.1007/978-3-032-12162-2_6

This theory provides a structural support and a whole logic of its own to the study of evolutionary processes. In fact, this approach was first used in the field of biology, starting with the application of game theory to the process of biological evolution. From there, it was expanded to analyse social behaviours and regularities on their own merits.

The authors of 'evolutionary game theory' are clear that the social rules studied from this perspective should be viewed not only as stable strategies from a biological perspective, but also from a cultural perspective. Therefore, the survival of these institutions is not due to their capacity for biological survival and reproduction, as some authors of evolutionary psychology might argue, but rather because they enable individuals who adopt these strategies to thrive within a given social context and specific incentive framework.

We will analyse evolutionary game theory in detail and its application to social rules and cooperation. However, we will first briefly review the basic notions of game theory in order to analyse the differences between the 'classic' version of this theory and the evolutionary version, to which we will devote ourselves.

6.1.2 Review of the Basic Notions of Game Theory

The term 'game theory' (GT) was coined in the 1940s by John von Neumann and Oskar Morgensten, who began to explore and publish their ideas in this area. GT has since evolved into a broad discipline that is applied to the analysis of the behaviour of people, animals, and even robots and computers. Initially, its application focuses on the behaviour of individuals in market contexts, such as exchanges (von Neumann and Morgensten, 1944). It is then expanded to apply to all individual decisions in environments where the results of the actor's actions depend crucially on the actions of other actors.

Therefore, GT works with models where individual decision-makers are conceived as **'players'** who elaborate a course of action to be carried out. This course of action is interpreted as a **'strategy'**, taking into account the possible behaviours and outcomes of other relevant individuals in that context, whether interacting directly with them or not. These strategies and decisions are evaluated within a **'payoff matrix'**, which provides a specific incentive framework. This framework enables actors to assess the **'outcomes'** of each strategy within its respective context. GT thus proposes a series of notions that will allow this theory to be applied to different scenarios in which individual strategic behaviour is analysed.

Firstly, a distinction is proposed between **cooperative games and non-cooperative games.** The former consists of games in which players can communicate with each other and negotiate outcomes. In this type of game, given the possibility of 'negotiation' between the players, the theoretical speculation then moves on to the analysis of possible coalitions between the participants and the conditions for their stability. Non-cooperative games are those in which players are unable to reach prior agreements. As a result, their decisions are analysed separately. A classic example of this is the 'Prisoner's Dilemma', a scenario and game that has been used to analyse many different situations. The results and consequences of this game have provided a valuable opportunity for a thorough examination of the assumptions underlying the theory, as well as for re-evaluating the methodology of its application.

A second relevant distinction is between **zero-sum games and positive-sum games**. The former are characterised by a balanced outcome, with the gain or loss of one player being exactly counterbalanced by the gain or loss of the other participant. In contrast, the latter are those games in which both players can benefit simultaneously, with a net profit, even if the distribution of that profit may be unequal.

The final distinction between types of games is between **one-shot games** and **repeated games** where participants interact on several occasions. The latter is very important for evolutionary game theory.

The **strategies** conceived by the participants may consist of a single decision or a complete pattern or plan of action for each situation in the game. In effect, the strategy can be regarded as a predetermined rule that fully specifies how one will respond in each possible circumstance. Among the strategies, we differentiate between **dominant strategy (or dominance),** which is the strategy of one of the players that is profitable for him independently of the strategy of the opposing player. In other words, the player always 'wins' whatever the strategy chosen by the other player. This could lead to an equilibrium of the dominant strategies in the game. Conversely, the **dominated strategy** is one that never succeeds, i.e. it occurs in a context where another strategy is always at least as effective. By establishing whether dominated strategies exist, we can eliminate a number of inferior strategies until there is, if possible, only one left to choose from.

In addition to this basic vocabulary, it is worthwhile recalling here some central notions of 'classic' game theory that will be relevant to fully understand the differences with the evolutionary version of game theory, its innovations and consequences, and then to analyse its possible application in the field of law. One of these fundamental notions is that of the **Nash Equilibrium.**[1] This 'equilibrium' refers to those situations where no individual player benefits from modifying their strategy, provided that the other players maintain their own strategies. That is, it is a solution that assumes that each player has selected their best strategy and that, all parties are aware of the strategies adopted by the other players. In this way, as long as no one changes their strategy—which would require the rest of the participants to re-evaluate theirs—everyone will maintain the successful strategy they have already chosen.

A classic example of this type of equilibrium is the choice of a traffic rule. From an external perspective, the choice between having all drivers drive 'on the left' or 'on the right' is indifferent. However, an agent who is playing a strategy and observes that all other participants are following the same strategy is highly incentivised to maintain their original approach. Otherwise, he would risk being killed quickly by causing a multiple crash. If we were to present the strategies of two possible participants and their outcomes in a very simple matrix (see Fig. 6.1), the same conclusions would be reached.

It should be noted that the 'Nash equilibrium' is not synonymous with the 'Pareto optimum' concept, which is more frequently encountered in economic science.[2] In terms of Pareto efficiency, the optimum will be reached once the initial allocation of goods across a set of individuals

---

[1] This notion, developed by the mathematician John Forbes Nash Jr., was proposed as a conceptual solution for non-cooperative games.

[2] This is a notion proposed by the economist Vilfredo Pareto to reflect a situation of efficiency. Many label this notion of efficiency as 'minimal'.

	Drive Left	Drive Right
Drive Left	100, 100	0,0
Drive Right	0,0	100,100

Fig. 6.1 Traffic matrix

is completed, and the situation of one individual cannot be improved without harming the situation of the rest. A change towards a new allocation that improves the situation of one individual within that order would cause the situation of other individuals to be harmed. Therefore, such a change would not be desirable, leaving the scenario in this equilibrium situation. Optimising, in these terms, would imply being able to improve the situation of one individual without harming the situation of others.

6.1.3 The Prisoner's Dilemma

The prisoner's dilemma is a type of game[3] that exemplifies a 'one-shot' situation. In this scenario, two rational individuals evaluate the possible outcomes of all possible combinations of strategies. They conclude that the best strategy is not to cooperate, even though it is more convenient for both participants to do so in terms of net social benefit.

The game's premise is as follows: two individuals who have committed a crime are arrested and incarcerated separately, unable to communicate with each other by any means. The investigators have not presented sufficient evidence to convict them both of the main charge (for instance, armed robbery), although, given the evidence already collected, they could charge them both with a lesser charge (for instance, attempted

[3] First proposed by Merrill Flood and Melvin Dresher in 1950, it is formulated in its current version by Albert Tucket in 1992, incorporating the criminal aspect and its definitive name.

robbery), and they could be sentenced to 1 year in prison. The investigators offer each prisoner (A and B) two options: (a) remain silent or (b) 'confess', testifying that the other committed the crime and providing the evidence necessary to convict his partner, thus betraying him. The following 'payoff matrix' is also proposed (the numbers change in each example, but not the structure of the incentives):

- As stated above, if both A and B remain silent, they will each serve one year in prison on the lesser charge.
- If A betrays B but B remains silent, A will be released, and B will serve 20 years in prison, and vice versa.
- If A and B both betray each other, they will each serve 5 years in prison.

As they cannot communicate with each other, they cannot negotiate a common strategy. It is also implied that the detainees will not be able to reward or punish their partner more severely than their own prison sentence, and that their decision will not affect their future reputation.

It is important to note that the game is based on a series of assumptions that result in the above outcomes. Namely the assumptions are that: (1) that prisoners are rational individuals, and (2) that they are self-interested or selfish. Based on these assumptions, the possible responses of the prisoners, like those of any good 'homo economicus' seeking to maximise profits, are analysed. Given that betraying a partner offers a greater reward than cooperating with them in all cases—a dominant strategy—it is concluded that all prisoners will betray each other. Therefore, the only possible outcome for two purely rational prisoners is to betray each other, resulting in a 5-year prison sentence for both (see Fig. 6.2). This conclusion is of theoretical importance, since it appears to show that two individuals separated from each other, who are both seeking the best outcome for themselves, end up betraying each other when they would both achieve a better outcome by remaining silent.

This game shows us that situations that are not zero-sum arise in most economic, social or political games, and that conflicts of interest and possibilities for mutual advantage can be observed in these games. In

		Prisoner A	
		Confess	Remain silent
Prisoner B	Confess	5, 5	0,20
	Remain silent	20,0	1,1

Fig. 6.2 Prisoner matrix

this specific game, however, the conditions are such that both participants, by following their dominant strategies, arrive at an outcome that is less beneficial for both of them than if they had both followed a common strategy. In other words, the total net benefit would be greater if they both remained silent. However, they cannot reach this conclusion because they are forbidden to negotiate, and each player's dominant strategy is to 'betray'.

How could a 'Prisoner's Dilemma' situation be overcome? One proposal is to change some of the basic conditions of the game. In particular, it is suggested that participants should be able to communicate and reach an agreement. What would happen if we changed the assumptions of the game to allow the players to communicate and to play repeatedly?

If that is the case, we can turn it from a non-cooperative to a cooperative game. This would imply discussing the instances of a possible agreement and the conditions for the subsistence of such an agreement (Cfr. Dixit & Nalebuff, 1991, Part II, pp. 110 and ss). If the agreement were to allow the players to choose the best strategy for both, what are the chances of this agreement being fulfilled? What determines the balance between cooperation and confrontation in the realm of agreements? How can we ensure cooperation when the players are competing to achieve the most beneficial outcome for each other? There are several factors that make this type of agreement fragile. On the one hand, there is the individual incentive to betray; on the other hand, there is the level of credibility of each of the players, and finally, there is the inter-dependence of decisions.

With regard to the first of the 'threats' to the continuity of the agreement, the incentive for each player to default on any agreement appears to be an underlying condition of the agreement. As we have seen in the previous chapter, the free rider, for example, obtains the same benefits without incurring the costs. In reality, humans show a systemic bias towards cooperative behaviour in this and similar games, despite what is predicted by simple models of 'rational' selfish action. As outlined in previous chapters, the type of cooperation depends on the specific circumstances.

There is an alternative model based on a different type of rationality, in which people predict how the game would be played if they formed coalitions and then maximised their predictions. This model has been shown to make more accurate predictions regarding the rate of cooperation in this and similar games given only the payoffs of the game. In any case, the incentive framework should be analysed to determine which factors influence the participants' calculations in a way that compensates for that natural instinct to 'betray' an agreement.

And so, the second question arises: what are the most effective mechanisms for detecting non-compliance? (Dixit & Nalebuff, 1991, p. 108):

(a) **Detecting non-compliance:** Firstly, it is often challenging to detect a breach of the agreed terms between players. This is due to the fact that certain behaviours exhibited by the participants are not readily identifiable as instances of non-compliance, or alternatively, there are deficiencies in the precision and effectiveness of the dissuasive measures employed. This type of agreement is often illustrated by a deal between producers or sellers of a product or service, where they attempt to agree on maintaining high prices (Dixit & Nalebuff, 1991, p. 101). In such a 'cartel', it can be difficult to detect, at times, breaches by the participants. Let us consider the possibility that one of the cartel participants reduces their prices. Is this a strategic shift by the competitor, or a result of falling demand? Occasionally, non-compliance manifests in an indirect manner, which can make it challenging to detect. To continue with the example, a price agreement may be honoured, yet a 'promotional package' or other type of deal may be offered that obscures the final price of the product.

(b) **Law of Increasing Opaqueness:** With regard to this 'law', it is challenging to determine non-compliance by the parties to these 'collusive agreements' since these agreements focus on the most transparent dimensions of the goods or services, while competition (and possible non-compliance) moves to the less observable dimensions. As with the example above, the agreed price of a good or service is adhered to, but its quality or quantity may be altered (for better or worse), thus preventing competitors from easily detecting non-compliance with the agreement.

(c) **Difficulty in identifying the violator:** This challenge arises in cases where more than two participants are 'playing' and it is therefore more difficult to identify specifically who is breaching the terms of the agreement. In such cases, the requirement for punishment as a 'deterrent' for compliance with the agreement is essential. It is also noted that for punishment to have a real effect, it must be general and affect both guilty and innocent parties.

(d) **Non-compliance may consist of remaining passive:** In many cases of agreements between parties, non-compliance may simply result in doing nothing, making it difficult for competitors to identify and sanction any breaches.

In terms of the 'incentives' for cooperation, it is essential to consider the most effective mechanisms for sanctioning those who breach the agreement. Sanctions may arise from within the game itself or from external sources. Internal sanctions are inherent to the game's structure, for instance, in repeated games, a win in one move may result in a loss in the next. In contrast, external penalties are added to the original game in order to reduce the incentive to default.

As evidenced by the 'Prisoner's Dilemma', sanctions are ineffective in one-shot games. In such cases, it is not possible to find a solution that achieves mutual cooperation. In contrast, in repeated games, mutual cooperation can occur through the structure of sanctions that function as incentives. The collapse of cooperation naturally results in a loss of future benefits. If the cost is sufficiently large, it will deter cheating and maintain cooperation. It is also important to note that the benefits of non-cooperation are realised before the costs of terminating the agreement. The relative importance of gains and losses depends on the relative importance of the present with respect to the future. In the field of politics, for instance, the future beyond the next election is often of little consequence. It is therefore recommended that 'punishment must be guaranteed' be established as a principle to ensure the desired outcome.

On the other hand, there are specific characteristics that sanctions must meet in order to function as incentives to comply with agreements (and, consequently, to foster cooperation) (Dixit & Nalebuff, 1991, pp. 117–118): (a) **Simplicity and clarity:** a player considering non-compliance can easily and accurately calculate the consequences, (b) **Certainty:** it is vital that players have confidence that non-compliance will be punished and cooperation rewarded, (c) **The degree of severity:** sometimes the best form of deterrence is not the 'proportionality' of the sanction but the imposition of the highest possible sanction (given that the threat of punishment is sufficient to maintain cooperation it should not be a matter of concern if the punishment is excessive). However, if we do not ignore the risk of error, then the punishment should be as small as possible in order to have deterrent capacity.

It is also suggested that, in the case of repeated games, the best way to get out of 'prisoner's dilemma' situations is to incorporate a strategy that is clear and effective. Thus, authors, such as Robert Axelroad (1984, p. 20), propose that a strategy that meets all the requirements would be the so-called Tit-for-tat, i.e., do to the other what the other has done to you. The first move would be to cooperate and then to imitate the opponent's action in the previous period, i.e. to cooperate or not according to the last move of the other player.

For this author, the 'tit-for-tat' strategy fulfils four principles as a successful decision rule: (a) **Decency:** in this case it means that it is never the first to defect, which would avoid unnecessary conflict, (b) **Provocability:** at the same time the rule never lets an offence go unpunished, so it serves to dissuade the other player from persisting in defection when he tries to use it, (c) **Leniency: it does** not hold **a** grudge for long and is willing to restore cooperation and (d) **Clarity: it is easily recognisable**

and once recognised, it is easy to realise that the best way to carry it is to cooperate with it.

Finally, there may be some reservations about implementing the 'tit-for-tat' strategy. These issues may arise from potential misunderstandings or misjudgements among participants. As the error would be transferred from one to the other in a 'bounce' effect, this could lead to the failure of the strategy. In this sense, the strategy is 'too provocative' and, if misjudgements are endemic, it could be dangerous to use such a simple strategy.

Given that the strategy starts with cooperation, it has the potential to avoid the prisoner's dilemma entirely. However, what happens if one party has a misperception of the other's move? When there is a possibility of misunderstanding, this strategy allocates half of its time to cooperation and the remaining half to non-cooperation. Once misunderstandings arise, they are as likely to accumulate as they are to be cleared up. Therefore, as the probability of error rises, it becomes challenging to sustain cooperation in a prisoner's dilemma scenario.

In this sense, the so-called tit for tat strategy would appear to be a good candidate, but it is too quick to punish someone who has a good record of cooperation. Therefore, a strategy that is more discerning, that is more lenient when non-cooperation appears to be the exception and punitive when non-cooperation appears to be the rule, would seem to be necessary. In this regard, it is essential to consider the 'history of actions' of the other party in the short, medium and long term when developing a strategy.

It is important to note that other authors may propose different strategies and models of game theory in which strategies compete in terms of frequency. In this sense, we will now examine the concepts introduced by evolutionary game theory and contrast them with those of classic game theory.

6.2 Evolutionary Game Theory (Skyrms, Alexander)

6.2.1 Basic Notions

evolutionary game theory (EGT) offers a compelling option for contemporary social sciences. It combines the modelling current of traditional game theory with the evolutionary, dynamic element of biology and experimental disciplines. With the contribution of John Maynard Smith and other authors (Alexander, 2021), this theory began to apply the dynamics of the strategic game to the processes of biological evolution, introducing the idea of studying the frequency of strategies present in certain populations. John Maynard Smith, an evolutionary biologist and geneticist, was among the first authors to combine game theory and biological evolution. He also emphasised the role of the gene as a unit of biological evolution, a theme that was later taken up, as we have seen, by Richard Dawkins and subsequent authors.

The EGT, which was originally designed as a theory for the field of biology, was quickly adopted by social scientists. This theory states that the performance or fitness of a given strategy depends on its frequency, thus introducing a strategic aspect to evolution.

One of its current representatives, Jason McKenzie Alexander (2021), who applies this approach to the study of the evolution of moral rules, understands that this interest in EGT on the part of social scientists, despite its biological roots, is due to three reasons:

(a) EGT's use of the term 'evolution' may not refer to a biological evolution, but rather to cultural evolution, that is, the change in beliefs and norms over time.
(b) The assumptions of rationality underlying EGT are more suitable for social science modelling than those underlying traditional game theory.
(c) EGT provides the explicitly dynamic element that was lacking in traditional game theory.

6.2.2 The Two Approaches in Evolutionary Game Theory

In an introductory paper on this school of thought, Jason McKenzie Alexander introduces two approaches to EGT (Alexander, 2021). The first approach is rooted in the seminal work of Maynard Smith and Price, the first representatives of this approach, who pioneered the concept of **'evolutionarily stable strategy'** as the primary analytical tool. A strategy is said to be evolutionarily stable if it possesses the following property: if almost all members of a population follow this strategy, no mutant (i.e. an individual adopting a new strategy) could successfully invade the population. To be more specific, a strategy S is evolutionarily stable when: (1) S performs better playing against S than any mutant performs against S, or (2) a mutant performs just as well against S as S, but S performs better playing against a mutant than another mutant.

Of course, to arrive at this type of analysis we must be clear about the assumptions of analysis and the incentive or 'payoff' scheme of each of the strategies. Maynard Smith and Price offered, in this case, the example of the repeated 'Hawk-Dove game'. In this game (also called 'Chicken Game' in another of its versions) two players compete for a resource that is valuable for both—given that it improves their physical *fitness*. Two possible strategies are presented: the 'Hawk' which involves attacking the opponent relentlessly, until the resource is obtained, and the 'Pigeon' strategy which involves retreating and conceding when attacked. Given the assumptions and the incentive scheme of this game, it is argued that the Hawk strategy is the evolutionarily stable one.

The 'Chicken Game' version is similar in that it is a game in which two drivers are rapidly approaching each other with the danger of collision: one must swerve, or both may die in the collision, but if one driver swerves and the other does not, the one who swerved will be called a 'chicken', i.e. a coward. From a game-theoretical perspective, 'Chicken' and 'Hawk-dove' games are identical; the different names result from the parallel development of basic principles in different research areas. The term 'hawk-dove' is more commonly used in the field of biology and evolutionary game theory, and 'Chicken Game' in the field of political science and economics. The game has also been used to describe mutually assured destruction in belligerent escalations.

The second approach to EGT, as represented by authors such as Brian Skyrms (1996, 2004) or McKenzie Alexander (2021) himself, involves constructing an explicit model of the process by which the frequency of strategies changes in the population. This approach then studies the properties of evolutionary dynamics within that model. This view is exemplified by the well-known repeated 'Prisoner's Dilemma', which we have already examined. In this case, the incentive scheme will also be a relevant factor, but it is important to note the assumptions made about the population in question. The EGT analysis encompasses a range of factors, including the size of the population analysed, the relationship between generations, the change in frequency of strategies, and several others.

This approach to EGT provides a range of evolutionary mechanisms for mathematically modelling a population of individuals playing a game (for example, the Prisoner's Dilemma). One of the most important of these is the notion of ***replicator dynamics***. The EGT is able to determine which strategy is the most stable equilibrium over time.

Whilst these two approaches to EGT appear to generate comparable results in certain instances, it may be observed that what is identified as the evolutionarily stable strategy for the initial perspective can subsequently be shown to be the consequence of the stable equilibrium under the replicating dynamics perspective. In other cases, however, the application of each view may not result in the same outcomes. In this sense, this second version of the EGT incorporates elements such as the number of strategies present in the population at the beginning of the game and the structure of relationships between individuals in the population. These elements have the potential to influence the outcome of the analysis of the evolution of strategies.

6.2.3 Evolutionary Game Theory Applied to the Emergence of Rules

From the EGT perspective, the behaviour of individuals is explained on the basis of the existence of a set of social norms that all, or almost all, individuals follow. In this sense, authors who study a specific behaviour, in the context of this theory, will ask themselves whether there is a social norm—that is, a behavioural strategy—that explains the behaviour of individuals and, if so, why such a rule exists.

This is where the element of game theory becomes relevant. Game theorists represent situations where an individual must make a specific decision the outcome of which is also informed by the actions of other parties. Therefore, they model it by attempting to assume those conditions that can explain the individual's decision and the emergence of a social norm. In other words, social norms are explained as successful strategies in contexts of repeated interactions under certain conditions. At the same time, this analysis of the emergence of the social norm is carried out from the perspective of methodological individualism. In brief, human behaviour is explained as governed by a social rule, but this is understood as the consequence of a number of separate, individual decisions. The social norm does not arise from external forces, but rather, it is the outcome of multiple successful individual decisions.

We consider that one of the most valuable contributions of EGT is related to the study of the emergence of norms, be they moral, social or legal. We will present here an example of this type of analysis of norms, the analysis of the emergence of moral norms proposed by McKenzie Alexander. We find this analysis to be enlightening from two perspectives: (a) on the one hand, we will be able to introduce some of the most interesting conceptual tools proposed by the EGT; and (b) we will be able to observe some possible points of contact with the philosophical assumptions of Classic Evolutionism, which can be fundamental to our evolutionary vision of law.

6.2.4 The Agent-Based Model vs. the Replicator Dynamic

Brian Skyrms, a representative of the second 'approach' of the EGT, proposes in his article "Sex and Justice"(Skyrms, 1996, pp. 1–20) an explanation of the evolution of a series of rules. These include, for example, the rule of equal division (50% and 50%) or *fair division* based on the interaction between different strategies over time. To this end, it provides a model that shows, from an evolutionary perspective, what the 'laws of *replicator dynamics*' (Skyrms, 1996, p. 11) would be that would lead to the emergence of a given rule.

It is worth remembering that the **replicator dynamics** is a set of dynamic laws that describe how the distribution of strategies in a population changes over time. This dynamic allows us to identify certain strategies or sets of strategies that are fixed or stable, meaning that they do not change over time. In this way, certain equilibrium can be achieved within the given population: (a) An unstable equilibrium may be reached, where a small segment of the population deviates from the dominant strategy. In this scenario, the evolutionary dynamics will direct the population away from equilibrium. (b) Alternatively, a stable equilibrium can be attained, where if the small segment of the population deviates from the strategy, the evolutionary dynamics will restore the population to its original state of equilibrium.

By introducing these notions, Skyrms departs from the notion of the Nash equilibrium, as previously discussed at the beginning of this chapter. Skyrms's position is that other game theories that work with the idea of rational, self-interested agents and the notion of the Nash equilibrium conclude that there are several possible equilibria and fail to explain why one equilibrium is chosen over another. Instead, their evolutionary perspective enables them to observe that, when faced with the possibility of multiple equilibria emerging, some of these equilibria will prevail over time, thus becoming the norm. He claims, "Evolution selects from the infinity of equilibria in informed rational self-interest (the Nash equilibria) a unique evolutionarily stable equilibrium which becomes the rule or habit of just division" (Skyrms, 1996, p. 11).

However, despite the advantages that this version of replicator dynamics may have over other static explanations, there are a number of assumptions that this theory makes. These assumptions have met with several objections presented by Justin D'Arms (1996) and confirmed by Alexander. One of the key assumptions in the model is that the population under study is infinite and that the interactions between individuals are random. This means that there is no social structure or network of social relations.

In this sense, Alexander, while agreeing with the second approach of the EGT, leaves aside the perspective of replicating dynamics, replacing it with *agent-based models* and their dynamic stability. In his book *The Structural Evolution of Morality* (Alexander, 2007), Alexander proposes different evolutionary models for the study of the emergence of moral rules (Alexander, 2007, p. 25). Firstly, for this author, an evolutionary model must provide (a) a representation of the state of the population and (b) a specification of the dynamic law, that is, how the state of the population changes over time.

The **'dynamic stability'** proposed by Alexander, on the other hand, also differs from the notion of Nash equilibrium stability used by several authors, including Binmore (2005). The concept of 'dynamic stability' refers to scenarios involving more than two individuals interacting, in which all strategies are simultaneously perturbed. However, it is observed that there is a tendency of the players'choices to return to equilibrium (Alexander, Alexander, 2007, p. 280).

Alexander analyses, in particular, the case of the emergence of moral norms such as fairness, trust, cooperation and retaliation, being the thesis of his book that these norms, represented by heuristics, exist because it is in the best interests of the individuals who adopt them to comply with or follow them. In his terms: "The central claim of this book is that morality provides a set of heuristics that, when followed, serves to produce the best expected outcome, for each of us, over the course of our lives, given the constraints placed by other people" (Alexander, 2007, p. vii).

To this end, the author proposes (and in this he agrees with those who propose replicating dynamics) a conception of agents as individuals with *bounded rationality* and the evolutionary process as an exclusively cultural process.[4] Regarding the first characteristic, Alexander proposes the idea that agents act with 'bounded rationality' and challenges the assumption of the perfect rationality of the '*homo* economicus' perspective (Alexander, 2007, p. 5). Herbert Simon, (quoted by Alexander, 2007, p. 5), explains that the human mind has limited capacity to formulate and solve complex problems and it is very small compared to the size of the problems whose solution is required by objectively rational behaviour in the real world. Likewise, agents consider the future actions of other individuals when making decisions. That is, they have interdependent choice problems and formulate expectations regarding each other's actions.

Despite limited capabilities, individuals manage to solve most of the practical problems of everyday life by employing certain heuristics. These heuristics consist of rules that, although they cannot be explained or even articulated by agents, are useful for solving problems. Alexander refers to this as 'common knowledge' and, in his view, heuristics encapsulate this common knowledge in forms that are understandable and ready to be applied in contexts other than those in which they originated.

As discussed in Chapters 2 and 3 of this work, this knowledge, like the practical knowledge discussed by authors such as Hayek, cannot be translated into theoretical and formally or consciously transmissible knowledge. Rather, it is a 'know-how' in certain situations that is transmitted more through imitation than through theoretical mechanisms. In this respect, it is interesting to consider the potential connections between this concept of heuristics (i.e. certain 'intuitive' or 'automatic' rules that emerge spontaneously and, if they prove useful, are replicated in different, unforeseen situations) and the notions of institutions and rules of spontaneous origin already proposed by 'classic evolutionism', i.e. the tradition of Scottish Enlightenment thinking and Hayek.

In addition, Alexander proposes the application of 'agent-based models' to the study of the emergence of rules, with these models taking into account the structure of social relations and how this, together with

[4] In this sense, McKenzie Alexander does not consider genetic evolution or potential biological/cultural co-evolution in his analysis.

the incentive framework, influences the possibility of the emergence of moral norms.

Finally, and unlike the model proposed by his teacher Skyrms, Alexander posits a series of assumptions (Alexander, 2007, p. 35) which, we believe, are more realistic and more appropriate to be applied to the study of the emergence of norms (social, moral or legal) in real communities. These assumptions are:

(a) **Small populations:** in these proposed models consider groups that can vary in size from small groups to real-sized populations, but not groups of infinite numbers of agents (as assumed by other evolutionary models).
(b) **Limited interactions:** here, a more 'realistic' assumption is considered, in the sense that possible interactions between individuals are not purely random. Unlike other models that assume 'random' interactions between participants in a given population, this model considers specific relationship structures between participants, as well as limited interaction possibilities and a finite number of interactions between participants.
(c) **Key agents***:* this element is introduced, which we consider fundamental to understanding how this type of model is applied to the emergence, stability or the changing of rules. It is recognised that not all agents in the model play the same role or have the same influence with respect to the strategies of others in terms of strategy imitation. These 'key agents' are agents whose decision to adopt a certain strategy has a strong influence on the decisions of other agents.

Alexander defines these 'key agents' as "one whose adoption of a different strategy sparks a large-scale shift in the strategy frequencies found in the population. A key agent occupies an Archimedean point, enabling her single action to alter radically the future state of society" (Alexander, 2007, p. 35). We believe that the concept of 'key agents' is fundamental to understanding relationships within certain contexts or social networks. For example, consider the role of a religious leader in establishing a moral norm. In the case of law, we believe that judges, legislators and political leaders can be this type of 'key agent', whose influence on the emergence of a legal norm or the configuration of a legal order is greater than that of an ordinary citizen. For example, consider the influence that the decision of a supreme or the highest court can have on the strategies adopted by other legal agents (lower-level judges, lawyers, doctrinarians and citizens) based on that decision.

(a) **Non-determinism:** The author introduces the idea of innovation, or what we would call 'mutation'in biological terms, into his model. In other words, the possibility that some agents will introduce new strategies without being influenced by other agents or rules. In other words, the possibility of strategies emerging that were not present at the beginning, or 'time 0′, of the game. Therefore, no matter how much the author's model takes into account structure, incentives and evolutionary laws, it will never be able to precisely determine the final outcome of the resulting social order configuration. This implies that a purely 'deterministic' model of cultural evolution is inconceivable.
(b) **Heterogeneity of agents**: In contrast to other models that analyse the outcomes of repeated individual interactions, this model does not consider identical agents to be involved in the dynamics. Unlike the theories that include replicative dynamics, which presuppose homogeneity, this model assumes that, in addition to differences in strategies, agents may be heterogeneous with respect to interaction styles or the adoption of different learning rules, for example. In short, it does not assume that all agents will respond or act in the same way under the same incentives or conditions. It even assumes different 'learning curves', which we will examine in the next section. This assumption is also interesting in the context of applying this type of model to law, since we can assume that different types of agents—judges, lawyers, legislators, etc.—will exhibit different types of behaviour or learning curves in response to the same incentive scheme.

6.2.5 Learning Rules

In addition to these assumptions, Alexander's theory offers a series of learning rules that can be used to model how agents interact in the context of a community with a given social structure (Alexander, 2007, p. 39). Three of these learning rules are based on imitation and the fourth on the idea of 'best response' but adapted to agents with limited rationality. The proposed learning rules are as follows:

(a) **Imitate the best neighbour:** according to this rule, each agent, at the end of each generation, evaluates the results of its 'neighbours' and adopts the strategy of the one that has obtained the best result. It is assumed, in turn, that it will not change its strategy if it has no incentive to do so.

(b) **Imitate with probability proportional to success:** the agent compares his results with those of his neighbours. However, instead of ignoring those players who were better than him but who were not strictly the best, this rule assigns a probability above zero to each neighbour who performed better than the agent, indicating the likelihood that the agent will adopt that strategy (Alexander, 2007, p. 39).

(c) **Imitate the best average outcome (or utility):** the agent selects the strategy with the best average utility in the neighbourhood, selecting randomly in case there is more than one tied (Alexander, 2007, p. 39)

(d) **Best answer:** for this rule, the agent adopts the strategy that will result in the highest utility for the next generation, based on the assumption that none of the neighbours will change their strategy. If there is more than one such strategy, the agent will choose one at random. Expectations play a central role in this rule, since it considers the expected future success rather than the past success of a strategy. Furthermore, the rule takes into account the rationality constraints of the agents, as it assumes that they do not make strategic calculations to determine what strategies their neighbours will use in the future, but rather proceed on the assumption that

> neighbours will continue to act as they have in the past. (Alexander, 2007, p. 41).

This last rule seems particularly applicable to the case of the evolution, change and stability of certain social, moral and legal rules. Given that this would be the product of interactions between many players within a social structure, it is reasonable to assume that an agent, believing that others will continue to act as they have been doing, will adopt the strategy or rule that will produce the best future outcome.

6.2.6 Conclusions and Perspectives

Based on these models proposed by Skyrms, Alexander, and other authors of evolutionary game theory (EGT), we can now outline some preliminary conclusions regarding the application of EGT to the study of the emergence, stability and change of legal rules. First, these theories show us that certain rules will not emerge under any circumstances but that the incentive scheme is fundamental with respect to the emergence, change and stability of certain strategies or rules. For example, in the case of cooperation as studied by these authors, if the 'attractiveness of defecting' is very high, coordination mechanisms are unlikely to emerge.

Secondly, these studies suggest that the initial state of a population has a strong influence on the final outcome. Therefore, a community whose original population exhibits a high level of trust-based behaviours is more likely to see these behaviours become widespread. Conversely, if a certain strategy or rule does not exist in the original situation, it will be more difficult for it to emerge later within this population.

In turn, we consider the contribution of this theory to be fundamental with regard to the importance of 'key players', whose actions can change the outcome of the game. For example, in the fairness case studied by Alexander, the game changes when these key players appear, forever altering the assumption of symmetrical relations in other theories. As previously mentioned, this example is highly relevant to law, where legislators and judges can largely determine the range of possible strategies and the associated costs and benefits.

In short, we can conclude, with the EGT, that the interactions between individuals that can lead to the emergence of norms are conditioned by many factors, such as the number of individuals that make up a specific social order, the structure of their relationships, the 'special' roles of certain individuals, and the characteristics of each individual. When certain strategies prove successful—for instance, coordinating different individual plans or avoiding conflict—they are imitated or adopted by others looking to improve their performance.

Following Hayek's thinking, we could consider evolutionary game and learning processes taking place at an institutional 'meta-level', where strategies consist of complex institutional arrangements or set of rules. From this perspective, some populations might imitate those that have achieved more productive institutional arrangements. Hayek refers to this as a kind of group cultural selection between different orders of rules in some of his texts. The most successful order of rules survives because it allows the best coordination of individual action plans, as discussed in previous chapters.

With regard to the potential relationship between evolutionary game theory and classic evolutionism, it is worth noting the similarities between the two in terms of certain anthropological assumptions. Notably, both view agents as individuals with limited rationality who use 'frugal heuristics' to solve everyday problems. In this sense, it is easy to see the similarities with Hume's and Hayek's thinking regarding the importance of repeated actions and expectations in the emergence of rules and institutions.

On the other hand, classic evolutionism does not provide precise explanations of the mechanisms or processes by which social, moral or legal norms emerge and undergo trial and error. Given this shortcoming of classic evolutionism, perhaps we could adopt some current evolutionary theories, which share many of its epistemological assumptions, to 'complete' the picture of the evolution of social orders painted by classic authors. In this sense, we believe it would be interesting to explore the possible complementarity of thought with current evolutionism, such as that proposed by evolutionary game theory.

References

Alexander, J. M. K. (2007). *The structural evolution of morality*. Cambridge University Press.

Alexander, J. M. K. (2021). Evolutionary game theory. In E. N. Zalta (Ed.), *The Stanford Encyclopedia of philosophy* (Summer 2021 ed.) https://plato.stanford.edu/archives/sum2021/entries/game-evolutionary/

Axelroad, R. (1984). *The evolution of cooperation*. Basic Books.

Binmore, K. (2005). *Natural justice*. Oxford University Press.

D'Arms, Justin, (1996). Sex, fairness, and the theory of games, Journal of Philosophy, 93:12, pp. 615–627.

Dixit, A. K., & Nalebuff, B. J. (1991). *Thinking strategically: The competitive edge in business, politics and everyday life*. W W Norton & Co Inc..

Skyrms, B. (1996). *The evolution of the social contract*. Cambridge University Press.

Skyrms, B. (2004). *The stag hunt and the evolution of social structure*. Cambridge University Press.

von Neumann, J., & Morgensten, O. (1944). *Theory of games and economic behavior*. Princeton University Press.

7

Co-evolutionism

7.1 Introduction

We have already referred, in previous chapters, to some schools of thought and theories that study the evolution of rules and institutions as the joint product of biological and cultural evolution. In other words, they are not the result of one or the other process, but of the interaction between these two parallel and interrelated evolutionary processes. We will refer to this approach as 'co-evolutionism', and to illustrate this perspective, we will present the work of Peter Richerson and Robert Boyd. These two professors, along with a large group of researchers, are among the most prominent exponents of this viewpoint.

In this case we will refer to some of their works, such as "Natural Selection and Culture" (Richerson & Boyd, 1984) and their renowned book "Not by Genes Alone"(Richerson & Boyd, 2006) from which we will extract their main ideas.

E. M. Santanatoglia, *An Evolutionary Account of Law*, Palgrave Studies in Classical Liberalism, https://doi.org/10.1007/978-3-032-12162-2_7

7.2 Darwinian Model of Cultural Evolution

Richerson and Boyd begin by introducing the idea that natural selection is a general evolutionary mechanism. In other words, this mechanism applies not only to the evolution of genes, but also to cultural evolution, albeit indirectly, via genes that influence the creation and replication of cultural practices. Natural selection can also act directly on cultural variation, even though the behaviours favoured by each mode of selection may not necessarily be the same. In other words, to understand cultural evolution, we must consider all processes through which cultural variations are transmitted and modified, regardless of their origin (genetic or cultural), and through processes such as socialisation, imitation and learning.

They observe that Darwinian evolutionary theory is generally considered antithetical to theories invoking the inheritance of 'culturally' acquired variation. By contrast, Darwin maintained that the inheritance of acquired variation was important in nature and compatible with the action of natural selection. This view remained influential until around 1930, when Darwinism became associated with Mendelian genetics. However, today, there is a reconsideration of the consequences of the inheritance of acquired variation.

On the one hand, some social scientists use the analogy between genetic and cultural transmission as a basis for a general theory of culture, as discussed in previous chapters of this text. One example is the work of Dawkins, who not only explains the process of biological evolution in detail, but also elaborates on the theory of 'memes' to explain cultural evolution by analogy with biological evolution (Dawkins, 1989). Conversely, some biologists consider how culturally transmitted behaviour fits into the framework of neo-Darwinism. Finally, some biologists and psychologists use the formal similarities between genetic and cultural transmission to develop theories that describe the dynamics of cultural transmission.

Richerson and Boyd identify a common idea underlying all these approaches, unifying these works: social learning or cultural transmission can be modelled as a system of inheritance. Therefore, to understand cultural change, we should understand the microscopic processes that increase the frequency of certain culturally transmitted traits while decreasing the frequency of others. In this sense, all processes through which cultural variations are transmitted and modified would be considered in this way. Richerson and Boyd propose calling this resulting mode 'the Darwinian model of cultural evolution'because it resembles the neo-Darwinian theory of organic evolution.

They therefore propose considering the role of natural selection in cultural variation. Specifically, they ask how natural selection acts within a system of culturally transmitted variation when genetic inheritance is also at work.

7.3 Natural Selection and Culture

In this case, Richerson and Boyd provide us with a notion of culture that will allow the formation of their model of analysis. They say: "We define culture as information acquired by imitation or learning from other individuals and able to affect an individual's phenotype, usually his behavior" (Richerson & Boyd, 1984, p. 430). And they clarify that, although their definition emphasises that culture is a system for the inheritance of acquired variations, it is compatible with the anthropologist's definitions of culture.

They also argue that, in some respects, culture and genetics are similar. For example, certain behavioural patterns are difficult to distinguish with regard to whether they are culturally or genetically influenced, as in the case of IQ. In other respects, the two transmission processes can differ greatly, selecting for different phenotypic aspects.

Richerson and Boyd (1984, p. 430) claim that culture is transmitted when an individual observes the behaviour of others, or when a 'naive' individual is taught by a more experienced one. This means that behaviour modified through a trial-and-error learning process can subsequently be transmitted. In this way, they define culture as a system for the inheritance of acquired variation.

On the other hand, cultural transmission patterns differ from genetic transmission patterns. For example, other 'models' influence cultural transmission, such as peer or grandparent models, which are part of the transmission process. The terms analogous to the 'length of a generation' or 'mating system' are more varied and different than those of the genetic process. This is why these authors highlight differences in transmission patterns and emphasise what they refer to as 'asymmetries between the two systems'.

Finally, another feature of cultural transmission is that the 'inexperienced' individual who acquires different cultural items through this process is also an active (and not merely passive) participant in it. To some extent, individuals decide what to learn from others; however, a zygote cannot choose its genes.

7.4 The Forces of Cultural Evolution

The aim of the Darwinian view of cultural evolution (Richerson & Boyd, 1984, p. 430) is to understand cultural change in terms of the forces at work in cultural variation as individuals acquire cultural traits, use acquired information to guide their behaviour and act as models for others. In this sense, the term 'forces' refers to the processes that increase or decrease the proportion of people in society who hold particular ideas about how to behave.

Richerson and Boyd thus recognise three kinds of evolutionary forces affecting culture: (a) random forces, (b) decision-making forces, and (c) natural selection acting directly on cultural variation. Each of these forces will be briefly developed below:

(a) **Random forces:** this is the cultural analogue of mutation or drift in genetic transmission. Intuitively it would seem that random errors, individual idiosyncrasies and chance transmission play a role in behaviour and social learning.
(b) **Decision-making forces:** these forces involve biased or partial transmissions that occur when 'naïve' or inexperienced individuals voluntarily expose themselves to a variety of models, preferentially imitating one over the other. A second such decision-making force occurs when individuals modify existing behaviours or invent new ones through individual learning. If this modified behaviour is

then transmitted, the resulting force resembles the guided, non-random force of classical 'Lamarckian' transmission. When we discussed evolutionary game theory, we saw how some agents modified their strategy by taking into account the outcomes of their own strategy versus the outcomes of the strategies of other participants. Faced with better results from the strategies of others, they voluntarily change their own strategy via imitation or conscious learning processes.

All of these decision-making forces are 'derived', meaning that these decisions require rules, which must be derived from the actions of other forces. They may have been acquired during an earlier episode of cultural transmission, or they may be due to genetically transmitted traits that control the neurological machinery for acquiring and retaining cultural traits. These traits influence this decision. In the latter case, this specific hypothesis closely resembles some socio-biological hypotheses, which posit that the course of cultural evolution is determined by biological natural selection operating indirectly on cultural variation via decision-making forces.

(c) Finally, these authors consider the **third type of forces: natural selection.** This can operate directly on cultural variation since it is an extremely general evolutionary mechanism (Richerson & Boyd, 1984, p. 431). Richerson and Boyd support this assertion by pointing out that natural selection can operate on any system of inheritance, and that even Darwin was able to formulate a model of natural selection without a deep understanding of genetic inheritance.

Consequently, they argue that natural selection can operate on any inheritance system that possesses a few essential characteristics: a) the variations must be heritable, b) these variations must affect the phenotype and c) the phenotypic difference should affect the individual's ability to transmit the variation they carry.

Thus, in the case of natural selection applied to cultural transmission, variations would be transmitted by imitation or individual choice, rather than by sexual or asexual transmission, although this would not affect the basic argument. Here, we would be referring to a 'blind' force of selection of a phenotype—for example, a behaviour—that is due to a type of non-parental transmission, which we will discuss in more detail in the following sections.

Richerson and Boyd's conclusion is that Darwin had no problem imagining random variation, acquired variation and natural selection acting together as forces in organic evolution, and they see no problem in applying this analysis to cultural evolution.

7.5 The Model of Cultural Selection

Focusing on the idea of the application of natural selection to the domain of culture, Richerson and Boyd then offer a model that attempts to show the effects of natural selection on culture, transmitted through non-parental pathways. In this case, they propose a model in which a group of children, the 'offspring', are exposed to the influence of both their parents and their teachers and are culturally influenced by both in the development of different traits. These authors propose the following assumptions for their model:

1. 'Offspring' or 'naïve' individuals are 'enculturated' by two models: one from their genetic parents, and one from their teachers.
2. There are two variants of dichotomous cultural traits: C and D, which lead to the possibility of becoming a parent or teacher, respectively.
3. Parents have a weight of A, while teachers have a weight of 1-A.
4. Individuals characterised by different cultural variants have different probabilities of becoming parents (for example, the probability of C may be different from that of D).
5. Individuals characterised by different variants have different probabilities of becoming teachers (for example, the probability of D is different from that of C).

Thus, there are two different and potentially conflicting selection processes which act on cultural variants.

A. A process selects between individuals, allowing some of them to become parents and 'enculturate' children, in a way.
B. Another process selects among individuals as to who will be teachers and who will also be in a position to 'enculturate' children in a different way.

Therefore, different types of phenotypes can be identified that result from this selection process. The frequency of trait C among children after cultural transmission is calculated based on: (a) the frequency of C between parents, (b) the frequency of C among teachers, (c) the probability of the children, given that parents and teachers are both C, (d) the probability of the children, given that the parents are C and the teachers are D and (e) the probability of the children, given that parents are D and teachers are C.

Based on this model, its mathematical aspects, assumptions and combinations, the authors draw two conclusions. First, the equation expresses that the frequency of cultural variant C after transmission is a weighted measure of its frequency among parents and teachers, where the 'weight' reflects the relative importance of parents and teachers in transmitting the central trait in question. Assuming that individuals with cultural variant C are more likely to become teachers and individuals with cultural variant D are more likely to become parents, the equation can be used to predict the frequency of each variant in the population. Consequently, the frequency of 'C individuals' would be higher among teachers and the frequency of 'D individuals' would be higher among parents.

The second conclusion is that, given the model (and the equation), C could increase in the population if teachers were sufficiently important, even if D individuals are assumed to have higher genetic fitness.

For example, consider a child whose genetic parents have a 'natural talent' for music, such as absolute pitch, which is a genetically inheritable trait. Suppose the child has 'C' teachers who, despite not having a natural talent for music, are good educators in terms of musical instrument education and practice. Would this child be more influenced by their genetic predisposition or the educational process under the guidance of their teachers? In some cases, through phenotypic flexibility, imitative processes and more conscious decision-making, non-parental role models can strongly influence the behaviour of the 'naive' individual.

Basically, the model shows (Richerson & Boyd, 1984, p. 432) that selection acting on a non-parentally transmitted cultural variant can reduce Darwinian fitness. Some might argue that this effect is unlikely to be important since a cultural inheritance system with these characteristics or properties would not be favoured by selection and would only have evolved by chance. "Selection, the argument would run, ought to have acted to prevent such distorted cultural adaptations either by the creation of decision-making forces that counteract the effect of selection on non-parentally transmitted cultural variation or by preventing nonparental individuals from becoming important in cultural transmission" (Richerson & Boyd, 1984, p. 432).

But Richerson and Boyd consider that this argument is incomplete because it ignores the fact that individual decision-making can be costly compared with social learning. If costs are high, then selection will not favour these forces that fully compensate for the maladaptive effects of non-parental transmission. If non-parental transmission offers individuals advantages in information acquisition costs, then selection on the genes underlying the asymmetric transmission capacity will be favoured.

All organisms rely on various modes of phenotypic flexibility. This can be exemplified by trial-and-error learning. An individual performs 'experiments' to determine the nature of their local environment, and then modifies their behaviour based on the results of these experiments and inherited learning rules. However, conducting these experiments and setting up the cognitive machinery takes time and resources that could be used for other components of fitness. Therefore, phenotypic flexibility is more useful in variable environments than in constant ones.

Many authors argue that cultural inheritance is adaptive because it reduces the cost of acquiring useful information about how to behave. For instance, when it is costly, selection acting on genes can reduce the importance of individual learning and the need for force. In such contexts, a combination of a limited decision-making ability and effective cultural transmission may be the most effective means of acquiring adaptive 'information'.

On the other hand, non-parental individuals may make better role models than parents because they may have greater skills and knowledge. However, accurately discriminating between adaptive skills and maladaptive inclinations can be costly and time-consuming. In contrast, using simple, low-cost decision-making rules to bias the choice of models or behaviours to imitate can increase the naive person's skills at the tolerable cost of imitating maladaptive behaviour.

Analysing the evolutionary consequences of a variety of simple bias rules suggests that non-parental transmission may be habitually adaptive, especially in variable environments.

7.6 Culture and Darwinian Explanations

All the points discussed so far lead Richerson and Boyd to these 'Hypotheses on the interaction between genes and culture in human evolution':

1. "Culture acts as an inheritance system.
2. Various evolutionary forces will act on culturally transmitted variants. The directional forces include decision-making forces and natural selection.
3. If the pattern of cultural inheritance includes nonparental or otherwise asymmetric transmission, natural selection on cultural variation can increase cultural variants that are not favored by selection on genes.
4. Selection on genes can, however, favor nonparental transmission because this mode of transmission has its own advantages.
5. The capacity for a particular form of cultural transmission will be favored by selection on genes whenever the net fitness advantages exceed the costs. Information costs will frequently favor weakly biased imitation of models, even nonparental models, because the effort needed to accurately separate adaptive from maladaptive behaviors is high".

Richerson and Boyd then conclude that if these hypotheses are correct, there would be no reason to expect any particular human trait in any society to conform to the predictions of standard Darwinian theory. In order to understand human behaviour, we must analyse how the system of cultural transmission interacts with social and environmental contingencies in order to create behavioural patterns. Furthermore, to comprehend the evolution of human behaviour, it is imperative to grasp how the system of cultural transmission has evolved, and how genetic selection affecting this system has favoured or enabled its development.

The authors propose as an example of genetically maladaptive effects the demographic transition in industrial nations over the last century. In this case, natural selection acts on variations that are non-parentally transmitted, showing that families with more resources and time for child-rearing choose to have smaller families, while those with fewer resources choose to have larger ones. This may involve different patterns of parental and non-parental inheritance.

However, it is interesting to note that real human decisions are often underpinned by simple rules, such as, choosing to imitate people who appear happier or more successful. While these simple rules can capture many of the benefits of non-parental cultural transmission, they can also expose individuals to significant costs if selection acts directly on non-parentally transmitted traits.

Richerson and Boyd also argue that, while the hypothesis that selection on non-parentally transmitted cultural variation can reduce genetic fitness is logically consistent, whether it is correct is an empirical question (Richerson & Boyd, 1984, p. 433). In addition, a number of empirical objections can be raised in this regard. For instance, if decision-making forces are weak when faced with the quantity and complexity of culturally acquired behaviour, natural selection acting directly on cultural variations may be an important force of cultural evolution. Furthermore, cultural variation can even be transmitted by parents. When observing significant differences between individuals or groups of people, their cultural history may be a relevant factor. However, this does not preclude the fact that human behaviour can generally be predicted by considering which cultural trait optimises genetic fitness.

While all of these hypotheses are plausible, they are not necessarily correct. In each case, a hypothesis could be constructed to suggest that the behaviour in question, which is considered to be maladaptive, is actually genetically adaptive. There are examples to support a range of hypotheses, from socio-biological to more culturalist ones.

7.7 Conclusions: Co-evolutionism and Law

Although these authors have not worked directly with the evolution of legal rules and institutions, we consider their views on the possible biological and cultural evolutionary explanations, and their interrelationships with respect to cultural behaviours, to be relevant.

Towards the end of their work "*Not by Genes Alone*" (2006, p. 237), they place special emphasis on studying the relationships between the different disciplines of the natural and social sciences, and the interrelations between them. For these authors, the explanation of human culture ultimately rests on understanding the genetic and cultural processes that generate it. However, these processes are closely linked, as the way in which we think, learn and feel biologically directly affects which cultural variants are learned, remembered and taught, thereby influencing which variants persist and spread.

Likewise, some Darwinian conceptual tools, such as the notion of natural selection, are fundamental to understanding some generalised features of human behaviour. For instance, they argue that people value their own children more than those of others because this feeling was favoured by natural selection in the evolutionary past. However, they also emphasise the importance of cultural inheritance, which, being subject to its own natural selection, favoured variants that allowed for greater survival and the tendency to be imitated by those who adopted them.

The complex ways in which genetic and cultural evolution interrelate are now studied by multiple disciplines, including social psychology, experimental economics and many others. All of these disciplines explore some of these relationships, but many questions remain, such as the relationship between micro-evolution at the level of individual behaviour and more macro phenomena, such as large-scale cooperation.

In this sense, Richerson and Boyd (2006, p. 245) argue for the need for a synthetic theory of human behaviour that can reconcile the fields of biology and social science, as well as the different traditions within each field. They consider the value of an evolutionary theory of culture and argue that many of their hypotheses have succeeded in explaining social patterns that had previously been documented by social scientists. They believe that they have provided a framework—the evolutionary one—that allows for the integration of data from diverse disciplines and schools of thought within the social sciences. They also believe that enormous controversies within the social sciences have found natural resolutions within the evolutionary framework. We will consider some of these observations and conclusions in the final part of this book, where we will present our own evolutionary account of law.

References

Dawkins, R. (1989). *The selfish gene*. Oxford University Press.

Richerson, P. J., & Boyd, R. (1984). Natural selection and culture. *BioScience, 34*(7), 430–434.

Richerson, P. J., & Boyd, R. (2006). *Not by genes alone. How culture transformed human evolution*. The University of Chicago Press.

Part III

Evolutionary Account of Law

8

The Bricks of an Evolutionary Account of Law

8.1 The Philosophical, Anthropological and Psychological Assumptions About Agents

Having analysed the main classical and contemporary evolutionary views on institutions, we will now propose our own vision of law as an emerging order. To achieve this, we will take various elements, or 'bricks', from different theories and views, which we believe can be combined to form the basis of our vision of law. In this sense, we will make our own philosophical, anthropological, and psychological assumptions about the interrelated agents that constitute this phenomenon explicit, where possible.

Firstly, we will consider a very 'thin' notion of human nature, as presented by authors such as Hume and Smith, which we discussed in the first part of this work. Here, we present what we have seen of Hume's portrayal of the objective and subjective aspects of human nature. The objective aspect is represented by the 'innumerable wants and needs' experienced by the individual, as well as the scarce resources available to meet these needs. Thus, Hume assumes 'scarcity'to be the

E. M. Santanatoglia, *An Evolutionary Account of Law*, Palgrave Studies in Classical Liberalism, https://doi.org/10.1007/978-3-032-12162-2_8

defining objective characteristic of the individual in relation to their natural surroundings.

In addition, there are the two subjective characteristics—self-interest and limited generosity—which we have already explored. Thus, in Hume‘s terms, self-interest is not seen as a negative disposition or an evil attribute. Rather, he tries to expose how individuals tend to care more for themselves than for others, even though this self-interest includes a natural concern for those close to them, such as family and friends. On the other hand, limited generosity is exhibited as a tendency to be more generous to people who are closer to us than to strangers. Both aspects allow us to observe scarcity as both an objective characteristic and a characteristic of our own limited human nature in terms of our physical and sentimental capacities.

In Chapter 1, we also examined how Hume illustrated the challenges individuals faced in 'pre-social' or 'state of nature' societies. Fundamentally, they would have to face the limitations of strength, the inability to achieve excellence in any particular skill or ability, and the lack of security. These difficulties are solved by the remedies that living in society provides: first, the combination of forces that increases strength; second, the division of labour that improves abilities; and third, mutual aid that provides security.

As discussed in the first chapters, we consider this analysis of human traits in the context of scarce resources to be quite accurate and applicable to the study of human behaviour. In everyday life, we observe that individuals are faced with a limited supply of goods that would satisfy their numerous needs and desires. At the same time, people generally care more about themselves and their loved ones than about strangers. However, neither Hume nor the other Scottish authors present a scenario in which selfish individuals in their natural state are completely isolated and must create artificial bonds with each other. Instead, they present a vision in which individuals have feelings for each other, such as sympathy, and can spontaneously form groups, such as families or small communities. The problem that arises is the possibility of establishing common rules with people outside this close circle. This is where the views of Adam Smith and Adam Ferguson 'enter the scene', offering insight into the mechanisms by which individuals, through trial and error, develop institutions that enable them to coexist peacefully, even with those with whom they have no direct relations or shared projects. In conclusion, these classical authors gradually guide us from explaining coordination (or even cooperation) in small, homogeneous groups—among acquaintances who keep an eye on each other—to explaining cooperation in large, anonymous groups.

In addition to this perspective on human nature, our theoretical proposal will consider other subjective 'constraints', such as bounded rationality and dispersed knowledge, both of which are fundamental to a profound comprehension of the law. The 'bricks' previously introduced in Chapters 2 and 3 serve as a foundation for the subsequent discussion. For instance, it has been examined how Hayek has proposed several ideas related to the issues of rationality, knowledge and information in individual decision-making processes within complex social orders. The following four points summarise the author's thinking on the subject:

(a) **Knowledge is dispersed in society:** there is no complete and coherent core of knowledge available to each person. Individuals have pieces of knowledge that enable them to act and make decisions. This diffusion of knowledge applies not only to technical or scientific knowledge, but also to practical knowledge, the know-how of certain activities or skills, and the interaction of people with different knowledge is what defines the profile of that particular social order.

(b) In addition to technical or scientific knowledge, it is also fundamental to understand the **specific knowledge of the particular circumstances of time and place** that inform individual decision-making processes. In the course of everyday life, individuals base their decisions on specific knowledge and information relevant to their individual circumstances. This specific knowledge of 'time and place' is generally not considered by the social sciences when explaining the rationality behind human interactions.

(c) **The transmission of knowledge:** Hayek also believes that the transmission of both knowledge of specific circumstances of time and place and 'practical knowledge' from one person to another is impossible. This represents a significant difference with respect to scientific knowledge. In this context, he observes that certain social devices, such as the price system and certain abstract legal principles, effectively concentrate dispersed knowledge and information, thereby providing valuable guidance for human actions and decisions.

(d) Consequently, **the human and rational capacity for knowledge is limited**: no human mind can concentrate all the knowledge produced by the social order. Each individual makes decisions by considering fragments of such knowledge. As we have analysed, the social order has spontaneously produced a series of social devices that help people in their decision-making, such as language, prices and abstract legal rules. However, each person makes decisions and interprets the information provided by these social devices in specific circumstances of time and space, with their own subjective abilities and values.

As we will see in this chapter and the next, these considerations about how knowledge and preferences are formed in the process of individual decision-making question some of the assumptions of other theories, such as 'rational choice theory', opening the door to the current and active debate about the extent to which calculative instrumental rationality can explain all human behaviour.

This is also related to the notion of 'bounded rationality', which was introduced in Chapter 6. When criticising the notion of 'homo economicus' and his perfect rationality, Herbert Simon says: "*The capacity of the human mind for formulating and solving complex problems is very small compared with the size of the problems whose solution is required for objectively rational behavior in the real world -or even for a reasonable approximation to such objective rationality*" (Simon cited by Alexander, 2007, p. 5). As previously noted, both 'classical evolutionism'and 'evolutionary game theory' rejected the notion of a decision-maker with a purely rational mind and complete knowledge in these interdependent games. The following chapter will revisit this debate and the notion of rationality that will be adopted for the purpose of formulating our evolutionary account of law.

However, before we debate the extent of human instrumental rationality, we will examine two classic debates in the philosophy of the social sciences. These debates have gained importance in recent years and directly influence the evolutionary approach that we are proposing. The first is the debate between 'methodological individualism' and 'methodological holism', and the second is the discussion between the '*homo economicus*' and '*homo sociologicus*' models.

8.2 First Methodological Debate: Methodological Individualism vs. Methodological Holism

The first debate to be considered is that between 'methodological individualism'and 'methodological holism'. After presenting the main points of view of both positions, we will attempt to address the following questions: What is the view proposed by the different variants of evolutionary thought? Is there a methodology that can integrate both of these approaches?

8.2.1 Methodological Holism

Methodological holism, as well as methodological individualism, can be found in the work of some of the most important historical references in the social sciences and philosophy. Firstly, we should consider one of the most significant proponents of methodological holism: Émile Durkheim. This author, one of the founding figures of sociology, defined the subject of sociology as the science of social facts.

In his "The Rules of Sociological Method" he offers his concept of 'social fact', which is central to understanding his methodological position. He defines social facts as: "(…) a category of facts which present very special characteristics: they consist of manners of acting, thinking and feeling external to the individual, which are invested with a coercive power by virtue of which they exercise control over him. Consequently, since they consist of representations and actions, they cannot be confused with organic phenomena, nor with psychical phenomena, which have no existence save in and through the individual consciousness. Thus, they constitute a new species and to them must be exclusively assigned the term social. It is appropriate, since it is clear that, not having the individual as their substratum, they can have none other than society, either political society in its entirety or one of the partial groups that it includes–religious denominations, political and literary schools, occupational corporations, etc. Moreover, it is for such as these alone that the term is fitting, for the word 'social' has the sole meaning of designating those phenomena which fall into none of the categories of facts already constituted and labelled. They are consequently the proper field of sociology" (Durkheim, 1982, p. 52).

In short, Durkheim is giving a definite notion of social fact as coercive and external, that is, originating outside the individual. Moreover, their coercive force depends upon the existence of groups. In this sense, the social fact has its own existence, independently of the individuals who 'embody' it each time. From this perspective, it could be argued that the character of social reality does not need to reflect the characteristics of the individuals belonging to the group. Therefore, social facts exist independently, not as the simple sum or collection of individual facts, but as objects in their own right, with their own existence and characteristics that make them worthy of study.

From a Durkheimian perspective, the belief that an individual can, through their own decision, transform a social fact is considered naïve. They are independent of one individual manifestation or another (cf. Suicide) and even individual motivations for action become practically irrelevant for the purposes of the study of 'social facts'. The latter are closely linked to the social rules that underpin each group or sub-group and that define the limits of individual action.

Therefore, the social fact becomes conceptually independent. When explaining an individual's behaviour from a sociological perspective, reference should be made to the social facts that have determined it. To understand an individual's actions or decisions, it is essential to consider the group they belong to and the applicable social rules. This analysis enables us to 'deduce' the reasons behind an individual's behaviour.

8.2.2 Methodological Individualism

In contrast, methodological individualism is a position supported by prominent philosophers and social scientists, including Max Weber, Karl Popper and Friedrich Hayek. In this case, we will take the proposal of John Watkins, a disciple of Popper and one of the most stringent proponents of methodological individualism. In his work "Historical Explanation in the Social Science" (Watkins, 1994), the author proposed the five theses of methodological individualism, namely:

1. **The Ontological Thesis:** According to this view, all social entities are merely aggregate composites of individuals. Watkins defines it this way: "(...) the ultimate constituents of the social world are individual people who act more or less appropriately in the light of their dispositions and understanding of their situation".

2. This is followed by **the Meaning Thesis,** according to which all social concepts must be definable in terms of concepts referring only to individuals, their relations and their behaviour.

3. **Explanatory Thesis:** For Watkins, there are no independent social explanations—all social facts and law-like behaviour must be explainable only in terms of individual facts, i.e. facts about individuals, their motives, powers, beliefs and capacities.

Watkins says: "There may be unfinished or halfway explanations of large-scale social phenomena (say, inflation) in terms of other large-scale phenomena (say, full employment); but we shall not have arrived at rock-bottom explanations of such large-scale phenomena until we have deduced an account of them from statements about the dispositions, beliefs, resources, and interrelations of individuals (The individuals may remain anonymous and only typical dispositions, etc. may be attributed to them)" (Watkins, 1994, p. 442).

4. **Regulative Thesis:** Any social scientific theory must be compatible with a certain set of principles to be given. Theories that fail to conform to these principles must be rejected. Here we observe that Watkins adopts a strongly normative position, establishing a criterion for distinguishing when there is a scientific theory.

5. **Law-reduction thesis:** All law-like regularities that hold between social entities can be derived from law-like regularities that hold between individual constituent entities.

Watkins's argument is that, since individuals are the ultimate constituents of society, each social institution or event must be studied through the specific configurations of individuals, their dispositions, situations, beliefs, etc. Otherwise, we will only be left with 'incomplete or half-finished explanations' of large-scale social phenomena. Watkins also considers that regularities in social life could be explained in terms of models that exhibit such regularities as the result of 'self-evident' psychological material (1994, p. 442). We would then need to identify specific individual dispositions and how these generate a typical or regular process (similar to Weberian ideal types).

In conclusion, taking into account the five theses, we can say that, from a very strict methodological individualism, there are no social facts independent of the subjects that make them up. Conversely, from an ontological perspective, to a more methodological and even normative standpoint, the notion that only individual facts exist and that these, when combined and added together, constitute larger phenomena or social facts, is consistently emphasised. It is crucial to always bear this aspect in mind, and as such, it would be inappropriate to discuss 'macro' notions without also referencing the 'micro' elements that comprise them.

8.2.3 Comparison of the Two Methodologies

Returning to the point about how to explain an individual's behaviour or individual actions, even as an elementary component of a larger social phenomenon, we can then say that each of the methodological positions proposes inverse paths.

From the perspective of methodological holism, the behaviour of individuals must be explained by being deduced from:

(a) Macroscopic laws that apply to the totality of the social system as a whole. As illustrated by Durkheim's study of social rules, whether group-based or sub-group-based, this concept provides a framework for understanding how individuals adhere to specific guidelines when making decisions.
(b) Descriptions of the positions (or functions) of individuals within that whole. In this sense, the concept of 'role' becomes pivotal in explaining the range of behaviours permitted for an individual based on their specific position within the group.
(c) Consequently, from the perspective of methodological holism, if we wish to comprehend the behaviour of an individual, it is imperative to first identify the groups to which that individual belongs (women or men, young or old, of this or that nationality, of this or that religion, etc.). Once the group(s) to which the individual belongs has been established, the social rules that govern that group and its subgroups should be studied, in order to understand that behaviour by following those rules. Finally, it is essential to understand the specific role that each individual occupies in the group, as this determines the limits of actions allowed or forbidden for that role. For instance, when analysing the behaviour of an individual belonging to a specific religion, the permitted or prohibited behaviours may vary depending on whether they are a religious leader within that community or simply a devout follower of its guidelines.

If, on the other hand, we take the opposite standpoint—that of methodological individualism—and want to understand social processes and events, they should be explained by being deduced from:

(a) The principles that govern the behaviour of the individuals involved. In this sense, we should then try to understand their motivations, the structure of the individual decision-making process, the features of their cognitive apparatus or its possible limitations, the influence of affects or other elements on the reasoning process, etc. This will enable us to understand the characteristics of the actions that make up the basic elements of the social process to be studied.

(b) The description of their situation. Similarly, the specific circumstances of the subject at the time of action, their relationship with the context, and their interaction with other individuals, become very relevant. A significant part of the outcomes of individual actions are dependent not only on the motivations or objectives of the agent, but also on the interaction of that individual and their action with other individuals. Therefore, while the unit of study for methodological individualism is the individual, it is important to note that this does not exclude the analysis of the individual's relationships with other subjects and the context. This is crucial in order to understand how the sum of these actions can delineate the specific form of the phenomenon or social process under study.

8.3 Evolutionism and a Moderate Individualism: The Resolution of the Dichotomy Between Methodological Individualism and Holism

We believe that the dichotomy posed by the strictest positions of both methodologies could be overcome by the evolutionary account of law that we are proposing.

Thus, we will try to answer questions such as: Does the evolutionary account of law necessarily imply a methodological holism, given that it appears to have a whole as its object of study (social orders or institutional frameworks)? But aren't these orders the result of individual actions and interactions?

Some interpreters of Friedrich Hayek's work claim that his view of 'self-generated' social orders necessarily implies a holistic point of view (De Sousa, 2005, p. 124; Heath, 1992, p. 28). That he would have moved from his strict methodological individualism, as manifested in his early work such as 'The Counter-Revolution in Science' (1952) to a more holistic stance in his more mature work such as 'Law, Legislation and Liberty' (1983). In fact, some complexity theorists (McGlade & Garnsey, 2006) consider that complex systems, studied from an evolutionary perspective, entail the use of a holistic methodology. However, we believe that the evolutionary account of law that we propose—and also Hayek's mature work—calls for a moderate methodological individualism.

Furthermore, proponents of these visions have advocated for an individualistic methodology in different ways. It has been acknowledged by several writers that Hayek, in conjunction with Popper and Watkins, is considered to be among the foremost proponents of methodological individualism in the twentieth century. It can be argued that this individualism was a reaction to a particular view of social facts, such as that proposed by Durkheim. This implies maintaining a position equidistant from both radical methodological holism—as advocated by Durkheim—and extreme methodological individualism—as proposed by the early Hayek or Watkins.

The question arises as to why, despite our support for the individualistic approach, we should consider a shift away from this radical methodological individualism. This strict position merits several resistances, which we will now analyse.

Strict methodological individualism proposed a compositional method for the social sciences, by which, through the observation of the attitudes of individuals whose combination allows us to reproduce a complex phenomenon, which generally cannot be studied by direct observation. Should we proceed, we may encounter certain fallacies and logical problems.

On the one hand, when explaining the characteristics of social wholes (in our case, legal orders) from the properties of their parts, we run the risk of falling into the fallacy of composition. Under this fallacy, it is assumed that all the individual properties can be distributed from the parts to the whole without major problems.

As previously stated, we believe that we are unable to make such a 'leap' because the characteristics that can be attributed to individuals who, in their interactions, produce a social phenomenon, cannot be attributed to such phenomena. For instance, asserting that individuals are 'selfish' or 'self-interested' does not apply to the societies, moral orders or legal systems that they compose or bring into being. As we mentioned in the first chapter of this work, using Mandeville's words, we may even encounter individual characteristics that contradict the characteristics of the phenomena they produce. Therefore, we may observe individuals who are 'ungenerous' or even 'very selfish' or 'miserly' towards others, who produce prosperous and wealthy communities and thus benefit third parties without having foreseen it or wished it.

In this line of thought, we are also confronted with the criticism of several authors including Kincaid (1994, p. 500), who objects to methodological individualism, particularly to what we have seen as the Fifth Thesis proposed by Watkins for its reductionist method. He presents three reasons for this criticism:

(A) <u>The possible multiple realisations of social events:</u> the reduction of social terms to individual terms would require the possibility of an exact or very precise equivalence between the social terms and the individual terms, but if one of them fails (in this case the individual), all the bi-conditional conditions would fail. Thus, since the individual terms are realisable in multiple ways as representing the social, equivalence between the social term and the individual term cannot be established as required by the thesis.

(B) <u>Individual actions have indefinitely many social descriptions depending on context.</u> The archetypal case is when we observe an individual taking the life of another. What is the significance of this action? Is it an act of homicide? Is it the application of a death penalty? Or is it an act of war in a war context? Kincaid believes that this problem could be solved by offering fewer specific notions of individual behaviour, including broader contexts. However, how can we describe this context without using 'holistic' terms? In this case, the thesis would leave us lacking resources, as we would be unable to make use of any social notions.

(C) <u>Any workable individualist social theory will in all likelihood presuppose social facts.</u> Here the author notes that, in describing the relevant context of an individual action, we often refer to social roles or types of individuals, not to particular individual actions. Thus, even if we recognise their individual origin, we cannot describe them without reference to some social terms.

Considering these critiques and resistances, we find that a 'moderate' methodological individualism—as the one embodied by the Scottish Enlightenment authors—would allow us to understand evolving social phenomena. It implies:

1. That every social event, such as the emergence of a legal order, is not the direct and deliberate consequence of the actions of individuals, but the unplanned result of multiple individual interrelationships. Therefore, it is not possible to fully explain the characteristics of the whole by merely describing the characteristics of the individuals who unintentionally produce that outcome. This approach helps avoid the fallacy of composition that could arise from a strict and naïve methodological individualism, such as the one demanded by Watkins.
2. This 'moderate' individualism thus represents an ontological thesis that provides a genetic explanation of social facts, since all objects of social theoretical research are the product of human actions and are not completely independent of this individualistic 'genesis'.
3. Consequently, it is not necessary for any theory that aims to explain or describe a social fact to be translated into individual statements or 'reduced' in any way. If social facts are the consequence, perhaps unintended, of individual actions, beliefs, etc., it is not necessary to try to have a perfect translation of every social theory into individual statements of any kind in order to have a good explanation of the phenomena.

So, is it possible to be a methodological individualist without falling into the fallacy of composition and the problems presented by Kinkaid? Yes, we are confident that these challenges could be overcome, along with the majority of the discussions and objections to MI, since these criticisms are attacking a literal interpretation of Hayek's 'compositional' method and Watkins'radical position. The evolutionary view we propose calls for a more moderate form of methodological individualism, one which even Kinkaid would be willing to accept (Kincaid 1994, p. 509).

The apparent paradox between the study of (social, legal) orders as totalities and methodological individualism in evolutionary theory is resolved simply by perceiving the notions of individual and society (seen as a spontaneous order) as co-dependent. As with Hume and Hayek (later), this view does not attempt to explain society as a simple sum of isolated individuals or as the mere generalisation of individual properties. The 'outcome' of individual interactions may be much more complex than the mere sum of those interactions and may have its own properties, different from the properties of the individuals who contribute to its emergence. Furthermore, it can be studied in its own right, with no need to refer to individual terms or to translate it into individual actions at each step. However, it is crucial to remember that individual actions are the origin and support of these orders, meaning that without them, we could not have order. This perspective differs significantly from Durkheim's approach, as it does not consider these social facts to be entirely independent, external and coercive. On the contrary, they are dependent on individual actions, are endogenous and can be changed as individuals change in their beliefs, desires and interrelationships.

More recent authors, such as Richerson and Boyd agree that the more Darwinian view of concepts allows us to fluidly relate individual and collective phenomena, eliminating the need to choose between 'macro' and 'micro' levels (2006, p. 247). Indeed, they recall that biological theory includes genes, individuals and populations, and that in these models, what happens to individuals affects the properties of populations. These authors believe that if we add culture to this consideration, Darwinian tools are still very useful in helping us to create links between phenomena across different levels of organisation. They conclude: "Individuals seem to be hapless prisoners of their institutions because, in the short run, individual decisions don't have much effect on institutions. But, in the long run, accumulated over many decisions, individual decisions have a profound effect on institutions. Evolutionary theory gets right the basic structure of the relationship between individuals and the collective properties of their societies" (Richerson & Boyd, 2006, p. 247).

In the following chapter, we will present a detailed analysis of how orders can evolve across three distinct levels: biological, individual and social. In all of them, individuals are the foundation of the evolutionary process, but only in one of them is the individual an active and conscious agent of change, that is, in the individual learning process. In other evolutionary processes, whether biological, social or institutional, although the individual is a central part of the process, they are not a conscious or isolated agent and cannot control it completely, even if they wanted to. This does not imply that the analysis of the individual's specific manner of acting and making decisions is not pivotal to comprehending how these processes occur.

8.4 Second Methodological Debate: *Homo Economicus* and *Homo Sociologicus*—Agent's Motivations

Having reviewed the debate between methodological individualism and holism and having concluded with the possibility of continuing our study by means of a moderate methodological individualism, we now turn to a second methodological debate.

This debate also has its history, but it has taken on particular value in the face of the new evolutionary schools of thought in the social sciences, which were the focus of the second part of this book. If we adopt a perspective that recognises human action and individual motivations as a first step towards comprehending social phenomena, then two clear, and even dichotomous, models emerge from the social sciences themselves. On the one hand, the model that will be referred to herein as '*homo economicus*', a concept strongly represented by the agent model proposed by classical microeconomics. Conversely, *the* '*homo sociologicus*', a concept derived from disciplines such as sociology and anthropology, represents an idealised subject that differs significantly from the preceding model.

Before we proceed with the debate, it would be opportune to review some classical notions offered by Max Weber. In the context of social sciences that aim to explain the structure of individual actions and decisions, we present the 'classical' classification of social actions proposed by Max Weber, a framework that we consider to be highly useful. Weber's classification of individual actions is based on the motivations or meanings behind them. We will then examine the definitions of action and social action, and the classification proposed by the author in 'Economy and Society' (Weber, 1997).

8.4.1 Action and Social Action for Max Weber

It is important to note that, for Weber, 'action' is understood as that human conduct which the agent or agents themselves see as subjectively significant (subjective meaning). Such conduct may be internal or external and may consist of the agent doing something or refraining from doing something. In turn, a 'social action'is defined as a conduct in which the meaning attributed to it by the agent(s) implies a relation with respect to the conduct of another person(s). Social action can be related to the past, present or future behaviour of other people.

In this sense, the 'other persons', considered in the subjective sense, can be particular individuals known to the agent, or a group of indefinite size, whose members are not known to the agent.

Of course, not every kind of action and not every kind of external behaviour is a 'social' action. For example, when the meaning of this action results simply from expectations about the behaviour of material objects. Consequently, social action should not be identified with: (a) many people acting together in a similar way or (b) one person acting under the influence of the behaviour of other people.

A very good example Weber proposes of a 'social action' is that of the use of money in society (1997, p. 18). The term 'currency' refers to a medium of exchange that is accepted by agents in transactions, based on the expectation that a significant number of other individuals, with whom the agent has no personal connection, will be willing to accept that particular currency as a medium of exchange in the future. In this context, the subjects are not known to the agent and are not present at the time of the action. However, the agent takes them into account when accepting money as a form of exchange for a good or service.

8.4.2 Four Types of Social Action for Weber

In the domain of social actions, Weber distinguishes four 'ideal types' of action. Actions can be (Weber, 1997, p. 20, 1978, p. 28):

1. **Means-ends rational action:** this type of action is determined by the agent's expectations of behaviour, both of objects in the external world and of other people and using these expectations as 'conditions' or 'means' for the achievement of rationally weighed and pursued ends of one's own.
2. **Value-rational action:** this type of action is determined by the agent's conscious belief in the value—ethical, aesthetic, religious or otherwise—of a given conduct, without any relation to the result. In other words, the agent acts in accordance with the principle that animates it, not for any specific outcome (even if the consequences of the act that he considers right may harm him).
3. **Affectual action:** this type of behaviour is especially driven by the agent's current affections and sentimental states. His is an emotional decision, made without full consideration of the potential consequences or underlying principles.
4. Finally, **traditional action** is determined by a custom or tradition that is deeply rooted in society.

Weber also considers the rationality of each of these types of social action, which will be very useful for the issue of the rationality of action that we will analyse in the next section of this chapter.

Therefore, he establishes that the first type of action, i.e. rational action according to ends, is the 'most rational' of the four types of action. This is because it involves the agent establishing a goal and evaluating alternative ways to achieve it and finally choosing the most efficient way to reach that goal. This type of action is easily 'rationally re-constructible' by the observer and clearly implies the use of an identifiable instrumental rationality.

The second type of action, which, according to Weber, is of a weaker rationality, is still within the realms of reason. The agent affirms a value in choosing the action, but, in contrast to the first type, this is more difficult for the observer to understand rationally, since it would have to coincide with the agent's value framework.

Weber's third type of action, affectual action, would already fall into the realm of irrationality. In this scenario, the agent is driven by strong emotions or feelings and does not consider the potential consequences of the actions, nor the values that motivate them. Instead, they act impulsively.

Finally, for Weber, traditional action is the most irrational of all. He thus describes a 'gradation' of rationality between the most rational (purposeful) and the most irrational (traditional) actions. In the latter case, the agent does not evaluate the consequences of their actions or the values that motivate them, and they are not moved by their own feelings. Instead, they carry out the action because they were taught to do so, or because it has always been done that way, or because everyone does it that way. This overrides their own criteria, ends, values, etc.

This classification, along with the underlying view of the rationality of actions proposed by Weber, remains highly relevant in the contemporary context. This is due to the resurgence of interest in the debate in light of recent theoretical developments, including rational choice theory, behavioural economics, and various psychological theories of decision-making procedures in the human brain. We will see some of the implications in the next section of this chapter.

8.4.3 Desires and Opportunities

On the other hand, we bring here the analysis of individual behaviour proposed by Jon Elster (2007, 3rd part), who proposes to analyse action from the perspective of desires and opportunities.

In this author's opinion, the first step in understanding individual behaviour is to conceive the whole spectrum of possible actions that the individual could perform, in the abstract. We then consider the action we observe against this large range of possible actions as the result of two successive filtering operations:

1. **First filter:** Elster conceives it as consisting of all the physical, economic, legal and other constraints facing the agent. The set of opportunities is constituted by the actions that are compatible with all these restrictions. Opportunities are defined as the options or means available to the agent.
2. **The second filter** would be represented by the mechanisms that determine which of the actions in the opportunity set is actually carried out. The agent selects the course of action that is expected to deliver the best results, based on their 'desires or preferences', which in turn define what the agent considers to be possible.

As Elster himself proposes, desires and opportunities are not always independent of each other, as is sometimes assumed. Furthermore, this approach is not exhaustive. While I may have the opportunities to take the most appropriate action to fulfil my desire, I may not have the 'fitness' to identify the correct action. In other cases, this inability may be situated at an earlier stage, where the agent would lack the opportunity or the desire to acquire the ability.

8.4.4 Opportunity-Based Explanations

Elster distinguishes between two types of behavioural explanations, those that are opportunity-centred and those that are desire-centred. Although behaviour is the joint result of desires and opportunities, its variation over time can be explained largely on the basis of opportunities.

Indifference curves: If we consider a consumer with a specific desire to consume a certain good or service, for example to listen to a concert, they must allocate their income between that good and a selection of everyday consumer goods. This will be influenced by relative prices and income. Should prices change, consumers may adjust their income distribution; however, they will never consume more than their total income.

Even if the second filter (wants) could be anything (in this case, attending that concert), the consumer would still be severely constrained by the first filter of opportunities.

In this regard, some economists propose the **'equal desires'** hypothesis, asserting that individuals possess similar desires and preferences, with differences arising from differing opportunities. In cases where a preference depends on an ability or aptitude (e.g. enjoying classical music), it is claimed that this aptitude depends on the opportunity to acquire it, and the desire to acquire it is assumed to be uniform across the population.

It is thus argued that opportunities are more fundamental than desires, since they are easier to observe, not only by specialists but also by other members of society. It is clear that opportunities are fundamental because of their potential to influence behaviour. It is more straightforward to alter circumstances and opportunities than it is for people to change their opinions (although this argument is more about the costs and benefits of alternative policies than it is about relative explanatory power).

8.4.5 *Homo Economicus* and *Homo Sociologicus*

Finally, we will introduce the basic features of the Homo Economicus and Homo Sociologicus models.

We will commence by following the analysis proposed by Boudon (Boudon, 2010) which sets out various ways of explaining individual behaviour. In the social sciences (economics, sociology, political science, etc.), Boudon contends that, while these fields seek to elucidate collective phenomena, they are compelled to elucidate individual behaviours, as these ultimately constitute the foundation of collective phenomena.

In this way, he adopts the methodological individualism that has been discussed already, according to which (according to its strictest version) social phenomena are 'composed' of individual phenomena and, in order to explain the former, it is necessary to deduce them from the principles that govern the behaviour of the participating individuals (their beliefs, dispositions, resources, interrelationships) and the description of their situation. Boudon also adds that, within this explanation of individual behaviour, one can appeal to motives of the 'why' type (efficient causes) or to motives of the 'in order to…' or 'what for' type (final causes).

As a result, we are confronted with the two models mentioned above, which offer divergent insights into the individual and their motivations.

8.4.5.1 Homo Economicus

For this model the following are the most salient characteristics of the individual:

- Selfishness or self-interest is the defining feature of human nature.
- Utility maximisation is the expected action of a rational, self-interested individual.
- The assumption is made of a strict individual rationality, with requirements on preferences and decision-making processes.

This archetype of the individual was initially applied to the field of market transactions, but was later adopted by other disciplines and contexts, such as politics and law. Among them, we can highlight some versions of the 'law and economics theory', which brought this type of analysis to the study of different branches of law.

From this perspective, these characteristics appear to provide a comprehensive explanation of human action, orienting it towards the fulfilment of personal desires and goals. However, this view has been criticised for its limitations, with behaviours that cannot be explained by this model of individual action being observed.

8.4.5.2 Homo Sociologicus

In contrast, the *Homo Sociologicus* model proposes that the most distinctive features of human behaviour are as follows:

- Human nature is characterised by the ability of individuals to follow rules.

- Human action is defined by a set of social rules that act as both motivations and constraints.
- From this perspective, as previously mentioned, social roles are fundamental to understanding human behaviour, since they establish the range of 'valid' actions and decisions that the individual might consider in a specific social context.

8.4.6 The *Homo Economicus* and the Evolutionary Theory of Law

Based on the distinction presented above, we will introduce here the considerations of Phillip Pettit who in his paper "The virtual reality of Homo Economicus" (Pettit, 1995, p. 308) presents the debate and proposes a solution.

Thus, Pettit sums up the economists' view of agents' minds in this way: "(…) economists present human agents as relatively self-regarding creatures who act with a view to doing as well as possible by their predominantly self-regarding desires. These desires are usually assumed to be desires for what is loosely described as economic advantage or gain: that is, roughly, for advantage or gain in the sorts of things that can be traded. But self-interested desires, of course, may extend to other goods too, and there is nothing inimical to economics in explaining patterns of behaviour by reference, say, to those non-tradable goods that consist in being well loved or well regarded" (Pettit, 1995, p. 314).

It is notable that this vision of agents, as described by Pettit, finds expression in the field of legal theory through the school of 'law and economics', also called 'economic analysis of law'. In its most classical form, the school assumes that agents act as 'homo economicus'. This involves calculating the costs and benefits of following or violating rules, evaluating the efficiency of certain institutional arrangements and finding the solution to legal conflicts through economic analysis. But what could we say from an evolutionary view of law, such as the one we are presenting?

Firstly, we can see that, from the assumptions of human nature we have been working with, we can agree in general terms with the 'homo economicus' view. Our evolutionary approach establishes self-interested individuals, guided by their desires and goals. However, there are some key differences to note:

(a) First, in our evolutionary view—and from the Scottish school to the present day—human 'selfishness' includes concerns about others, such as family and kin, therefore others are considered in the evaluation of the act. This natural inclination and sympathy for others implies the capacity to generate groups and small societies. In other words, it appears that our assumption of human nature is more comprehensive than the 'homo economicus', considering a wider range of factors as potential motivations for action. Furthermore, the structure of social relations and the role of certain individuals (such as leaders or arbitrators) influence individual decision-making processes.
(b) Our conception of 'self-centeredness' does not necessarily include a conscious utility calculus as implied by the *'homo economicus'* perspective. A view of the individual with sympathetic inclinations towards others, limited knowledge and limited rationality replaces the agent proposed by the *'homo economicus'* view, which makes it more difficult to claim that individuals act 'purely rationally' with full information.

Continuing with Pettit, he also observes that the 'homo economicus' conception of the agent's mind may clash with the view generally adopted by the everyday view of human action. This 'common sense' perspective encompasses a range of concerns that are not fully addressed using a hyper-rational, individualistic viewpoint, such as social norms, expectations of others, merit, friendship and shared history. This represents a challenge to the 'homo economicus' view. However, Pettit believes he has a vision capable of reconciling these two models and refers to this as the *'virtual reality of homo economicus'*. In Pettit's terms "(…) whereas ordinary folk conform in most contexts to the picture of the common mind, the economic mind is still *implicitly* present in such contexts" (Pettit, 1995, p. 317).

In Pettit's virtual-actual model, the agent does not consistently prioritise self-interest considerations in the deliberation and decision-making process. This concern practically influences the cases of decisions that 'sound' certain 'alarms' at the moment when the agent's interests may be compromised, and then self-interest considerations and cost/benefit evaluations of different courses of action will appear on the scene.

At Pettit, we primarily operate in accordance with rules, common patterns and the tastes of others. However, in situations where our most fundamental interests or assets are at stake (e.g. life, physical integrity, our most important assets), the 'homo economicus' perspective surfaces, and we begin to evaluate our actions based on cost-benefit analysis. He believes that this reference to a virtual self-regard, although not useful to explain the emergence or survival of every behavioural pattern, could be useful to explain "the resilience of that pattern of behaviour under various shocks and disturbances" (Pettit, 1995, p. 324).

Finally, he concludes that explaining human behaviour in terms of virtual self-interest, even in cases of non-market behaviour, allows us to reconcile the economic and common-sense explanations.

We find Pettit‘s proposal very interesting, where both models (HE and HS) coexist, with *'homo sociologicus'* acting in everyday life, and 'homo economicus' in virtual mode, ready to act when the agent of action himself is in danger. However, our evolutionary perspective challenges Pettit‘s assertion that self-interested concerns can solely explain the resistance of social norms and institutions, but not their emergence. The broader conception of 'self-interest' that was proposed encompasses the idea that, because individuals have discovered the benefits of living in society, they can pursue common interests with people outside their immediate social circle. As demonstrated, the emergence of legal rules and institutions (and even moral and social rules) can be attributed to self-centred human behaviour, not always deliberate, considering that individuals have concerns that extend beyond the economic perspective.

Secondly, the evolutionary account of law provides a framework for understanding the dynamics of strategies and norms. It is important to note that, due to its ability to consider individuals with changing beliefs, expectations and social frameworks, 'rational' responses can be very different in each context. We will address this issue in more detail in the following section.

Finally, our evolutionary view of law differs from the 'homo economicus' view by considering that "Man is as much a rule-following animal as a purpose-seeking one" (Hayek, 1983, p. 11), which presents us with the problem of the 'homo sociologicus' view that we will discuss in the next section.

8.4.7 *Homo Sociologicus* and the Evolutionary Theory of Law

As we have seen, the '*homo sociologicus*' model describes human beings as 'rule followers'. Those who propose '*homo sociologicus*' readings of individual action align closely with a 'holistic' view of society, giving social norms a significant place in their analyses. In the context of groups that define the identity of subjects, individual actions become comprehensible only when viewed through the lens of the social norms that are characteristic of each group. Therefore, these social norms are pivotal because they are not only constitutive of the particular society, but also of the individual actions of the human beings who live in it. Social norms, therefore, indicate the range of permissible actions and the punishment for non-followers within the community.

As previously mentioned, Weber's (1978, p. 28) classification of social action comprises four 'ideal types': a) means-ends rational actions, b) value-rational action, c) affectual action and d) traditional action. Hollis recommends taking up this classification, broadening the notion of rationality proposed by Weber. In this way, Hollis (1994, p. 151) suggests—based on Weber's ideal types—that not only 'homo economicus', action guided by instrumental rationality, but also 'homo sociologicus', typically represented in the role of the bureaucrat, could represent the 'rational' type. That is, in his words: "whereas for *homo economicus* to be rational is to calculate, for *homo sociologicus* to be rational is to follow a rule". So, in this interpretation of Weber's ideal types, the scope of rationality is broader and encompasses both explanations, without dismissing the sociological explanation as irrational.

Moreover, Hollis, referring to Hume's discussion of 'the origin of justice and property' (1994, p. 192), calls for a more complex moral psychology to understand the emergence of rules and promises between strangers. He thinks that certain relationships or negotiations between individuals—such as the 'Centipede Game'—(Binmore, 2005, p. 71) can be better explained from the point of view of '*homo sociologicus*' than from that of '*homo economicus*'. In fact, Hollis criticises 'rational choice theory' (Hollis, 1994, p. 184) since, in his view, it works with ideal types that lack a particular psychology, treats preferences as given, makes the origin of preferences irrelevant, and only concentrates on how these preferences produce certain choices. We will discuss these issues of individual rationality in more detail in the next chapter.

We agree with Hollis in that "choices can be individual and reasoned, without necessarily being instrumental" and that, in most cases, both views are necessary to understand human behaviour. He states that "Yet we have not been reworking the notion of choice simply to have it swallowed by the notion of rule-following. The starting image was of two filters, with the normative context creating a menu of options and then the particular choice made by rational calculation. The upshot, I think, is that the filters coalesce. Strategically rational choices depend on normative expectations, which themselves depend on what it is strategically rational for a social agent to choose. Sel, roles and reason cannot be disentangled" (Hollis, 1994, p. 195). Our evolutionary view of rules provides an understanding of human psychology that incorporates these normative considerations. This conception is more aligned with Hollis's view of the 'intelligent' rule-follower than with the pure view of the rational, maximising agent.

Hollis also suggests using Wittgenstein's 'language games' to understand human action in a social context. These are the rules that an individual follows as part of a larger 'game' formed by the interaction of several individuals. These rules, created by the participants, are reinforced through repeated adherence. There are constitutive rules, which determine the boundaries of the game, and regulative rules, which establish the 'moves' permissible within it. He states "… I would like to make an ontological suggestion about a social world where choices are strategic and rules are constructed in the course of following them" (Hollis, 1994, p. 197).

This proposal has similarities with our evolutionary view in that it states that rules evolve gradually and change according to players' behaviour since they are not always fully aware of the consequences of their actions. However, there are also some differences:

Firstly, 'language games' do not describe human nature, nor do they explain why individuals interact or how these games and their norms emerge and disappear. In contrast, the evolutionary view implies a thin yet substantive notion of human nature, shedding light on the possible origins of social norms and institutions.

Secondly, the 'language games' proposal offers no notion of human nature and therefore does not allow us to expect any specific behaviour or resulting rules. On the contrary, the evolutionary view provides a framework for understanding human nature, enabling us to form expectations about possible behaviours and the rules individuals may follow within a social order. For instance, we might anticipate that people would prioritise the well-being of their family and friends over that of strangers, and act accordingly.

Thirdly, Hollis's interpretation of 'language games' appears to portray a social world in which individuals are conscious of the rules they establish or adhere to. They seem to understand the meanings attached to their actions or words, and how these meanings differ from those of other 'language games'. By contrast, the Hayekian view of spontaneous orders and the social dynamics studied by current evolutionism and evolutionary game theory entail a view in which individuals are not fully aware of the consequences of their actions. While they may occasionally set out to consciously create a system of norms or modify an existing rule (for example, when a bill is introduced), they often unknowingly create or change rules through their actions. Social and legal orders are games played by individuals who are not aware that they are 'players' in such games.

8.4.8 Evolutionary Theory and the Resolution of the Dichotomy Between *Homo Economicus* and *Homo Sociologicus*

As we have said, this evolutionary view of the emergence of rules, and of legal norms in particular, enables us to reconcile a dichotomy in social thought. There are two almost antagonistic conceptions of human action and its social context that can influence our view of law. Indeed, some legal theories implicitly or explicitly adopt these conceptions. We will discuss the main arguments of each view, their influence on legal thought, and finally how the evolutionary explanation of law, as set out in the theory of spontaneous orders, might resolve this dichotomy.

In summary, on the one hand, we have the 'homo economicus' view, which describes the decision-making process of rational individuals seeking to maximise utility. This view highlights egoism or self-interest as a defining characteristic of human nature, and rationality (utility maximisation) as one of the ways in which this characteristic expresses itself. Initially applied to market transactions, this view was subsequently extended to explain actions in non-market contexts. From this perspective, these characteristics appear to offer a 'complete' explanation of human action as behaviour oriented towards satisfying one's own desires or goals.

In contrast, the 'homo sociologicus' view introduces us to the study of human action in a social context. Here, human action appears to be influenced by the social norms or rules of a particular society, acting as motivations or constraints, or by the characteristics or demands of the social role played by the individual at a given time. This establishes the range of 'valid' actions and decisions that can be considered. Thus, human nature could be defined as the capacity to follow rules or play a role within a social structure.

The contradiction between these two views of human action depends on the idea that they are mutually exclusive: either individuals are always goal-oriented, taking into account their own desires without considering their context or other human beings, or they are blind followers of established rules, without their own criteria, who do not take into account their own desires and goals. We believe that our evolutionary view allows us to combine these two perspectives.

In conclusion, our evolutionary view reconciles the 'homo economicus' and 'homo sociologicus' perspectives. While individuals are self-interested, this does not mean that they do not form necessary relationships with others or recognise the mutual need to resolve coordination conflicts. They may be motivated by various factors, such as self-interest, sympathy for others, or learning mechanisms that enable them to imitate or adopt more successful strategies. Their actions produce regularities that are often internalised as rules, making them more effective. These rules also adapt individuals to the changing desires and goals of others. By following these rules, individuals also reinforce expectations regarding their own and others' actions. In conclusion, individuals are rule followers of rules that are created involuntarily by their own selfish behaviour and the interrelationships between them.

References

Alexander, J. M. K. (2007). *The structural evolution of morality.* Cambridge University Press.

Binmore, K. (2005). *Natural justice.* Oxford University Press.

Boudon, R. (2010). *La racionalidad en las Ciencias Sociales.* Ediciones Nuevas Visiones.

De Sousa, F. (2005). Hayek and individualism: Some question marks. *History of Economic Ideas, XIII*(2), 111–127.

Durkheim, Emile. (1982). *The rules of sociological method.* Simon & Schuster. (Original work published 1895)

Elster, J. (2007). *Explaining social behavior: More nuts and bolts for the social sciences.* Cambridge University Press.

Hayek, F. A. (1952). *The counter-revolution of science.* The Free Press Glencoe.

Hayek, Friedrich A., (1983). *Law, legislation and liberty* (I vols.). The University of Chicago Press. (Original work published 1973)

Heath, E. (1992). Rules, function, and the invisible hand. An interpretation of Hayek's social theory. *Philosophy of the Social Sciences, 22*(1), 28.

Hollis, M. (1994). *The philosophy of social science: An introduction*. Cambridge University Press.

Kincaid, H. (1994). Reduction, explanation and individualism. In M. Martin & L. C. McIntyre (Eds.), *Reading in the philosophy of social sciences* (pp. 497–515). Massachusetts Institute of Technology.

McGlade, J., & Garnsey, E. (2006). The nature of complexity. In *Complexity and co-evolution*. Edwards Elgar Publishing Limited.

Pettit, P. (1995). The virtual reality of 'Homo Economicus'. *The Monist, 78*(3), 308–329.

Richerson, P. J., & Boyd, R. (2006). *Not by genes alone*. The University of Chicago Press.

Watkins, J. (1994). Historical explanation in the social sciences. In M. Martin & L. C. McIntyre (Eds.), *Reading in the philosophy of social sciences* (pp. 441–450). Massachusetts Institute of Technology. Original work published 1957.

Weber, M. (1978). The logic of social action. In M. Weber & W. G. Runciman (Eds.), *Max Weber: Selections in translation* (p. 28). Cambridge University Press.

Weber, M. (1997). *Economía y Sociedad*. Fondo de Cultura Económica, Mexico City(Original work published 1922)

9

More Bricks to an Evolutionary Account of Law—Rationality and Levels of Evolution

9.1 Third Debate: Rational Choice or Bounded Rationality—Agents and Their Decision-Making Processes

In this chapter, we proceed to analyse a third methodological debate, which is fundamental to the evolutionary vision of law that we are proposing. Despite the potential for this topic to be explored as an independent issue, given the extensive and deep current bibliography on the subject, the present study will dedicate only a few pages to outlining the main and most current positions on it.

As will be evidenced in the forthcoming discourse, this reflection is closely associated with the considerations of the preceding debates. It refers to the rationality of agents when deciding on a course of action. It has been suggested that the 'homo economicus'model refers to an individual who possesses a strong instrumental rationality, which enables them to calculate the costs and benefits of each possible alternative course of action and to decide between them. Meanwhile, the 'homo sociologicus'model would appear to be describing instinctive or adaptive behaviours, with minimal intervention from (at least instrumental)

E. M. Santanatoglia, *An Evolutionary Account of Law*, Palgrave Studies in Classical Liberalism, https://doi.org/10.1007/978-3-032-12162-2_9

rationality. However, as demonstrated by Hollis' proposal, a rationality behind 'following the rules' can be posited.

As we shall see, 'rational choice theory' still has many followers today (albeit with different versions), and there are many authors in the fields of philosophy, psychology and economics who dispute its assumptions.

We will begin with a brief introduction to Boudon's different ways of explaining behaviour and then move on to the debate itself. In order to do so, we will first review the central notions of 'rational choice theory'(RCT), a theory that has marked the debate of the second half of the twentieth century and the beginning of the twenty-first century, not so much for its complete acceptance but for its influence on many other theories and disciplines of the social sciences. In order to provide some examples that are pertinent to this paper, we should note that many of the fundamental concepts of RCT have had a significant impact on the early versions of 'law and economics' and classical 'game theory'.

In the other direction, we will provide a concise overview of the views that question these assumptions of rationality. This will include Herbert Simon's 'bounded rationality'and current versions of behavioural economics, as well as the 'homo heuristicus'proposed by Gigerenzer. Finally, we will conclude with the assumptions of agent rationality adopted by the proposed evolutionary view.

9.1.1 Behaviour, Action and Choice

We have already explored the way Weber or Elster, at different times, propose to explain human behaviour. In his work, especially the essay dedicated to 'Rationality in the Social Sciences', Raymond Boudon also refers to the various ways in which the social sciences approach the study of human actions and their motivations, with particular reference to the question of the rationality of agents (Boudon, 2010).

He begins by proposing a series of basic definitions that provide a clear framework for the discussion. Firstly, he defines behaviour as any bodily movement whose origin is internal to the agent (thus not merely responding to an external stimulus). In this class, he differentiates between reflex behaviour (e.g. falling asleep) and intentional actions driven by desires and beliefs. These actions may or may not be preceded by explicit decisions. For instance, when planning a driving route for the first time, the decisions are explicit. On subsequent occasions, however, they are not.

Boudon also notes the distinction between actions, decisions and choices. He distinguishes between decisions and actions, stating that the former can have causal efficiency even if they do not lead to an action. That is, not all decisions lead to actions, for example, when I decide not to do something. Choice, on the other hand, is a decision between alternative paths. While all choices are decisions, the converse is not true.

On the other hand, the author notes that social sciences offer explanations for behaviour by appealing to efficient causes, other than neurological ones. These include (a) Cultural causes: for example, explaining how an individual internalised a belief under the effect of socialisation, (b) Biological: when a behaviour is interpreted as the result of a process of adaptation to the natural environment, or (c) Psychological: when an act is presented as the effect of the instinct of imitation that supposedly dominates the human being.

Moreover, he explains that there are two types of behavioural explanation:

1. Rational explanation: which explains the individual's behaviour by his or her intention to satisfy a desire or achieve a goal.
2. The A-rational (or irrational) explanation: which explains it by forces that are more or less beyond the control of the individual.

Finally, Boudon distinguishes three different types of 'behavioural theories' (Boudon, 2006), on which he has his opinions (he mostly holds the last one):

Type I: the 'rational-utilitarian theory', exemplified by the 'rational choice theory', which we will develop in the next title;

Type II: the 'causalist theory', which considers behaviour as the result of social, cultural or biological forces and which we have seen developed in the more extreme versions of holism and '*homo sociologicus*';

Type III is the 'rational psychology' or 'comprehensive rationality' theory. From his perspective, this theory overcomes the limitations of the other two theories of behaviour. In this sense, according to Boudon, the rational explanation of behaviour appears to satisfy the usual criteria of scientificity more effectively. However, the prevailing view that identifies rationality with the individual's pursuit of a means to fulfil their preferences is insufficient, as noted by Max Weber and Amartya Sen (1986) today.

9.1.2 Rational Choice Theory

Rational choice theory (RCT) is a model that aims to explain individual decisions by assuming that agents are rational (Abitbol & Botero, 2005; Elster, 2007). The hypothesis is that agents form rational beliefs, including beliefs about the options available to them. When we consider Elster‘s analysis of action, it becomes clear that it would not be necessary for RCT to classify the determinants of behaviour as subjective (desires) or objective (opportunities), given that this theory of rational choice is subjective in its entirety. In other words, the desires and opportunities under discussion would be those that the subject has the capacity to identify and include in his analysis of possibilities.

Furthermore, RCT establishes a number of requirements to affirm that a choice is rational. Firstly, it establishes the conditions under the agent's beliefs at the time of action. Secondly, it outlines the requirements for presenting the individual's preferences.

With regard to the requirements concerning the agent's beliefs, there are three conditions:

(a) Action must be optimal given the beliefs.
(b) Beliefs should be as well supported as possible, given the evidence.
(c) Evidence should be the result of optimal investment in data collection.

When then, are beliefs rational? Beliefs are rational when they are shaped by the processing of available evidence using procedures that, in the long run and on average, are the most likely to produce true beliefs.

Now, when will we have good evidence? What would be the optimal investment of resources (time and money) in acquiring further information? The determinants for RCT to establish that optimum are:

(a) The amount of information that is rational to collect is contingent upon the desires of the agent.
(b) Prior desires and beliefs determine the expected benefits of the new information.
(c) The expected costs of new information, which are determined by prior beliefs, can also sometimes be accurately estimated.
(d) The optimal search for information may also depend on the results of the search itself.

It can also be assumed that learning processes take place in which the agent identifies the optimal point in the search for further information to form beliefs.

These conditions imply several theoretical consequences. On the one hand, a belief is not rational if it is the result of two processes biased in opposite directions that exactly neutralise each other; that is, it cannot be the product of a contradiction. On the other hand, action should be caused by desires and beliefs that make it rational, it is not enough to do the right thing by chance.

This leads us to consider that RCT, through these conditions, detects some common errors when analysing human actions. Among others:

(a) To infer the rationality or irrationality of processes from the optimality (or not) of outcomes. Deviating from the rational course of action is a sufficient condition for outcomes, but not a necessary one.
(b) To assert, for instance, that instinctive reactions of fear are rational, despite the fact that all that can be said for certain is that they are adaptive. This feeling is not rational in the strict sense, since it is not the product of the machinery of rational decision-making. However, it does remeasure rationality, in that it is the very behaviour that such machinery would have produced had it been applied to the situation.

On this last point, it is interesting to note the approach to RCT of some authors who study the behaviour of individuals (human and non-human). These authors also support RCT, arguing that it reflects well the results of adaptation processes. While it may not offer a 'correct' explanation of how individuals make decisions in specific contexts, the final outcome of the evolutionary process is often very close to the outcome of a strict application of RCT.[1]

On the other hand, we find the requirements established by RCT with respect to agents' preferences. In this sense, the primary requirement for optimality is that the selected action must be the most effective means of satisfying the agent's desires, given their beliefs about the available options and their consequences. However, in order for this requirement to be satisfied, RCT is based on a series of assumptions about the agent's individual preferences (a topic which has been much discussed in recent times, as has been noted).

In summary, we can say that RCT assumes:

(a) Self-interest or selfishness on the part of individuals. Thus, it is clearly on the side of '*homo economicus*' in the debate analysed above.
(b) It is also assumed that agents have perfect information at the time of the decision, i.e. the rational ability to evaluate all alternatives.
(c) With regard to agent preferences, the RCT assumes that these satisfy the following characteristics:

[1] In this sense, several papers were discussed at the International Conference: "Evolution, Cooperation & Rationality" which was organised by the University of Bristol. UK on June 27–29, 2011: https://research-information.bris.ac.uk/en/projects/evolution-co-operation-and-rationality/ At this conference—in which we were pleased to participate with a paper—distinguished professors such as Ken Binmore (UCL/Bristol), Peter Godfrey-Smith (Harvard), Samir Okasha (Bristol), David Papineau (King's College), Elliot Sober (Univ. Wisconsin-Madison) and several others exposed their ideas. A number of them, from biological disciplines or who supported different 'adaptationist' theories ended up defending RCT as a theory that allows explaining, at least, the results of the adaptation processes. On the other hand, those professors who work more with economic and mathematical models of understanding the motivations of human behaviour, coincided in observing the limitations of RCT in explaining these phenomena.

- Reflexivity: preferences must be comparable with themselves. Although a trivial assumption, it allows the following assumptions to be made.
- Transitivity: assuming three options A, B and C, if the agent prefers A to B and B to C, he must also prefer A to C. If transitivity does not apply, it is possible that the person does not have an optimal choice. The issue that may arise is that, as preferences undergo cycles, this choice may be repeated indefinitely and lead to the person's downfall through a series of staggered improvements. What justifies describing an agent with intransitive preferences as irrational is not so much the absence of an optimal option, but the fact that he may accept an offer that makes him worse off.
- Completeness: all actions can be ranked in an order of preferences, although there may be some indifference between two options. That is, for any two outcomes, the agent must be able to articulate whether he prefers the first to the second or vice versa, or whether he is indifferent to either of them, e.g.: utility values (continuity).

These conditions will allow us to order the preferences into a stable and coherent set, conditions that are also imposed in order to make of RCT a theory that allows us to predict the course of action of the agents. To summarise, preferences cannot be contradictory and should be consistent over time, at least during the course of the actions being analysed.

9.1.3 Limitations of Rational Choice Theory

Considering these general characteristics and requirements of RCT, it is evident that a number of criticisms and limitations have been presented (Boudon, 2010; Elster, 2007). Here, we will only allude to two of these critiques: indeterminacy and hyperrationality. These critiques lay the foundation for the theories of bounded rationality and heuristics that we will discuss in the next section.

- **Indeterminacy:** Given the structure of the RCT and its claim to be a predictive theory, one could argue that it demonstrates a certain weakness in predicting agents' actions in certain cases. This is because it cannot make unique predictions about what an agent will do in a given situation for several reasons:

(a) The agent is indifferent between two equally optimal options. In non-trivial cases, the two options may differ in several dimensions, and these differences are compensated for.
(b) Consumer preferences may be incomplete.
(c) There are situations of uncertainty or ignorance (non-risk) in which expected returns cannot be compared.
(d) Difficulty in determining the optimal investment in data collection (grey areas).
(e) There are even more important cases that we will see as strategic interactions. In these cases, each agent must form beliefs about what the others are likely to do based on his own reasoning, knowing that they appeal to similar reasoning (game theory).

- **Hyperrationality:** In certain cases, the appeal of 'being rational' may result in the adoption of irrational behaviours. As previously stated, one such scenario could be when individuals, in their pursuit of further information to support their beliefs or address other similar issues, disregard the costs associated with the decision-making process. Thus, agents ultimately 'lose' by aspiring to optimise their decision to the greatest extent possible.

- **Cases against the 'canons of rationality'**: There are many other cases in which, according to Elster's terms (2007, pp. 215–220), the 'canonical principles of rationality' are violated. That is to say, there are cases in which individuals choose to behave against what RCT would predict. A substantial number of these cases are currently being discussed in the relevant literature, and some of them will be referred to in the following title. It is interesting to note that, in empirical observation, these cases often fail to adhere to the most fundamental assumptions of the RCT structure. For instance, they do not always align with the principle that an individual will always prefer more to less or that, in a choice between two unfavourable options, a rational agent will always prefer the lesser of two evils. The following are a few examples (Elster, 2007, pp. 217–220).

(a) **The paradox of voting:** Given that no national election (e.g. for president) is won by a single vote, an individual's vote makes no difference to the outcome and may incur 'costs' or inconvenience to the voter. Despite this, large numbers of people turn out to vote in these elections (even in cases where elections are not compulsory).
(b) **The credit card paradox:** When considering the option of paying in cash or with credit cards (at the time of their introduction), any price difference must be presented as a discount for paying in cash. This is because consumers are generally more inclined to use the card if the difference is not presented as a surcharge for paying with a card, but as a discount for paying in cash even though the options are logically equivalent.
(c) **The sunk cost fallacy:** We often make decisions, even those that may be disadvantageous or incur a higher cost, because we take into account an already assumed 'sunk' cost; one that is already incurred anyway and will not change the outcome of the current action. Elster provides the following example (Elster, 2007, p. 218): "If you buy tickets for an event and heavy snowfall makes it burdensome to get there, you might still go even though you would have refused the tickets had they been offered to you free". This type of reasoning has even been applied to cases of much greater political or social relevance and is therefore often referred to as the 'Concorde fallacy' after the costly Anglo-French aircraft project of that name or the 'Vietnam fallacy' after the United States' reluctance to withdraw from that country.

These are just some of the cases that are now being put forward as 'counterxamples' to rational choice theory, and which have given rise to some of the theories that we will now discuss.

9.1.4 Bounded Rationality

This 'classical' view of individual rationality proposed by RCT is confronted by a number of alternatives that attempt to understand the structure of the individual decision-making process from the perspective of a less rigorous and more comprehensive rationality. Indeed, in many cases, the presented alternatives are justified by the results of experiments or, even, by the mere empirical observation of the forms of individual behaviour in various situations (market or non-market). As illustrated, in many cases the results of these observations differ from the predictions of the RCT model.

It could be argued that this would not be too much of a concern if we only conceived of RCT as an abstract model for explaining how individuals make decisions and not as their actual description. That is, although we often act without being aware of the whole decision-making process, RCT would allow us a 'rational reconstruction' of this process.

But the problem arises when one tries to use RCT as a model for predicting individual behaviour. It is at this point that we begin to see discrepancies between the agents' behaviour and the expected behaviour according to the RCT guidelines. A paradigmatic example, which has given rise to many theoretical reflections in recent years, is the case of the 'Centipede Game' (Elster, 2007, pp. 337–340). According to the rules, two participants are presented with two piles of coins. For example, one pile may contain two coins and the other may contain no coins. In each turn, the player must choose between (a) taking the larger pile and leaving the smaller pile to the other player or (b) passing both piles to the other player. In the latter case, each time a player passes both piles to their opponent, both piles grow by one coin. If the game reaches one hundred moves and neither player has chosen option (a), the game ends with neither player winning anything. As this is an alternating game, it is not usually shown in the form of a payout matrix, but rather in an extended or 'tree' form. Given the maximum spread of one hundred plays, the drawing has one hundred branches, or 'a hundred legs'.

This game serves as a good example of instances where the predictions made by theories such as RCT do not correspond to the actual outcomes of the game. In that case, given the structure of the game, if we were to follow RCT, individuals should not play beyond the first move, given the 'backward induction' that would lead participants to consider that it is better to stop at the first move. However, in this case, the overwhelming majority of players play to the end or until a few moves short of a hundred moves. It therefore follows that the deviation from the expected 'equilibrium' is significant (Elster, 2007, p. 338). Elster considers that this may be due to uncertainty regarding the game in human decisions that appear to be 'irrational', given that in most cases in everyday life individuals are not sure how many moves or future interactions with the other players will occur in the future, and they adopt a 'today for you, tomorrow for me' approach that works in most cases.

According to this line of thinking, the notion of 'bounded rationality' will be reviewed, as originally proposed by Herbert Simon (2000). This proposal, initially oriented to the domain of business administration and later expanded to numerous other fields, attempts to delineate the process by which 'decision-makers' arrive at decisions in real-life scenarios. Simon's observations reveal that several of the assumptions underpinning RCT are not met. For instance, the assumption that agents make decisions in contexts of perfect knowledge or complete, stable and coherent preferences is not always valid.

As we have introduced in chapters 6 and 8, Simon outlines the '**principle of bounded rationality**' according to which "The capacity of the human mind for formulating and solving complex problems is very small compared with the size of the problems whose solution is required for objectively rational behavior in the real world -or even for a reasonable approximation to such objective rationality".

And so, he lists some of the most important limitations that individuals have in making decisions according to RCT standards. Simon, then, proposes that the rationality of individuals is limited by **(a) the available information (b) their cognitive limitations and (c) the finite amount of time they have to make a decision.**

With regard to the first limitation, we have developed the issue in some detail in previous chapters, for example, the issue of dispersed information studied by Hayek. In our current age, the significant volume of information being produced and disseminated at any given moment makes this point particularly relevant. It is difficult to imagine a situation in which an individual can gather all available information for the purpose of making a decision. It is reasonable to conclude that most decisions, including both consumer and personal decisions outside the market, are made with incomplete information.

This is also related to point (c), since no individual has infinite time to make a decision. Even if he had a lot of time, this would lead us to some of the questions we have already discussed with respect to RCT, i.e., what is the optimal allocation of resources to make the 'optimal' decision (in this case time or effort for information search)? In many cases, the decision-maker may choose a course of action with incomplete information if the decision-making process is too time-consuming. As we will see, this also impacts today's debate on the use of heuristics by agents, which allows them to make quite accurate and efficient decisions with little information.

Finally, with regard to point (b)—that is, cognitive limitations—we will elaborate on this point in the next section, taking into account the contributions of Kahneman and other authors who have studied this issue in detail.

In reality, individuals are unable to find an optimal choice; rather, they simplify the available options, satisfying rather than optimising the decision, seeking a satisfactory solution rather than an optimal solution. In Simon's terms, the objective is to reach a 'satisficing' decision, a combination of the words 'satisfy' and 'suffice'. This is a satisfactory and sufficient solution, but not necessarily 'optimal'. In order to make decisions in such situations, individuals make use of heuristic methods. We will now turn to this alternative.

9.1.5 Expectations and Heuristics

This discussion about the limitations to individual rationality brings us closer to the debate around the role of expectations in the individual decision-making process. As discussed in previous chapters, **expectations** are assumptions about the future that can be confirmed or discarded upon disappointment. The degree to which they are evidence-based or rational may vary.

As outlined in Chapter 6, expectations are a fundamental aspect of game theory. For instance, in the notion of **Nash equilibria.** A Nash equilibrium is a set of correct and stable expectations held by the players with respect to the behaviour of the other players. This is a scenario where each player has no incentive to adjust their strategy, provided that the others do not alter theirs. This solution concept assumes two things: first, that each player has adopted their most effective strategy, and second, that all players are aware of each other's strategies.

In this context, it is worthwhile to introduce the concept of 'heuristics'. This term has been used in different contexts with slightly different meanings. For instance, in the field of the philosophy of science, Imre Lakatos' proposal is well-known. This proposal defines heuristics as a set of methodological rules offered by each research programme. According to Lakatos, these rules are not necessarily mandatory and can be positive or negative, suggesting how to proceed and what problems to avoid when generating solutions and hypotheses within a theory or research programme (Lakatos, 1978, pp. 47–52).

Here, however, we are referring to the most common usage of the term in current literature, which defines a heuristic as a practical or informal procedure, technique or art for solving specific problems. A common example of such procedures is the way we learn to catch a flying ball with our hands. In this case, the focus is not on theoretical or computational aspects (we should be machines for calculating speed, curve, wind impact, deflection, etc.), but rather on a straightforward technique for observing the ball and using our hands to catch it underneath.

It can thus be seen how evolutionary game theory considers that individuals with limited rationality make use of certain heuristics (common knowledge) to solve everyday problems. These rules encapsulate this common knowledge in an easily understandable form and are ready to be used in contexts other than those in which they originated. In a similar manner, the Scottish authors explained the establishment of certain rules and institutions.

We will shortly discuss the treatment of heuristics and especially the proposal of a 'homo heuristicus', but first we will introduce some notions of psychology and behavioural economics that can help us to better understand the process of individual decision-making.

9.1.6 Systems 1 and 2

It is worth introducing some of the concepts that behavioural psychology studies have contributed to in recent years and which have impacted economics and the social sciences in general. In economics, for example, it led to the birth of 'behavioural economics'and the emergence of disciplines such as 'behavioural law and economics'.

Its most notable proponents include Daniel Kahneman, Richard Thaler and Cass Sunstein. The former two were awarded the Nobel Prize in Economics for their contributions to the field of behavioural psychology and its applications to economics. These findings have influenced the study of law through 'behavioural law and economics' and related theories.

It is therefore important to emphasise that the incorporation of the biological and neurological study of human behaviour into the social sciences, as discussed in the second section of this work, has brought an empirical element to the debate on the rationality of agents. This was also part of the 'biological turn' discussed in Chapter 4.

In this sense, we believe that these theories, as well as 'evolutionary game theory' with its simulations and 'field experiments', and the 'experimental' variants of philosophy and the social sciences, i.e. 'experimental philosophy' and 'experimental economics', offer a very interesting renewal of the speculative philosophical approach to this fields. It is no longer just a matter of the 'rational reconstruction' of decision-making processes, nor of attempting to provide a logical framework for the 'intuitions' that motivate us. Nor is it a matter of constructing neat abstract models that explain, step by step, how we 'suppose' our brain to work at any given moment.

Today, we have many more tools to observe how individuals act and make decisions in different contexts, and to track how our brains work in specific situations—even using brain scanners. Many explanations of how this process occurs are currently being tested, combining biology and neurology with psychology, decision theory, strategy, economics and even law, as we have already discussed. This enables us to consider how our brains function when faced with an external rule, and how individuals with limited rationality can create, recreate, apply and interpret rules. However, as this topic could be the subject of another work in its own right, here we will only present some very general ideas.

In his famous book "Thinking, Fast and Slow" (2001, Ch 1 to 3), Daniel Kahneman shows us how our brains do not always work in the same way. Although he refers to these as 'System 1' and 'System 2', he does not suggest that we have two brains, but rather the brain exhibits two distinct modes of operation for different situations. Thus, he proposes that:

– System 1: those thought processes that are intuitive, automatic, experience-based and relatively unconscious, and
– System 2: more reflective, controlled, deliberate and analytical thought processes.

System 1-influenced judgements are rooted in impressions arising from easily accessible mental content. Conversely, System 2 is responsible for monitoring and checking mental operations and overt behaviour, though it does so with limited success.

We could draw an analogy between this theory and Pettit's approach to the 'virtuality' of homo economicus, as discussed in Chapter 8 (Pettit, 1995). As we have seen, for this author, we generally act in accordance with social rules or imitate behaviours of the environment, until the situation confronts us with the possibility of our interests being affected, and then the 'homo economicus' appears. In this scenario, the two systems, 1 and 2, seem to coexist. System 1 is constantly operating, providing rapid and automatic responses to various situations and problems, and justifying its actions. In contrast, System 2 is only active when a situation merits careful calculation and a more thorough justification for a specific course of action.

It is interesting to reflect on the relationship between the *homo sociologicus,* heuristics and legal rules in this context. It may be that by following the group or acting in accordance with social rules without further analysis, we are not being 'blind followers of rules' but rather complying with heuristics, as procedures that help us to solve problems and resolve everyday situations. In this context, it is pertinent to consider the number of times legal rules (as in other cases, social or moral ones) are perceived as these heuristics. Without questioning them in detail every time we follow them, these heuristics allow us to carry out a plan, achieve a goal or enhance coordination with others. This is without questioning or analysing their benefits on a case-by-case basis, for instance, the act of coming to a stop automatically upon the sighting of a red traffic signal.

Conversely, in cases that present a greater degree of difficulty and whose consequences may be more complex, we resort to speculative thinking, analysing or interpreting the rules in detail. On occasion, this process has led to the questioning of the very rule itself, and the subsequent promotion of reform. The subsequent chapter will provide a more detailed analysis of some of these cases.

In addition, Kahneman presents his 'prospect theory', which refers to the manner in which agents make decisions in contexts under risk. This element of risk 'reveals' a series of tendencies in thinking, biases and regularities in the behaviour of individuals, which differs from those predicted by RCT views and the homo economicus model. The author differentiates between 'Econs'—that is, individuals as seen from the homo economicus model—and 'Humans'as seen from the behavioural psychology proposed by him (Kahneman, 2013, pp. 269–271). A typical and very simple case to observe the conclusions of the 'prospect theory' is the loss aversion of most individuals. The example under analysis is that of a game where the outcome of a coin flip is predetermined. In the event of the coin showing tails, the participant loses $100, whereas in the event of the coin showing heads, the participant wins $150. It is interesting to note that the vast majority of participants choose not to participate in the game, despite the fact that the expected gain is greater than the loss. The prospect of losing $100, which they have already acquired, often discourages individuals from participating. In this sense, the 'expected utility theory' would tell us otherwise, believing that the individual's decision would only be based on the final expected wealth (Kahneman, p. 283).

Kahneman thus exposes the problem of what he calls 'thinking errors'. The author presents a range of cognitive biases, fallacies and heuristics that have been observed in a variety of experiments, along with the errors that individuals tend to make based on these biases. For instance, cognitive biases frequently result in the erroneous estimation of the personal probability of disease, or the tendency to seek confirmatory evidence that corroborates one's preconceived hypotheses or beliefs, a phenomenon known as 'confirmation bias'. As has previously been outlined, there is also a significant body of evidence to suggest that individuals are less willing to lose something they already have than something they do not yet possess (Kahneman, 2013, pp. 278–288).

From this perspective, he also promotes the idea that, in the face of some of these biases and 'errors' in thinking, some kind of 'nudge' is necessary for individuals to make decisions that may be more beneficial or correct. This line of thinking has had a significant impact on public policy in recent decades and has led to the development of 'behavioural law and economics', a theory that will be analysed in more detail shortly.

9.1.7 Behavioural Economics

It is worth mentioning here too the 'behavioural economics'just cited. Many authors within this school of thought present experimental and fieldwork-based works, in which agents do not act as predicted by the RCT or the *homo economicus* model. In this sense, they establish the foundations of a new economics based on the observation of how individuals act 'in reality' rather than on the basis of ideal models of behaviour, which do not always correlate with empirical observations.

One of the most prominent exponents of this current of thought is Dan Arieli, who, in his work "Predictably Irrational: The Hidden Forces

That Shape Our Decisions" (2008) presents many examples of experiments where agents do not make economic decisions as predicted by neoclassical economics, the homo economicus model or RCT. He cites the example of 'arbitrary coherence' (that we have already discussed in Chapter 3), that is, choices made by agents that are based more on past decisions—that function like 'anchors'—than on current desires or values (instrumental rationality). We may often make concessions in terms of money, time or other resources in order to maintain personal consistency. Therefore, Arieli proposes that the relationships observed in the market between demand and supply are not based on our preferences but on our memory.

Arieli provides numerous additional examples illustrating patterns in our thought processes that can, at times, deviate from rationality, though they are often reiterated and predictable. Among other cases, he comments on how the fact that one of the proposed options is free influences on the choice of consumption. The influence of what is free (or, in other words, the value of zero) changes the whole structure of the choice as RCT would predict it (Arieli, 2008, Ch. 3, 'The Cost of Zero Cost', p. 49 and following on from that). We often accept free products, even when we do not usually consume them or are not convinced by them. As demonstrated by a range of experiments, the discrepancy between two cents and one cent is significantly less than that between one cent and zero. The value of free goods encourages consumers to make decisions about products they would not have otherwise considered, thereby shifting the entire demand curve.

All these new theories and experimental work try to show, on the one hand, the main criticisms of RCT and the theories that support a strongly calculative rationality as the basis of individual choices. To this end, they provide numerous examples of the most diverse that show how individuals act in reality and how many of the predictions of RCT are not fulfilled, such as the case of the Centipede Game or the zero price effect, both of which have already been discussed. Thus, Arieli, commenting on another experiment regarding how individuals are influenced by the choices of others when ordering in a restaurant, shows that people are guided more by their 'social prestige' or their attempt to show individuality and originality rather than by satisfying their taste, and he concludes with the following[2]:

These novel theories and experimental work seek to illustrate the primary criticisms of RCT and the theories that support a strongly calculative rationality as the basis of individual choices. To this end, they provide numerous examples of diverse cases that demonstrate how individuals act in reality and how many of the predictions of RCT are not fulfilled. Examples of this include the Centipede Game and the zero price effect, both of which have already been discussed. In commenting on a related experiment concerning the influence of others' choices on individuals when ordering in a restaurant, Arieli, draws the following conclusion:

> "But there's a bigger lesson that I would like to draw from this experiment-and in fact from all that I have said in the preceding chapters. Standard economics assumes that we are rational -that we know all the pertinent information about our decisions, that we can calculate the value of the different options we face, and that we are cognitively unhindered in weighing the ramifications of each potential choice".
>
> The result is that we are presumed to be making logical and sensible decisions. And even if we make a wrong decision from time to time, the standard economics perspective suggests that we will quickly learn from our mistakes either on our own or with the help of 'market forces'. On the basis of these assumptions, economists draw far-reaching conclusions about everything from purchasing trends to law and public policy.
>
> But, as the results presented in this book (and others) show, we are all far less rational in our decision-making than standard economic theory assumes. Our irrational behaviours are neither random nor senseless - they are systematic and predictable. We all make the same types of mistakes over and over again, because of the basic wiring of our brains. So, wouldn't it make sense to modify standard economics and move away

---

2 Idem 288, Chapter 13, p. 239 (own translation).

> from naive psychology, which often fails the tests of reason, introspection and - most importantly - empirical scrutiny?
>
> Wouldn't economics make a lot more sense if it were based on how people actually behave, instead of how they should behave? As I said in the Introduction, that simple idea is the basis of behavioural economics, an emerging field focused on the (quite intuitive) idea that people do not always behave rationally and that they often make mistakes in their decisions". (Arieli, 2008, p. 239)

Thus, Arieli, like many others, shows how subjects use heuristics to solve common questions and how cognitive biases and even possible errors generated by individual behaviour appear. This information obtained from empirical observation and these theories 'feed' our model of the agent with incomplete information and limited rationality. Furthermore, it provides valuable insights into the decision-making processes of these agents within the legal sphere.

9.1.8 Behavioural Law and Economics

As we have seen, Sunstein and Thaler incorporate Kahneman's psychological findings and behavioural economics into 'law and economics'. This provides us with an economic analysis of law that is no longer based on neoclassical economics, RCT and the idea of profit maximisation by the agent but is instead based on the behavioural economics referred to in the previous section. Consequently, a new interpretation of legal rules—and of the public policies that they seek to promote—is offered, based on how individuals interpret these rules and how they motivate action.

In other words, as well as considering the concrete consequences of establishing a legal rule, these authors also analyse how these rules are presented to 'users' and how they interpret them through their cognitive processes, biases and errors of thought, deciding whether or not to carry out the actions they 'suggest'.

Among many other biases, it is interesting to analyse how rules are presented to citizens, a concept known as 'framing'. For example, although the legislator's intention is the same, the effect of a rule presented as a prohibition or a 'punishment' differs greatly from one presented as a 'reward' or a positive incentive (a point that Hume made many years ago). Consider, for instance, the 'credit card paradox' discussed at the beginning of this chapter: it has been widely observed that the rule 'pay in cash for a 10% discount' has a much more positive effect on buyers than the rule 'pay with a credit card for a 10% surcharge', with the former being interpreted as a 'prize' and the latter as a 'punishment'.

Taking into account the empirical data obtained from many experiments, these authors suggest alternative ways of presenting public policies to make them more effective in achieving the desired results. They propose the concept of a 'nudge', which involves providing individuals with 'soft' and non-coercive incentives to make 'better' decisions and move towards the objectives of the public policy. Thus, by way of example, these authors propose 'guidelines' for people to choose the healthiest foods in cafeterias, through food placement, and public policy 'incentives' designed to encourage individuals to save more for the future. They argue that these 'nudges' can lead individuals to act in their own best interests.

As previously mentioned, these authors have developed these ideas in several papers in 'behavioural law and economics', in which they expand on these biases and apply them to the legal field (Sunstein, Jolls & Thaler, 1998). In this direction, they indicate not only their support for the bounded rationality hypothesis, but also for 'bounded self-interest' and 'bounded willpower' (Sunstein et al., 1998, pp. 1476–1480). Furthermore, they explore how these hypotheses imply various biases and errors in the decision-making process of legal actors. They analyse, among other things, how individuals can often be less 'self-interested' than the traditional reading suggests, or how laws or judicial decisions can have different effects depending on how they are drafted or framed. These biases often result in errors in the responses of individuals to these rules or policies, thereby suggesting the potential for 'shaping' behaviour not through strong incentives (such as prohibitions) but through subtle 'nudges' that guide individuals towards what is ultimately beneficial for them (even if they are not fully aware of it). Consequently, the transition from neoclassical economics to behavioural economics as the basis for the economic analysis of law has the potential to significantly impact the interpretation of legal principles and the practical outcomes of policies enacted through legal frameworks. As previously mentioned, this theory is now known as 'nudge' and has been extensively applied to public policy (Thaler & Sunstein, 2012). As previously discussed, this exemplifies a recurring relationship between theories of human limitations, social, political and legal theory, and the formulation of public policy.

9.1.9 Homo Heuristicus

Finally, we turn our attention to the proposal by Gigerenzer and Brighton (2009), who introduce the concept of 'homo heuristicus'. This 'ideal type' does not reflect a more limited or less sophisticated form of instrumental rationality; rather, it demonstrates the mechanisms that individuals develop to find quicker and more efficient solutions to a series of situations than 'homo economicus'. In contrast to the views of Kahneman, Thaler and Sustein, Gigerenzer and Brighton adopt an 'optimistic' perspective on the widespread use of heuristics by individuals.

In this way they develop the notion of a '*fast and fr*ugal' heuristic according to which the rationality of a decision depends on the structure found in its environment. In this way, it is observed that individuals are 'ecologically rational' when they make the best possible use of their limited information-processing capabilities, applying simple and intelligent algorithms that allow them to arrive at near-optimal inferences.

Compared to the notions of 'h*omo economicus*' and 'h*omo sociologicus*' that we have already analysed, h*omo heuristicus* appears as a model that overcomes this dichotomy. According to it, individuals use different paths to make decisions and act under uncertainty and the already discussed limitations of reason. It proposes that less information, computation and time can actually improve the accuracy of decisions as "Homo heuristicus has a biased mind and ignores part of the available information, yet a biased mind can handle uncertainty more efficiently and robustly than an unbiased mind relying on more resource-intensive and general-purpose processing strategies" (Gigerenzer & Brighton, 2009).

9.1.10 Heuristics and the Law

In another of Gigerenzer‘s works, he and Christoph Engel consider the specific relationship between heuristics and the law (2006). With reference to the background of the movement of the economic analysis of law, which sets out rational and utility-maximising agents, these authors propose here the need for a new interdisciplinary view that connects law and psychology.

To this end, they begin by defining *heuristics* as “simple strategies that professionals and laypeople use when making decisions with limited time and information” (Engel & Gigerenzer, 2006, pp. 1–2). These decisions enjoy characteristics such as simplicity, transparency and limited research requirements. In this sense, the authors insist that these decisions are often “better than rational ones” and allow for the development of reciprocal altruism, recognition, trust, etc.

They also argue (along with Simon and other authors) that heuristics are necessary in situations where the world does not allow for optimisation. Thus, they argue that, for many ‘real world’ problems (as opposed to theoretical optimisation problems) “optimal solutions are unknown because the problems are computationally intractable or poorly defined. Important issues such as what to do with the rest of your live, whom to trust, or whom to marry are typically ill-defined; that is, there is uncertainty about the goals, about what counts as an alternative and how many alternatives there are, and what the consequences might be and how to estimate their probabilities and utilities reliably” (Engel & Gigerenzer, 2006, p. 3).

However, in the face of such challenges, individuals do not remain paralysed. On the contrary, we find answers in habit, in imitation of others, in trust in institutions, reputation or good name. In this alternative view, heuristics are necessary because of the complexity of the external world. Our internal cognitive limitations enhance our performance rather than detract from it. Rationality, thus, addresses (from the perspective of ecological rationality already referred to in the previous section) the question of whether heuristics are adapted to the structure of the environment. In this way, heuristics are revealed as simple rules that allow for the exploitation of both evolved and developed abilities to act quickly and the structures of the environment to act frugally and efficiently.

With regard to the relationship between heuristics and the law, the authors emphasise two pivotal issues for the proposed interdisciplinary research programme to explore: on the one hand, heuristics as law and, on the other hand, heuristics as facts to be considered by law (Engel & Gigerenzer, 2006, p.4).

With regard to the first, heuristics as law, some questions are raised, such as whether current law, or the practice of generating and applying law, can be interpreted in terms of heuristics, or whether law could improve if it were open to the idea of heuristics.

In relation to heuristics as facts to be taken into account by the law, the authors posit that heuristics impact the behaviour of two distinct types of actors: those who make and apply the law, and those to whom the law is applied, such as the general public. They say: "Rule generation and rule application can react to heuristics used by the public, and both can themselves be the result of heuristics at work. Understanding these heuristics is relevant for the law in two respects. First, the law must properly reconstruct the governance problem to which it responds. If people rely on heuristics rather than optimisation, this may diminish or increase the social problem. Second, designing a good rule is not enough. The legislator must also ensure that the rule has the intended effect. The law must therefore anticipate how people are likely to react to its intervention. Again, this assessment will vary, subject to the heuristics upon which people rely" (Engel & Gigerenzer, 2006, p.4). In this sense, heuristics can help make new rules and the process of applying them can also be capitalised on by heuristics.

Finally, a comparison is made between the analysis proposed by the economic analysis of law—in its most classical version, anchored in versions of rational choice theory—with some broader versions of rationality and the ecological rationality proposed by them. It is concluded on the advantages of an evolutionary view that encompasses both the cognitive abilities of agents and the analysis of the environment. They propound that "An evolutionary perspective emphasizes that heuristics are anchored in the evolved abilities of the brain (e.g., the ability for pattern recognition and reciprocal altruism) and in the structure of the environment and exploits both to obtain good results" (Engel & Gigerenzer, 2006, p.10). Thus, for these authors, the evolutionary view could help us understand heuristics as 'better than rational' solutions.

In concluding their proposal, Gigerenzer and Engel raise several questions and controversies that may arise from this new field of study linking law and psychology. In this sense, they argue that law poses a challenge to psychology that is related to the impact of institutions on the understanding of the adaptive behaviour of subjects. In a similar manner, psychology can offer insights into the role of the mind in comprehending the design and impact of institutions.

9.1.11 Agents' Rationality—Conclusions

As illustrated in this section, the debate surrounding the rationality of agents in the social sciences remains unresolved. Whilst some schools and theories continue to adopt the traditional '*homo economicus*'model—which assumes rational behaviour based on maximising benefits, without giving much attention to issues of uncertainty or cognitive limitations—others have explored more comprehensive views on utility or the potential to understand the decision-making process from the perspective of certain elements of '*homo sociologicus*', such as imitation or adapting to the environment.

Consequently, there has been a proliferation of novel theories that examine the mechanisms of brain functioning from neurological, psychological and social perspectives. These theories highlight the limitations and inaccuracies in our thought processes. Among them are those, such as Kahneman, Thaler and Sunstein, who promote public policies that 'indicate' or 'promote' to subjects the 'best' decisions or actions, which they believe individuals cannot reach on their own, given their cognitive limitations and the use of heuristics instead of rational decisions. In contrast, other authors, including Simon and Gigerenzen, posit that the employment of simple, fast and frugal heuristics is a virtue rather than a defect. These heuristics enable individuals to make decisions more efficiently with less information, fewer resources, less time and more accurate results.

As will be evidenced in the following and final chapter, the standpoint adopted concerning the agent's rationality debate, as well as the preceding methodological debates (seen in Chapter 8), will furnish us with the most salient features of the agent as perceived by the evolutionary perspective. This perspective appears to offer a unifying explanation for the diverse aspects of the subjects examined in this section. Moreover, from an evolutionary approach, decision-making can be conceptualised as a biological, individual and social process.

This approach enables us to understand the diverse decision-making strategies employed by individuals in response to varied challenges and environments as sophisticated survival tactics. In some cases, individuals will utilise instrumental rationality to evaluate the efficiency of different alternatives in the pursuit of a shared objective. This process enables the calculation of optimal resource utilisation. However, in other cases, agents may decide 'automatically' based on intuitions, imitations, previous experience, habits and so forth. This automatic decision-making can be influenced by internal or external factors. It is evident that these heuristics are adapted not only to the conditions of the environment in which they develop, but also to the limitations of the human brain and psychology. Furthermore, it is hypothesised that these heuristics may change according to the point of 'learning' in which the subjects find themselves.

9.2 Three Levels of Evolution of Rules and Institutions

We have gathered a large number of the elements necessary for our evolutionary account of law. We have also analysed a large number of theories that propose evolutionary readings of rules and institutions from different perspectives, including biological, cultural and co-evolutionary viewpoints. This analysis has been conducted throughout the book. In this context, it is pertinent to inquire about the predominance of these processes and the potential for interrelationships between evolutionary dynamics across diverse levels.

However, to provide a comprehensive overview, we are interested in integrating three levels of analysis: firstly, all aspects of biological evolution and how we can understand rules and institutions as sophisticated survival strategies on the part of individuals. In this regard, we have analysed several theories, including the account of the process of biological evolution provided by Richard Dawkins and the proposal of evolutionary psychology. We have also considered several conjectures from current neuroscience that will have much to teach us in this respect. Secondly, all elements pertaining to the cultural evolution of rules and institutions at the level of social strategies. This perspective, previously explored by Hayek and more recently by the authors of co-evolution, demonstrates how, perhaps unconsciously, we integrate institutions and rules as strategic mechanisms that facilitate lowering transaction costs and uncertainty regarding other individuals' behaviour, as well as enabling the formulation of personal plans. Finally, the level of individual learning—studied by theories such as evolutionary game theory—through which we can observe how subjects behave, develop strategies, evaluate the results of each strategy, etc., and adapt their behaviour to these circumstances.

We can therefore consider rules and institutions to be the result of three distinct learning processes, occurring on three levels: biological, social and ultimately individual. These processes shape the way in which they develop. We should bring in Viktor Vanberg, who has proposed this idea of the three levels of evolution in several passages of his work (Vanberg, Vanberg, 2011, pp. 3–5 and Vanberg, 1994, pp. 58–59, 80–106). Vanberg proposes that a process of 'trial and error', of variation and selective retention, is at play in all cases. However, he also suggests that each of the processes—biological evolution, cultural evolution and the process of individual learning—has its own 'logic'.

In the context of biological evolution, genetically encoded behavioural dispositions or programmes take shape and are what we usually refer to as 'human nature' in the biological disciplines. As previously stated, this process is currently being studied and is related to the explanation of specific rules and institutions by theories such as 'evolutionary psychology'. It is evident that we, as individuals, are not aware of this evolutionary process, despite playing a leading role in it (or our genes, as some biologists would say). However, our behaviour is largely influenced by the range of possibilities that inform our nature in a biological sense.

In the context of cultural evolution, social learning is a gradual process involving experimentation with different cultural solutions in response to challenges or conflicts. While individuals may act independently, the unintended consequences of these actions can sometimes lead to the emergence of social regularities. These regularities feed one's own and others' expectations and contribute to the development of a social fabric. This learning takes place through the emergence of habits, shared traditions and rules of conduct, and is what we usually refer to when we speak of 'human cultures'. It is evident that individuals who make decisions based on calculative or bounded rationality, evaluating outcomes or following rules, or following emotional impulses or moral conditioning, do so within the range of possibilities that the cultural environment represents to them. A variety of theories of cultural evolution of social rules are currently being studied, including the 'memes theory' and co-evolutionism.

Finally, the individual learning process, which each subject undergoes throughout their life and from which their personal repertoire of behavioural dispositions is formed, operates on the basis of a genetic inheritance with which they are born and takes place in a social environment characterised by a particular cultural inheritance. In essence, while the study of individual behaviour and its motivations is a distinct field of research, the biological nature of these subjects and their specific cultural context can provide valuable insights into the range of behaviours considered by the individual.

It could be argued that these biological and cultural evolutionary processes form part of the framework (of payoffs, incentives, expected outcomes, etc.) that guides the decision-making process of individual agents between one strategy or another. Many theories, including Alexander's evolutionary game theory (Alexander, 2007), which we analysed in Chapter 6, take many of these elements into account. For instance, the bounded rationality of agents and the use of heuristics to solve a series of situations are considered, as outlined in the empirical and experimental study of the human brain (Kahneman, 2013 & Co), as well as the influence of the 'network of social relations' in models that simulate the emergence of complex phenomena from the interactions of a large number of agents connected in a specific way (agent-based models).

In this sense, and as proposed by many contemporary thinkers working in the field of co-evolution, human behaviours, motivations and the potential consequences of actions, as well as the interaction of decisions with those of others, could be analysed as the product of three levels of evolution interacting and, in some cases, influencing each other.

9.3 The Unit of Evolution of Law

In light of the preceding chapters' discussion and the three levels of evolution's thorough examination, the question that now arises is: what constitutes the 'unit' of evolution in law? In a manner analogous to the ongoing debates concerning evolution at the gene, individual, and group levels, this discourse could also be extended to the domain of law.

In considering the question of the 'unit' of study in the case of law, several alternatives could be posited. These include individual behaviours or strategies, general principles, specific rules, institutional arrangements, or complete normative orders. In this sense, it can be argued that, although the fundamental elements of legal orders may be the specific rules or institutions, or even the individual actions or behaviours of the agents, it would be of interest in this case to study the resulting 'emergent order'.

In conclusion, in the case of law, the 'legal order'may be observed as an object of study in its own right, which is the emergent or product of the interaction of millions of individuals in the process of evolution (across the three levels of this evolution). The behaviour of these individuals and their interactions produce regularities, principles, rules, and so forth. This process gives rise to a state of affairs at a given moment, which in turn allows them to create expectations and formulate action plans (a notion that has previously been proposed by Hayek). These ideas will be explored in greater depth in the following chapter; however, it is pertinent at this stage to introduce the approach to the object of study.

As we have seen, the evolutionary view applies both to the 'elements'—understood as the specific rules and institutions in this context—and to the order as a whole. The present study proposes to continue this research by examining this order at all levels, with the ultimate aim of formulating a comprehensive view of the whole that exhibits an order with its own characteristics (which are not necessarily confused with the characteristics of the elements that compose it). This issue will be addressed in the final chapter of this work.

References

Abitbol, P., & Botero, F. (2005). Teoría de la elección racional: estructura conceptual y evolución reciente. *Colombia Internacional, 62*, 132–145.

Alexander, J. M. K. (2007). *The structural evolution of morality*. Cambridge University Press.

Arieli, D. (2008). *Predictably irrational. The hidden forces that shape our decisions*. Harper Collins Publishers.

Boudon, R. (2006). *What behavioural theory for the social sciences?*, Centre d'Études Sociologiques de la Sorbonne, 2006. https://dialnet.unirioja.es/servlet/articulo?codigo=2993759

Boudon, R. (2010). *La racionalidad en las ciencias sociales, ediciones nuevas visiones*. Buenos Aires.

Elster, J. (2007). *Explaining social behavior: more nuts and bolts for the social sciences*. Cambridge University Press.

Engel, C., & Gigerenzer, G. (2006). Law and heuristics: an interdisciplinary venture. In *Heuristics and the Law* (pp. 1–16). MIT Press.

Gigerenzer, G., & Brighton, H. (2009). Homo heuristicus: why biased minds make better inferences. *Topics in Cognitive Science, 1*, 107–143.

Kahneman, D. (2013). *Thinking, fast and slow*. Farrar, Straus and Giroux.

Lakatos, I. (1978). *The methodology of scientific research programmes. Philosophical papers, volume I*. Cambridge University Press.

Pettit, P. (1995). The virtual reality of 'homo economicus'. *The Monist, 78*, 3.

Sen, A. K. (1986). Los tontos racionales: una crítica a los fundamentos conductistas de la teoría económica. In F. Hahn & M. Hollis (Eds.), *Filosofía y teoría económica*. Fondo de Cultura Económica.

Simon, H. A. (2000). Bounded rationality in social sciences: today and tomorrow. *Mind Society, 1*, 25–39.

Sunstein, C. R., Jolls, C., & Thaler, R. H. (1998). A behavioral approach to law and economics. *Stanford Law Review, 50*, 1471–1550.

Thaler, R., & Sunstein, C. R. (2012). *Nudge: improving decisions about health, wealth and happiness*. Penguin Books.

Vanberg V. J. (2011). *Darwinian paradigm, cultural evolution and human purposes: On F.A. Hayek's evolutionary view of the market*, Papers on Economics and Evolution, No. 1119, Max Planck Institute of Economics.

Vanberg, V. (1994). *Rules and choice in economics.* Rutledge Publishers.

10

Law as the Outcome of a Permanent Process of Emergence, Stability and Change of Rules and Institutions

10.1 The Bricks of Our Evolutionary Account of Law

10.1.1 Introduction

We have devoted the previous two chapters to analysing and discussing some of the methodological and epistemological foundations of our theoretical proposal. In this section, we will combine these factors here in order to make explicit—as far as possible—the assumptions of our vision of law. In this sense, we will then refer to our position in relation to methodological questions, in particular in the debate we have already developed on m*ethodological individualism* vs. m*ethodological holism.*

The present study will also make explicit the assumption on human nature, i.e. the type of agent that is presupposed and the position adopted in the debate between *homo economicus* and *homo sociologicus*. Furthermore, the standpoint that is adopted in the debate on the rationality of agents that has been previously advanced will be examined.

In essence, a methodological position of moderate methodological individualism is adopted. It is further assumed that the *homo economicus*

E. M. Santanatoglia, *An Evolutionary Account of Law*, Palgrave Studies in Classical Liberalism, https://doi.org/10.1007/978-3-032-12162-2_10

and *homo sociologicus* aspects of agents are combined; the former manifests itself more frequently in specific circumstances, while the latter is exhibited in the remainder of situations, where individuals tend to behave in a more adaptive way. Consequently, the conception of a more flexible *homo economicus* and an intelligent *homo sociologicus* is proposed. In this sense, and as was analysed in the previous chapter, we posit a vision in which individuals possess a limited instrumental rationality and tend to utilise heuristics—paths that represent solving situations through quick responses, without counting on large amounts of information and without complex rules of cost/benefit calculation.

10.1.2 Methodological Conception: An Evolutionary Account of Law and a Moderate Methodological Individualism

As discussed in Chapter 8, we contend that the more stringent positions of methodological individualism and methodological holism, which are presented as mutually exclusive, can be superseded by a moderate individualism that is perfectly compatible with the evolutionary perspective proposed in this work. As previously discussed in Chapter 9, the unit of study for the present theory is the 'legal orders'or 'institutional frameworks', that is to say, the specific combinations of rules and institutions that are in force in a given territory and at a specific time.

The present view implies an understanding of law as a self-generated order based on the three levels of evolution—biological, social and individual—that were proposed in the previous chapter. However, this does not invariably result in the adoption of a holistic methodological perspective, as it is considered essential to acknowledge that, while these orders may possess their own characteristics, their existence and specific manifestation are contingent on individuals who, in their interactions, shape them. It is thus the intention of this study to enter into the minds of the individuals who make up the communities that produce these phenomena—self-generated orders—on the basis of moderate methodological individualism.

On the one hand, the evolutionary process is conceived from three levels: the biological, the social and the individual. It is thus understood that many of the rules and institutions that individuals adopt as sophisticated (biological or cultural) survival strategies are not necessarily the result of conscious decision-making. Rather, these may be the result of selection mechanisms at both the biological and the social level. Nevertheless, this does not prevent us from recognising the individuals involved in these processes (even in the discourses of justification of those rules they did not consciously choose) and highlighting the role they also play in the processes of individual evolution.

As was concluded in Chapter 8, the tension between the status of social or legal orders as totalities and the possible application of methodological individualism is resolved by always bearing in mind that the notions of individual and social/legal order are co-dependent. In this sense, Hayek had already proposed in his work "Law, Legislation and Liberty" (1983, 1973, Ch. 1, p. 17) the relation of mind and society as two planes in a process of permanent co-evolution. In this manner, individuals are presented as the 'producers' of orders through their actions and the support of these orders, without being reduced to them.

It is therefore postulated that, from the standpoint of moderate methodological individualism, law can be understood as an evolving social phenomenon. This implies that, as stated by the 'classic' evolutionary view and reaffirmed by the new evolutionary schools, order is observed as the unintended product of individual interactions. In this sense, and as was stated in Chapter 8, the present study puts forward a hypothesis concerning the origin, or genesis, of legal order. Furthermore, it is argued that, in moving away from strict methodological individualism, it will not be necessary to translate all propositions about orders into individual statements.

We believe that the evolutionary perspective provides a more comprehensive understanding of this interaction between levels, as Richerson and Boyd have previously noted. This approach allows us to fluidly relate individual and social phenomena without having to choose between the 'macro' and the 'micro' view. In this sense, the evolutionary perspective we are proposing for application to law enables us to understand how changes in the behaviour, beliefs, motivations or expectations of individuals in a community modify the profile of the rules and institutions that arise from their interactions. It also allows us to understand how the institutional framework influences and modifies the range of possibilities of individual behaviours, beliefs, motivations and expectations.

We quote here again Richerson and Boyd's paragraph on the subject: "Individuals seem to be hapless prisoners of their institutions because, in the short run, individual decisions don't have much effect on institutions. But, in the long run, accumulated over many decisions, individual decisions have a profound effect on institutions. Evolutionary theory gets right the basic structure of the relationship between individuals and the collective properties of their societies" (Richerson & Boyds, 2006, p. 247).

In Chapter 9, it was demonstrated that not all evolutionary processes are conscious to agents. In this sense, the process of biological evolution appears to be a process that is practically blind to the agents involved. Meanwhile, the process of social evolution also exceeds the level of individual decision-making. Rather, it may be more related to the adoption of strategies by individuals, which are more or less conscious behaviours. One example of this is heuristics, which are quick, automatic actions on the part of individuals, although not totally 'unconscious'.

10.1.3 Anthropological and Psychological Assumptions: Human Nature Assumptions

10.1.3.1 Evolutionary Theory and the Resolution of the Dichotomy Between *Homo Economicus* and *Homo Sociologicus*

As was extensively discussed in Chapter 8, the models of the individual—the homo economicus and the homo sociologicus—have been central to the debate in social science and the philosophy of social science for the last fifty years. While the former appears to have absorbed the influence of theories such as 'rational choice theory' that emphasises the capacity of individuals to evaluate alternatives, foresee outcomes, calculate benefits and losses, and so on in a comprehensive manner, the latter connects not only with classical sociological and anthropological readings but also with current empirical explorations of how individuals incorporate social rules. Furthermore, they are concerned with the adaptation of individuals to different social environments on the basis of their interaction capacities, tacit rule following and so forth.

As outlined in Chapter 8, both of these visions have been the subject of extensive analysis and discussion. Within the framework of this debate, and in consideration of all that has been analysed in relation to rationality, the evolutionary view can sustain a position that reconciles both models.

Firstly, by moving away from the more extreme versions of these theories that make them mutually exclusive. Secondly, by relying on theories that attempt to explain the evolution of rules and institutions (both biological and cultural) and on those that examine the motivations of individuals when deciding to take a course of action. To obtain a comprehensive understanding of the individual and their actions, it is necessary to consider all aspects. Consequently, we propose a reconciliation of theories that explain the emergence of rules and institutions on a biologically based evolutionary foundation, such as evolutionary psychology or co-evolutionary theories, with those that focus on individual learning processes that have 'macro' consequences in terms of frequencies, such as evolutionary game theory. Therefore, as posited by Hayek, it can be concluded that "Man is as much a rule-following animal as a purpose-seeking one" (Hayek, 1983, 1973, Ch. 1, p. 11).

It is evident that in certain situations, such as the purchase and sale of a significant asset, individuals will deliberately evaluate all available options, taking into account a range of factors including costs (monetary, in kind, opportunity costs, etc.) and benefits (monetary, in kind, expected, etc.). They will also attempt to gather all relevant information and may even calculate the costs of incorporating more data to inform the decision. In the meantime, they act and make small (or big) everyday decisions almost constantly. These include how to get somewhere, how to make a small transaction, and how to address a colleague. These decisions do not involve long, rational disquisitions on alternatives and the evaluation of results. Instead, they are quasi-automatic behaviours, guided by heuristics, that have been incorporated almost unconsciously. These allow individuals to solve a large part of the daily questions that they face with very little cost and little information. Therefore, we adopt a balanced perspective on human nature, recognising that it is not solely driven by rational self-interest or completely adaptive, in the sense of blindly following social rules.

This also informs our view of law. We envisage agents who will not blindly follow any externally imposed rule, regardless of the authority or legislator imposing it (as many theories that focus on the production and application of legal rules in the strict sense appear to presuppose). Nor do we envisage an agent who is overly calculating, who only considers norms in terms of constraining their actions to the extent that they incur a cost, specifically a cost that is not outweighed by the benefit of compliance. This type of agent is the one that some theories of law—such as, for example, some versions of realism or the strictest readings of the economic analysis of law based on RCT—seem to conceive of. It is evident that neither of the two 'pure' models provides a comprehensive understanding of a significant number of everyday actions (even within the strictest field of law) that are predominantly influenced by mutual expectations arising from repeated interactions and reciprocal altruism, rather than by strict adherence to rules or pure calculation.

The proposed evolutionary vision, which conceives law within self-generated or spontaneous orders, allows us to combine both views. As previously outlined, we understand individuals to be self-interested, yet this does not imply that they are unable to recognise coordination conflicts, that they do not have legitimate concerns for others, or that they are incapable of establishing necessary relationships with other individuals. Furthermore, as we shall see, these relationships—and the regularities that emerge from them—may be motivated by various factors, including self-interest, sympathy for each other, and learning mechanisms that allow them to imitate or adopt other, more successful strategies. These regularities are often internalised as rules because they have been shown to be more effective or better adapted to individuals' changing desires and goals. As previously mentioned, individuals' compliance with rules serves to reinforce others' expectations of their actions and vice versa. We can therefore conclude that we are presupposing individuals who, given the processes of interaction and internalisation, follow rules and that these rules are, in turn, the unplanned product of their own self-interested behaviour and interrelationships with all other individuals. The concept of conceptual co-dependence between individuals and self-generated orders (e.g. legal orders) is therefore proposed, along with the idea that both co-evolve and influence each other.

These assumptions are also related to the last 'brick', which is related to our assumptions about agents' rationality, as discussed in Chapter 9, and which we are now going to turn to.

10.1.3.2 Bounded Rationality

In the preceding chapter, we thoroughly analysed the theoretical explorations of the agents' rationality assumptions. As we have seen, some schools of thought—influenced by the homo economicus model and rational choice theory (RCT)—continue to operate under the assumption of an agent with full use of instrumental rationality and profit maximisation. These views do not pay much attention to possible cognitive limitations or to the characteristics of decision-making under situations of supreme uncertainty, among others. In parallel, a number of other current theoretical proposals emphasise the limitations and errors of our decision-making processes, putting forward various views on the bounded rationality of agents or the use of two differentiated mechanisms. One approach is based on instrumental rationality, aligning with the requirements suggested by RCT. The other approach allows for the resolution of decision-making situations through mental 'shortcuts' or heuristics.

In the context of these theories, some authors view these 'cognitive biases' with concern, as a natural tendency for agents to make reasoning errors, as illustrated by Kahneman, Thaler and Sunstein. These authors propose that public policies should help individuals to make 'better' decisions on the basis of suggestions, cues or nudges. In contrast, other authors who observe the same reality deem it advantageous for agents, such as Simon or Gigerenzer. They interpret the use of heuristics as allowing agents to make more efficient decisions, with less information, fewer resources, less time and better results.

As we have done with the other points, we now present the final methodological 'brick' to provide a foundation for our evolutionary theory of law. It is evident that the evolutionary perspective has the capacity to encompass the diverse aspects of the problem discussed in this section. From a business perspective, the theories based on this view—from biological, social or individual perspectives—allow us to consider the different forms of decision-making put into practice by individuals and observed by behaviourist theorists as different sophisticated survival strategies in the face of various environmental challenges.

In some cases, individuals will use instrumental rationality to evaluate the efficiency of different alternatives towards the same goal, allowing them to calculate the most effective use of their resources. In other cases, agents will decide 'automatically', based on intuition, imitation, previous experience, habits, etc. These heuristics appear to adapt not only to the environmental conditions in which they develop, but also to the limitations of the human brain and psychology. Furthermore, they may change according to the point of 'learning' at which the subjects find themselves.

When we apply this to the field of law, we can observe certain general rules or institutions that are often repeated in various societies (e.g. rules that exclude those who attack other members of the group or 'traitors' from society). It is possible to hypothesise that these are the result of biological survival strategies that have been moderately successful in different natural and social contexts. It is evident that, despite significant cultural differences, there are certain similarities in the structure of the institutional response to specific behaviours.

Contrastingly, we can observe a broad spectrum of normative and institutional responses to other situations more closely related to specific cultural and individual differences, as evidenced by various forms of inheritance law structures. These rules, which are likely not driven by a demand for biological survival but rather by a need to adapt to diverse social environments and individual learning processes, may exhibit greater diversity and sensitivity to environmental nuances.

It can therefore be observed that individuals often rely on certain automatic and generalised responses when confronted with certain circumstances. These responses are probably the most efficient given the information available. In other cases, significant energy, time and calculation are dedicated to deciding how to act or solve a specific case that may respond to a specific need of the individuals under that environment. However, these cases have not found a general response by biological or social evolutionary processes previously.

10.2 The Theoretical Antecedents of an Evolutionary Account of Law

We have devoted several chapters to analysing the schools of thought and authors that preceded us in this attempt to explain law as the product of an evolutionary process. Firstly, we have dedicated ourselves to what we call 'classical evolutionism', which is comprised of the authors of the Scottish Enlightenment, such as David Hume, Adam Smith and Adam Ferguson, as well as contemporary authors, especially Friedrich A. Hayek. These authors postulated the first ideas in relation to the evolutionary vision of rules and institutions.

In this line, we have analysed in detail the Scottish Enlightenment's particular conception of the origin and evolution of institutions related to law and justice. We have also examined the work of Friedrich A. Hayek, who, in the twentieth century and situated within the framework of the discussion of his time, follows the Scottish tradition and offers an evolutionary vision of law. Indeed, he even gives this vision the name of 'evolutionism' and confronts it with 'constructivism', which he defines as the idea that, through reason, we can design, construct and modify social orders according to our preferences and principles. From his perspective, this 'constructivist' mode of thinking exerted a pernicious influence on the ideological landscape of the early twentieth century, posing a grave threat to individual liberties and the evolution of established institutions. In this sense, it could be argued that arbitrarily designed and imposed change has the potential to be more damaging than inaction or any impediment to change. While Hayek explicitly departs from conservative positions (Hayek, 1978, Proscript: Why I Am Not a Conservative, p. 397), he believes that the rules and institutions which underpin a society should be subject to change in accordance with the shifting patterns of interaction among individuals, and not to be dictated by a centrally imposed master plan designed by a select few.

Following a detailed analysis of the background provided by 'classic evolutionism', we have provided a comprehensive overview of the authors and theories that have offered evolutionary views in the social sciences over the last fifty years. We have covered a wide range of theories, from the 'meme theory' to evolutionary psychology and from evolutionary game theory to co-evolutionism. In each of these cases, we have also tried to propose the application of these theoretical proposals to rules and institutions in general and to the legal order in particular. In addition to the appealing perspectives they offer on the social world, we consistently prioritise discerning their precise insights concerning law and legal systems.

What can we learn from these proposals? In addition to the methodological 'bricks' we have already analysed, how can we explain the emergence, continuity, change and even collapse of the rules and institutions of law from this perspective? In what ways can the legal order be understood as a self-emerging order based on the notions offered by these schools of thought?

Firstly, we can argue with Hume that legal rules and principles are not the natural outcome of our virtues, such as the sympathy or generosity we feel for others in certain circumstances. Indeed, legal principles and rules, such as the 'pacta sunt servanda' principle, which establishes that contracts and treaties must be respected by the parties as 'law between the parties', or today's sophisticated systems of private property, cannot be seen simply as the product of natural virtuous inclinations that men feel towards their fellow men. Such rules are part, then, of what Hume calls 'artificial virtues'. This definition entails the idea that they do not arise simply from human nature, but from the interactions of individuals in given circumstances.

Hume's 'three universal rules of justice' (Hume, 2000 (Book III, part III, section i))—stability of possession, transfer by consent and fulfilment of promises—demonstrate how rules can emerge gradually and acquire force slowly. These rules are not only the result of a mutual 'common sense of common interest', but also evolve in accordance with expectations of the behaviour of other individuals. Repeated experience persuades men of the disadvantages of not respecting the rules and reaffirms a sense of common interest and confidence in the future regularity of behaviour. In this way, Hume explains how individuals within a community, though they may be strangers to each other, can establish common rules.

We have also examined the contributions of Adam Smith and Adam Ferguson to this evolutionary perspective on rules and institutions. These authors provide a more general and historical standpoint, shedding light on the emergence of complex signalling systems and principles, including price systems and political institutions. These principles have given rise to expectations among subjects, thereby establishing the foundations for specific social regularities. The genesis of numerous legal institutions can be examined as the outcome of a process of historical trial and error that has resulted in the most effective rules for a given cultural context.

It was here that we observed the initial connection between Hume and evolutionary game theory, which explains the emergence of social rules as the result of decisions made as 'interdependent choice problems' (Alexander, 2007, p. 9). Both views concur on the significance of individuals' expectations of each other's attitudes and actions as the foundation for the emergence of common rules.

Furthermore, law serves as a precise illustration of the emergence of spontaneous orders, as theorised by Hayek. The legal order does not seek to satisfy a particular goal, but rather, it emerges as a general order at the intersection of various individual desires and plans. The establishment of abstract rules is not driven by the pursuit of a comprehensive objective. Conversely, these rules, as a general order, are the consequence of specific regularities in interdependent interactions.

As we have already seen, Hayek's description of spontaneous orders includes the idea that, slowly and imperceptibly, they produce (and are produced by) different kinds of rules. He thus distinguishes three types of rules (Hayek, 1983, 1973, pp. 41–43):

(a) abstract rules, inarticulate but also 'inarticulable' (that cannot be articulated).
(b) unarticulated but 'articulable' rules, i.e. that, in the face of demand, they could be articulated and.
(c) expressed and articulated rules.

Hayek claims: "Life of man in society, or even of the social animals in groups, is made possible by the individuals acting according to certain rules. With the growth of intelligence, these rules tend to develop from unconscious habits into explicit and articulated statements and at the same time to become more abstract and general. Our familiarity with the institutions of law prevents us from seeing how subtle and complex a device the delimitation of individual spheres by abstract rules is. If it had been deliberately designed, it would deserve to rank among the greatest of human inventions. But it has, of course, been as little invented by any one mind as language or money or most of the practices and conventions on which social life rests" (Hayek, 1978 p. 148).

In the case of law, we can consider the first type of rules—the abstract rules—as the implicit and internalised anthropological, sociological and philosophical assumptions of individuals in a specific society. In Hayek's terms, although these rules are not articulated or verbalised in any way, their existence can be discovered by observing the behaviour of individuals. Individuals, even if they are not consciously aware of it, act and manifest certain regularities in their behaviour, as if they were following rules (as Watkins would say, 'law-like behaviour'). Hayek's approach involves the recognition of tacit, non-conscious, non-articulable principles and rules that influence individual behaviour, as evidenced by the regularities in that behaviour. "Men generally act in accordance with abstract rules in the sense long before they can state them. Even when they have acquired the power of conscious abstractions, their conscious thinking and acting are probably still guided by a great many such abstract rules which they obey without being able to formulate them. The fact that a rule is generally obeyed in action therefore does not mean that it does not still have to be discovered and formulated in words (Hayek, 1978 p. 149). We will see how these ideas are related both to the three levels of evolution we have proposed and to various notions proposed by evolutionary game theory.

Meanwhile, the second group of rules, the unarticulated ones, operates implicitly in society but can be explicitly articulated when necessary. In the context of jurisprudence, legal principles that are capable of articulation yet remain implicit over time are those that must be 'discovered' by judges in complex cases. The present discussion does not intend to engage with the theory of 'hard cases' in any exhaustive manner, as this has been extensively studied by authors such as Dworkin (1978) and Hart (1997). In such cases, the judge is tasked with resolving a 'new kind of case or conflict', a challenge that extends beyond the scope of the legal system's explicit framework. In the context of Hayek's legal theory, the judge's role would not be to formulate an entirely novel solution, but rather to identify, within the existing legal framework, a response to the presented conflict that would harmonise with the rest of the legal order and its underlying principles. The solution to this issue may be found in the articulation of implicit rules, which are then rendered explicit and applicable to the case in question. It is imperative to take into account the expectations of the parties involved, as well as which of these expectations are likely to be frustrated or nurtured from the perspective of the judge.

The final type of rules consists of norms that, due to their requirement for generality and enforcement, are explicitly established through local, national or international legislation or through judicial decisions. It is generally accepted that such phenomena may be considered the articulation of a prior habit or regularity, encompassing abstract and unarticulated rules that have subsequently been formalised or positivised. These explicit positive rules also result in the incentives or benefits of different behavioural strategies being rendered 'public'.

In conclusion, law as a spontaneous order does not imply that all the rules that make up such an order necessarily have a spontaneous origin. Conversely, spontaneous orders may comprise a variety of rules from different sources with varying implications. Hayek also suggests that law is prior to legislation and cannot be reduced to it. Hayek emphasises that many theories identify law with legislation as the only source of law, forgetting the abstract rules of custom as its prior reason. Constructivist theories offer an artificially stable view of the legal phenomenon, overlooking the complex nature of social and legal change. Change is the driving force behind social and legal evolution, meaning that law cannot be studied using a static and formal model.

At this juncture, a concise exposition has been made on the salient elements from the preceding theories that have been posited for the study of law from an evolutionary perspective. In this sense, we understand our vision to be a continuation of a tradition of thought initiated by the authors of the Scottish Enlightenment and continued in the twentieth century by authors such as Hayek, that is, 'Classical Evolutionism'. In light of the influence that the 'biological turn' and novel evolutionary theories in the social sciences have exerted on this perspective, we have endeavoured to synthesise in the 'bricks' the assumptions that we take into account when proposing our own vision.

We will now attempt to describe the phenomenon of the emergence of legal orders. It is thus proposed that individuals act freely and are motivated by various reasons (interests, principles, tastes, etc.), but that the analysis of individuals cannot be reduced to basic or exclusionary models (such as *homo economicus* or *homo* sociologicus netus). It is further asserted that these individuals possess bounded rationality, employing various processes to make decisions, including heuristics. In this particular explanation of the emergence and development of legal orders, the evolutionary tradition of thought with its psychological, philosophical and methodological proposals will be taken into consideration, and the findings of the new evolutionary views of social phenomena will be incorporated.

10.3 An Evolutionary Account of Law

10.3.1 The Emergence, Stabilisation and Change of Legal Rules—The Rules as the Most Stable Strategies Inside an Evolutionary Game

10.3.1.1 The Emergence of Rules and Institutions

We have discussed the emergence of our rules and institutions in many sections of this book and we will consider now all the above-mentioned background.

In this sense, we can say that the new legal rules that allow us, for example, to know how we should make a sales contract with another individual, can originate either from an individual—for example, one of the parties proposing a strategy—or from a third party—for example, a 'court' or arbitrator—proposing a solution for a particular conflict. The origin of a rule can also be in the imitation of the behaviour of another individual from one's own community or from another community. There are numerous other potential 'genesis' for rules. It is even possible to consider chance as one of the sources of a specific strategy, understood as the 'first appearance' of a rule. To summarise, a particular response to a given situation can have various origins, including chance occurrences. As we will see in the following paragraphs, these specific forms of institutional response can 'settle' as the expected response of the agents and become positivised over time.

It is therefore worthwhile here to re-introduce the notion of a three-level evolution that we proposed in the previous chapter. As has been discussed, the human subject can be considered to be the protagonist of three separate evolutionary processes which occur in parallel: biological, social and individual.

The notion that the human subject is a 'protagonist' of the process of biological evolution has been challenged, as it is considered that genes are the ultimate unit of evolution. However, in a non-conscious way, humans are part of a process of biological evolution that requires, as a selection criterion, that of the greatest physical survival.

Furthermore, we are also part of various processes of cultural evolution, within the framework of the groups and communities to which we belong. It is through these processes, not always consciously, but sometimes with a certain degree of 'alertness' on the part of the participants, that certain institutional strategies become more prevalent, as proving to be more efficient in promoting a framework for the development and coordination of the individuals who live in them. In some cases, the process of cultural adaptation can result in the emergence and establishment of novel strategies, or the adoption, through imitation, of strategies developed by other communities.

Finally, the processes of individual evolution and learning, which appear to be mainly based on the behaviour and conscious decisions of individuals, as we have analysed through evolutionary game theory or certain aspects of co-evolution.

Consequently, when considering the genesis of the legal principles that constitute the current legal order of a community, it is conceivable that these principles may have originated from the need for biological, social or cultural survival, or individual survival, as the case may be. It is even conceivable to establish a correlation between the three types of rules proposed by Hayek and these three levels of evolution.

Firstly, abstract and more general rules—which are not necessarily conscious to individuals—may function as products of the process of biological evolution, marking a far-reaching path for us in terms of the adaptation of individuals to different natural and social contexts. These rules, which appear to be highly stable and generalised (shared by numerous diverse groups or 'societies'), have been shown to be more efficient and to guarantee biological survival in the long term. We can identify broad rules that address transgressions such as 'traitism' or 'cheating', resulting in the exclusion of those who break these rules from their respective groups. It is evident that, in the majority of societies, a set of rules exists that establishes such a criterion, even if it is not always explicitly reflected in a clearly defined positive rule.

It is also possible to relate this notion of abstract rules proposed by Hayek in the context of classical evolutionism to the idea of 'common knowledge' proposed by Alexander in the context of evolutionary game theory. In Alexander's view this common knowledge is related to the heuristics that have already been discussed, as he explains: "Heuristics encapsulate this common knowledge in comprehensible, and readily apprehended, forms, which can then be applied in contexts different from the one in which it was originally acquired" (2007, p. 5).

As we shall see in the following paragraphs, along with these abstract rules, individual behaviours are also motivated by explicit norms. However, it is all of these elements that make up a legal order (and not just laws in the broad sense). As Alexander—when discussing the view of individuals as rational machines—proposes "Since we are not these machines, we instead muddle our way through life relying on the less-than-perfect calculations derived from heuristics and rules of thumb" (Alexander, 2007, p. 5). In the field of law, it is notable that many individuals have an intuitive understanding of how to act in certain situations in order to respect the legal order, even if they have not received formal legal education or have not read a legal text or court decision in their lifetime. The majority of this information is transmitted in various ways through social interaction and informal learning (e.g. imitation) and is internalised by individuals in an unconscious manner.

Secondly, there are rules that are not explicitly articulated but can be made explicit in specific cases. We might consider these to be related to rules that emerge from the process of group cultural evolution. These rules may sometimes entail significant changes, but they are generally 'long-lived'. They undergo gradual change and are only challenged in the face of a 'crisis of the system'. We also find some rules or institutions that are shared by several groups or communities. In terms of public law, there are rules for organising powers or limiting the powers of the state, as well as rules that guarantee or protect basic individual rights. While not all legal orders share identical wording, and at times, these principles are not codified, they function as general guidelines that are articulated when the situation demands it.

Finally, there are the positive or more explicit rules, which are generally those that are conscious to individuals and the product of individual evolution and learning processes. These are narrower in scope, more capable of rapid change and have less overall impact. However, these rules often catalyse group cultic processes and are incorporated in a general way. We can consider, for instance, specific forms of contracting between parties, procedural strategies and even forms of conflict resolution. These solutions are initially devised by actors for particular cases. As we will see in the next section, these strategies often demonstrate remarkable stability over time and in different environments, and are gradually adopted as general solutions.

10.3.1.2 Stabilisation and Change of Rules and Institutions

Taking into account, then, this explanation of the emergence of legal norms, how can we explain the change and stability of these norms? We have already reiterated, at various points in this paper, the question of how certain solutions that are shown to be efficient for solving a given issue are presented in the following situation as a possible solution and how individuals generate expectations about them. Here we ask then, how, after the whole process of interactions and expectations described above, does a group of individuals find a rule and decide to change it afterwards? Or how can we explain the rapid change of some legal arrangements while others survive several generations and even major changes in context?

Considering this explanation of the emergence of legal norms, how can we account for the change and stability of these norms? It has already been noted on multiple occasions in this work that certain efficient solutions to specific issues are presented as potential remedies in the following situation and how individuals develop expectations regarding them. Following the process of interactions and expectations described above, how does a group of individuals reach a decision to modify a pre-existing rule? What factors can be identified as contributing to the rapid evolution of certain legal provisions, while others demonstrate resilience across generations and significant contextual shifts?

Classic evolutionism, as exemplified by Scottish authors and Hayek, does not offer a precise explanation of the process of rule change. Hayek's approach is based on a process of 'trial and error', drawing inspiration from Karl Popper's perspective on scientific thought. This concept is used to discuss the selection of rules within a society, without providing a specific learning rule. Furthermore, Hayek's analysis considers the case of competition between different institutional arrangements or sets of rules (complete legal orders). In this case, he proposes a kind of 'cultural group selection' whereby those legal orders that are better, in terms of giving individuals the possibility of following their life plans in a more complete and freeway, will succeed (or survive) over those that do not. He identifies certain individual rules or institutions, such as the rule of law or private property, that have proven more efficient than others in facilitating coordination between individual action plans. He also anticipates that these successful rule orders will be imitated by other communities.

Similarly, in the final three chapters of his "Law, Legislation and Liberty" (1983, 1973, p. 72 onwards), Hayek explicitly discusses the historical evolution of law and legislation, clearly distinguishing between them and asserting that the former is prior to the latter. He discusses specific legal institutions and even admits that legislation can modify the tendency of rules of spontaneous origin that may have emerged and whose consequences appear to us as undesirable. However, we believe that these ideas do not provide a clear framework for understanding the process of stability or change of specific rules or institutions. We believe that some of the new evolutionary theories dealing with rules and institutions can provide us with such tools today.

In this sense, we concur with Andreozzi (2005, p. 227) who considers that Hayek's ideas on rule selection can be related and even better explained by some models of evolutionary game theory (EGT). Although Hayek presents the case of rules that are open to free-riding as a problem for the explanation of the emergence and stabilisation of rules, Andreozzi believes that EGT mechanisms provide a way to show how group-beneficial rules can emerge and remain stable while being sustained through sanctioning within a population.

If we look at these mechanisms from the perspective of the three levels of evolution already discussed, we could say that there are mechanisms at the 'micro' level that could explain the stability or decline of different strategies at the 'macro' level. Thus, strategic decisions at the individual level can cause very relevant frequency changes in terms of repeated games and this, in legal terms, can mean that certain rules or institutions show certain levels of historical stability that are much higher than others that change rapidly.

Accordingly, we consider that the mechanisms studied by EGT can offer valuable insights into the selection, change and stabilisation of new strategies within a society or a legal order. As Alexander (2007, p. 25) explains, an evolutionary model provides, in principle, two key elements: (a) a representation of the state of the population and (b) a specification of the dynamic law, i.e. how the state of the population changes over time.

With regard to the second element, the dynamic law, we first find the 'replicator dynamics', which can be seen in the work of Skyrms (2004, p. 313) and is one of the most discussed dynamics in the realm of EGT. In this instance, we consider it unsuitable to implement this dynamic law within the domain of law, as its assumptions are not fully applicable to the legal field. For instance, as D'Arms (1996, p. 624) has observed and Alexander (2007, p. 33) has endorsed, the replicator dynamics theory postulates an infinite population and arbitrary interaction patterns among group members. Both assumptions could not be a suitable starting point for studying dynamics in the legal domain, since the societies or legal orders studied, although large, are made up of finite elements or agents and the relationship between agents in such groups is not random at all. Conversely, the relationships between agents are frequently replicated, with specific agents assuming pivotal roles in the social network (e.g., judges or legislators) that influence the strategies of others.

As previously discussed in Chapter 3, which focuses on Hayek's work, there are several authors and theories that highlight a close connection between Hayek's approach of studying law as a complex and spontaneous order and the contemporary models of complex systems studied by 'agent-based models' (Vriend, 1999). As previously outlined, these computational models, when applied to the modelled economy, observe phenomena as evolving decentralised systems of interacting autonomous agents. They are thus concerned with observing the spontaneous formation of global regularities in economic processes, such as the unplanned coordination of trade in market economies, and explaining them through bottom-up processes. In these processes, agents interact repeatedly and locally, through socio-economic institutions. Contrary to other theories, this interaction does not take place through imposed, top-down coordination mechanisms.

However, these models and methodologies are not limited to cases of market coordination, but are also applicable to other areas, such as morality. As outlined by Alexander (2007), this type of agent-based model, along with the concept of heuristics, can be employed to elucidate the process of the emergence of moral principles, such as cooperation and the rule of fair division.

As outlined in Chapter 6, these agent-based models and the various heuristics proposed by Alexander appear to be more suitable for the study of legal relations and their dynamics. Although agent-based models share certain features with replicator dynamics, such as the concept of agents with bounded rationality and the proposal of evolutionary cultural models, their assumptions differ significantly in many respects (Alexander, 2007, p. 34). This has implications for their potential application in the field of law.

We will now proceed to review the main assumptions of agent-based models in the context of EGT, considering their particular application to the realm of law:

(a) **Small population**: The size of the group can vary from small groups to the size of any real group. However, unlimited or infinite groups are not considered, and therefore the number of interactions, even if very numerous, is limited, and it is possible to reiterate relationships. In the legal sphere, we are considering orders that emerge from the interaction of a large group of individuals, but not of an infinite and random group. In this sense, this assumption could be a viable option within the legal realm.
(b) **Restricted interactions**: That is, non-randomness with respect to the possible interaction between individuals, allowing for the assumption that some interactions will occur more than others. By observing interactions repeatedly, we can identify patterns and structures in social relations. This, in turn, enables us to explain the emergence of regularities in rules and institutions. This is especially evident in the field of legal relations, where certain relationships

are more prevalent than others, such as those between partners or between legal agents and citizens of a particular area. In such cases, specific 'structures of relations' may emerge.

(c) **Key agents**: Alexander introduces the idea that certain agents play a distinct role within the structure of relationships. Key agents are thus defined as "one whose adoption of a different strategy sparks a large-scale shift in the strategy frequencies found in the population. A key agent occupies an Archimedean point, enabling her single action to alter radically the future state of society" (Alexander, 2007, p. 35). Consequently, the strategies employed by these agents are more extensively imitated than those of other agents, thereby impacting the trajectory of the overall order. When the interactions of these key actors are examined graphically, a 'node' is observed, given the concentration of relationships with other actors.

We consider this notion of the 'key agent' to be fundamental to understanding relations in the legal sphere. In this sense, it is clear that some agents play an essential role in shaping a legal order, since their decisions as judges, legislators or administrators will not only influence the strategies of others, but also establish, directly or indirectly, the payment schemes for each strategy. In this sense, while we recognise that all individual interactions form the basis for large-scale changes, some actors appear to exert more influence over others in the social structure, and this is something that the model of study should reflect. In the legal sphere, given the extent of its institutionalisation and formalisation, it is easy to identify some of these key actors, such as legislators, judges and civil servants.

(d) **Non-determinism:** These models also allow us to conceive of an amount of 'mutation', which, when translated into cultural language, means that some actors may propose new strategies without having been influenced by others on a regular basis. In other words, the possibility is conceived that, in addition to the strategies already put forward by the agents in the initial stages of the process, new strategies may emerge that were not present at the previous stage. It is important to note that the ratio of the frequency with which one or another strategy is employed by the group may change, and new strategies may emerge that have not been proposed by anyone before. From a legal perspective, we can talk about 'creation' or 'innovation' in the context of institutional strategies (akin to biological mutations). This occurs when an individual presents a novel solution or adapts an institutional approach that has been successful in other communities but hasn't been previously employed in this particular society.

This, in turn, implies that it is not possible to calculate or predict with certainty the outcome of a set of interactions in the future, since it is always open to mutations.

(e) **Heterogeneity of the agents involved in the dynamics.** As we have already seen and in contrast to the assumption of homogeneity of the agents of the 'replicator dynamics', this model proposes that actors in the legal world may exhibit not only different strategies but also different forms of interaction and individual learning.

In Chapter 6, we explored the various heuristics or learning processes proposed by Alexander (2007, p. 39) in his evolutionary game theory model applied to moral rules. It should be noted that some of these heuristics are based on imitation, while another is based on 'best response', but adapted to bounded rationality. We hereby recall them and explore their application to the legal domain:

(a) **Imitate the best neighbour:** This learning rule stipulates that, at the conclusion of each generation, each agent is required to evaluate the scores of its neighbours and adopt the strategy of the agent with the highest score. It is also assumed that the agent will not change strategies unless it has some incentive to do so. This rule can be applied to a wide range of legal agents. From ordinary citizens who determine their compliance with a given legal rule by assessing the results of the strategy they have chosen to follow, as well as the strategies employed by other agents in the relevant environment. He will thus imitate the agent who obtains the best results in his strategy. Furthermore, we can consider lawyers to be devising procedural strategies and studying previous cases to understand which of these strategies have worked best in that court.

(b) **Imitate with probability proportional to success:** As we have seen, this learning heuristic indicates that the agent will compare his scores with those of his neighbours, modifying his strategy only when a neighbour did strictly better, but assigning to each of the players who did better than him a different probability that he will adopt as his strategy. In other words, he will not merely consider those who have outperformed him; rather, he will also take into account all those who have shown superior performance, and will be inclined to adopt their strategies. Consider the actions of legal professionals, such as legislators, when formulating legislation to ensure its passage in the relevant chamber by a majority. He will probably consider several alternative strategies and select the most successful one, comparing it with other approaches implemented by other actors.

(c) **Imitate the best average payout:** Another approach to imitating the most successful strategies. In this scenario, agents select the strategy that offers the highest average payout in their community, and select randomly in the event of multiple ties. For instance, consider agents who are devising ways of making a sales contract without much technical legal preparation. It is probable that they will opt for the 'standard model' that has proven to be most effective for the majority of individuals within their community (perhaps without conducting a thorough analysis of the latest results among competing models).

(d) **Best response:** Finally, we recall this heuristic according to which agents adopt the strategy that will yield the highest payoff in the next generation, under the assumption that none of their neighbours change strategies (and in the case of more than one such strategy, players select a strategy at random). It is akin to an intergenerational Nash equilibrium. In this case, the role of expectations is pivotal, as it does not consider past success, but rather anticipates future success. However, it consistently assumes the assumption of bounded rationality, with agents operating under the presumption that other agents will continue acting in accordance with their past behaviours, without the need for explicit calculations. In this sense, let us consider an individual who devises a particular legal form for transferring property to their heirs. In this instance, the agent will give particular consideration to those strategies that are likely to be successful in the future (without necessarily taking into account past achievements), assuming that surrounding conditions will not change significantly.

As we have seen, we could apply all these heuristics or learning rules to the analysis of the behaviour of agents in the legal field. We often observe more conscious and calculated behaviour—perhaps on the part of 'key actors'—and other heuristics that are more based on assumptions and automatic behaviour. The final learning rule we are examining appears to be especially pertinent to the study of the evolution, change and stability of legal rules. As we have previously observed, its assumptions are consistent with the typical behaviour of agents in the legal domain, i.e. by considering expected future payments under the assumption that conditions will not change. Conversely, there is always the possibility of the emergence of a new strategy adopted by an unprecedented individual, in other words, the possibility of 'mutation'.

As discussed in Chapter 6, the notion of law as a game involves multiple players, and these evolutionary game theories can offer valuable insights into the evolution of legal rules, similar to how they are currently applied to the study of moral rules, such as cooperation, fairness and trust.

Applying the results observed at the time to moral rules, it could be said that the emergence and establishment of certain legal rules will depend on the circumstances and the reward scheme. The role of incentives is pivotal to ensuring the emergence and sustainability of certain rules and institutions (strategies) over time. As with cooperation, if the incentive to betray (e.g. violate the rule) is very high, it is likely that the coordination mechanisms, or the rule or institution considered valuable, will have a very difficult time emerging.

Moreover, the set of strategies that exist in the 'initial state' of the game appear to be highly influential on the final outcome. If a strategy is widespread in the original population, it is likely to spread. However, as we have seen, there is always the possibility of the emergence of a 'mutation', i.e. a strategy uninfluenced by any previous one. This would suggest that the institutions or rules present in a community at a given time may be pivotal to the evolution of strategies within that group in the future. It is more challenging for a new strategy, which has not been implemented before, to be adopted by the population than for one that is already widespread to continue to be successful.

Finally, as previously discussed, the role of the referee, or the 'key person' in a game, has the capacity to influence the outcome of a game. As we can see in the case of the moral rule of 'fairness', the game changes in cases where the role of the referee appears, changing the assumption of a symmetrical relationship. This consideration is particularly pertinent in the context of law, as it is a strategic 'game' in which there are explicitly designated agents in the roles of judges or arbitrators. These agents determine the range of possible strategies and the cost or benefit of following one or another strategy through their decisions.

In conclusion, it is clear that evolutionary game theory is a valuable tool for understanding how the heterogeneous rules that make up the law emerge from the interdependent interactions of a large number of individuals. It also highlights how the size of the group, the structure of relationships between group members and the specific roles they fulfil can influence the emergence, stabilisation and change of such rules. It can be observed that when certain strategies are proven to be successful, such as allowing coordination of different individual plans and avoiding conflicts, they will be imitated or adopted by those willing to improve their performance.

We may also consider raising this analysis to a 'meta-level' in which we can observe how entire institutional arrangements or sets of rules followed by one group can be imitated by others by similar means. This process of evolution will result in particular strategies and the legal rules and institutions that emerge from them proving more stable than others. As previously mentioned, we are referring to a 'dynamic stability' as proposed by Alexander (2007, p. 280). As previously outlined, this concept pertains to scenarios involving multiple interacting individuals, where the disruption of all strategies simultaneously leads to an eventual reversion of the players' choices towards a state of equilibrium (Gintis, 2006, p. 6).

If we apply this model of game theory, which operates at the 'micro' level by explaining the emergence of norms from individual interactions, to a three-dimensional evolutionary background, as we have suggested, we can consider agents choosing between strategies that may have emerged without their conscious participation, through processes of biological or cultural group evolution. From the interactions between biological and social/cultural evolution, each with its own selection criteria, the most stable strategies over time have been selected to guarantee the survival of the order or agents, as the case may be. Agents select from strategies that have already emerged from evolutionary processes preceding their own, although these were the unintended results of their own or other agents' interactions. These strategies are then fed back to them by their own conscious actions. Therefore, legal rules and institutions will not be the sole product of a process of biological evolution, of a cultural process of group evolution, nor of the more or less conscious decision of the agents interacting in the legal sphere. Rather, they will be the product of these three processes in a permanent interaction.

10.3.2 An Evolutionary Account of Law

We have arrived at a point where we are able to offer our version of an evolutionary account of law by combining all the bricks and elements presented. Firstly, we have our methodological 'bricks' and anthropological, psychological and epistemological assumptions: Our methodological conception proposes a moderate methodological individualism, and our assumptions about human nature imply a mixed nature that cannot be 'encompassed' by any exclusionary model. In summary, this is an individual who combines self-interest with adaptive capacity through different decision-making processes. Calculative rationality is used when warranted, while heuristics and imitative learning are employed at other times.

In addition to these bricks, our understanding of evolution extends to three distinct levels: biological, social (group) and individual. This comprehensive approach enables us to observe the outcome of these dynamic processes as self-emerging orders. These self-generated orders could then be studied both from 'classical evolutionism' and from more recent theories such as evolutionary game theory. Combining these elements and applying them to the legal field, we have offered here an explanation of the process of emergence, change and the stability of legal rules and can now offer a synthetic version of our evolutionary view of law.

Law reflects both coordination and conflict. Each individual has their own plans, based on a framework of beliefs, values and expectations of the actions and plans of others. These projects can often be coordinated, with each individual following their own plan without hindering the plans of others. However, in certain circumstances, different plans and mutual expectations can clash, resulting in conflict. Such conflicts often originate from misplaced expectations regarding each other's abilities to act in specific ways. As conflicts of a similar nature often arise in a community, and agents are subject to constraints on their rationality and capabilities, as well as constraints on each sphere of action, regularities in solutions also begin to emerge through implicit or explicit principles and rules.

It is therefore possible to regard these rules as more or less sophisticated survival strategies, whether biological or cultural in nature. We often manage to identify and analyse them only by observing certain regularities in the behaviour of individuals. Implicit rules are not always clear or easy to apply, and the need to make them explicit becomes evident in cases of specific conflicts. In other areas, such as morality and social rules, there is usually no authority to establish the final answer to such conflicts. However, within the legal sphere, legislative and judicial processes are in place to determine the limits of each individual plan and the legal response to mutual conflicts. It could be the subject of another paper to study the particular emergence of modern states as organs that concentrate much of the power to recognise, positivise and apply, through the monopoly of coercion, these norms. In the field of law, we can observe a certain stability not only in the strategies adopted by individuals, but also in the responses that are presented in the face of these legal cases as a process of conflict resolution.

Our evolutionary explanation of law begins with the idea that law is a dynamic and complex phenomenon. It is dynamic, because continuous change over time is a fundamental part of it. It is complex because it is composed of several heterogeneous elements combined and only observable through an intellectual approach. As previously analysed, we can gain an overview of the complex phenomenon, identifying trends or patterns. However, this information does not allow us to predict what will happen in a specific case.

Most legal theories tend to focus on explicit, articulate or codified rules, as if they were created ex nihilo by legislators or judges, through certain procedures. Some legal theories analyse whether the content of such rules conforms to certain moral prescriptions, such as some natural law theories. In other cases, the formal procedure followed for their creation is studied, for instance by legal positivism. Finally, the empirical aspects of the fact of prediction, creation and the application of such rules by courts are analysed, such as in some versions of legal realism. However, the evolutionary process that precedes and accompanies such a formulation is usually forgotten. This process, gradual and silent, involves different individuals following their own plans and trying to avoid clashing with each other. Through various attempts and mistakes, they establish principles of coordination. As illustrated by the three levels of evolution, some of these processes are not always conscious to their participants, which makes them difficult to reconstruct historically. However, it is the outcomes of these processes that ultimately shape the range of possibilities within which legislators, judges and other explicit rule formulators operate.

In our view, even legislators have no power to create laws from scratch. Just as Douglas North (1990) discusses 'formal and informal institutions', there is always a 'cultural humus' or framework of informal institutions that guides the creation of new legislation or judicial decisions. As outlined by Hayek, these are the abstract rules, or 'moral heuristics'as they are termed in evolutionary psychology, co-evolutionism and the 'homo heuristicus' theory. These are not prescriptive propositions in and of themselves, but rather a set of principles, values and indications of different kinds. They indicate the possible range of solutions that positive law could consider. We also consider these elements to be part of law because, although agents may not be conscious of them, they are internalised and motivate their actions. Including, in Hart's terms (Hart, 1997, p. 71), the 'internal' aspects of norms, these guidelines are as relevant for understanding law as positive norms, as they have the power to guide the individual's decision-making processes. Furthermore, these heuristics and implicit rules are important in their interactions with positive rules, which is evident in their influence on the interpretation and application of legal and judicial rules. In certain instances, they can even exhibit a greater force than positive rules. Their comprehension facilitates the elucidation of various normative phenomena, such as the distinction between rules that possess an immediate effect on reality and those that are neither put into practice nor applied, despite adhering to the formal requirements for their formulation. When a citizen, lawyer or judge must interpret and apply a particular norm or judicial precedent, they do so through a conceptual framework, formed by changing abstract rules, which are the result of biological and cultural evolution and their interactions.

Why is law an evolving phenomenon? As we have seen, the three evolutionary processes interact constantly to provide us with different types of solutions. On the one hand, there are those that are more automatic and adaptive, such as heuristics that are presented as quick solutions to repeated situations. These are the product of biological, cultural (or co-evolutionary) survival strategies. In contrast, explicit rules are the result of a more thoughtful calculation by agents in relation to others. These agents select the most efficient strategies for the specific case and context.

The former, which we also consider to be part of the legal order to be analysed, are not formulated or proposed by any central power or decision-making body, nor are they the product of an express pact or contract between individuals. Furthermore, they are not intentionally designed for any specific purpose. These are the result of a series of actions and decisions taken in different circumstances and contexts by different individuals, who, over time, have provided the basis for their emergence. These rules can change through variation in the beliefs, decisions and actions of individuals, and sometimes merely as the unintended consequences (positive and negative) of these. The latter can be regarded as explicit formulations and proposed solutions by citizens, legislators, judges and other rule-makers. Furthermore, they can be studied as the result of learning processes, such as those proposed by evolutionary game theory, which can explain some of these changes in individual strategies. However, it is crucial to acknowledge the interconnection between these explicit rules, which are often the result of individual strategies, and the two strong relationships they share with heuristics or implicit rules.

Firstly, they may be the rationalisation and positivisation of adaptive solutions that took place 'previously' as a product of the selection of biological or cultural evolutionary processes, as proposed by evolutionary psychology or co-evolutionism, among other theories. Conversely, those implicit rules that have not been codified provide a framework for interpreting and applying those that have been. This enables us to understand how, for example, two identical positive rules in different cultural contexts can have such divergent outcomes. Finally, even in the context of positive rules, it is important to acknowledge that, in the course of evolution, there have been numerous instances of rules or institutions that were initially designed to address specific issues between individuals that were subsequently proved to have had unintended consequences, such as resolving coordination problems or establishing a foundation for future interactions.

This heterogeneous set of rules, that constitutes the law, implies an incentive scheme, which is taken into consideration by individuals when deciding on a course of action. On the one hand, abstract rules represent a general limit to the range of possible actions. While they do not set specific costs and benefits for each strategy considered, they represent a broad boundary between actions that are within the limits and those that are outside them. For instance, certain principles that govern contract law and civil law in general, such as the principles of 'pacta sunt servanda' and 'good faith', initially emerged as moral heuristics before being incorporated into positive law. Whilst the exact nature of the action required is not specified, such as the precise contract to be signed or the signatory, it does outline the actions that are not permitted. One such example is the intentional harm of the other party to the contract. It is evident that acting in a manner that contravenes these principles could incur significant costs, even if these costs are not specified in detail.

Conversely, there is a more explicit payment scheme reflected in certain legal rules and decisions of judicial and administrative bodies. As these rules have specific objectives and addressees, they can function as instruments of a more robust prediction of what the outcomes of an individual strategy within a legal order might be. For instance, given explicit legislation governing liability, we can calculate the outcome of a breach of contract in different legal systems (i.e. the concrete results of a violation of the above-mentioned principle of 'pacta sunt servanda'). However, even in this instance, we will not be able to make an exact prediction. These positive rules must be applied in a specific context, and the context, with its abstract rules, will inform their interpretation and application.

We can now propose some conclusions about what a legal system is and how we can recognise it. Firstly, legal orders are conceived of as complex phenomena (Hayek 1983, p. 22), that is to say, the product of the interaction of heterogeneous elements in a specific social context. Among these phenomena, we categorise it as an emergent or self-generated order, the product of the three-level process of evolution that we have previously outlined.

As a legal order comprises various sources, the method of studying such an order cannot be reduced to a logical-analytical apparatus that would allow us to learn only the closed order of legislation. This being only a part of the legal order, it would be inaccurate to study it in isolation. We require an intellectual approach that displays its tendencies or patterns and its dynamic laws, and we believe that such notions are provided today by evolutionary theories. This evolution differs between communities, producing different orders. This is why similar pieces of legislation in different cultural contexts are interpreted and applied differently, and even contradictorily. The change and stability of certain legal rules within a social order is dependent on their ability to solve coordination problems or to provide better conditions for each individual to follow their plan.

What would be the consequences of applying the three-level view of evolution to rules and intuitions? The implications of applying the evolutionary view to law as a legal system and to rules and institutions separately are numerous. The first would be the view held by almost all thinkers with an evolutionary perspective, namely that a humble position should be adopted in the study and planning of social and cultural phenomena. This perspective indicates that our behaviour and its outcomes are not solely the result of our immediate decisions, but rather, they must be analysed within the framework of processes that extend beyond individual design. In many cases, they would be concrete solutions that proved to be more useful in the long term or 'evolutionarily stable' with respect to other possible institutional solutions. In this sense, and given our limited rationality and knowledge capacity, we will never be able to fully comprehend the complexity of these processes. Therefore, we will never be able to reduce them to a couple of variables to explain and predict them exhaustively.

Connected to the first conclusion, the second would relate to humility in the planning of public policies, given that this web of motivations is not so easily elucidated. If we regard individuals as adaptive subjects who will attempt to 'survive' in their specific physical and cultural context through trial and error of behavioural strategies (but not a fully conscious learning process), it is imperative to exercise caution when establishing incentives, nudges or other 'cultural artefacts' that seek to modify motivations and behaviours. There are various reasons for this, which we will only briefly outline here: (a) It should be noted that cognitive limitations and social constraints are not only suffered by those who 'receive' public policy, but also by those who propose it. (b) In many cases, we do not know and cannot imagine what the unintended consequences of the 'interventions' of the evolutionary process produced by the public policy under analysis might be. (c) The cumulative effects of the different interventions proposed by different public policies can result in us losing sight of what would have been the rules and institutions that would have been the spontaneous product of the interaction between individuals' actions. This 'data' could be very useful in determining which strategies would have been evolutionarily more stable given this genetic inheritance and social context.

In conclusion, the third proposal would extend an invitation, particularly to lawyers and jurists, to study a range of theories. These include evolutionary biology and psychology, behavioural theories, experimental studies in economics and philosophy, evolutionary game theory, theories of complex phenomena, agent-based models and many others. These theories imply new theoretical approaches to social phenomena. Integrating the contents of these theories with classical studies on legal and political rules and institutions would represent a significant innovation in terms of ideas, offering a novel approach to addressing long-standing issues in legal philosophy and doctrine. For instance, we must consider the kinds of anthropological, psychological, or epistemological assumptions we are making when describing subjects in relation to law. This includes whether we are assuming that the establishment of a new rule will imply a change in the motivation or behaviour of individuals. It also includes whether we are assuming that judges exercise a regulated and mechanical activity, a discretionary one, or an arbitrary one. Furthermore, we must consider whether subjects will respond to specific incentives set by rules in the same way in different societies or contexts.

10.4 Brief Comparison with Other Schools

In the field of legal theory, as Lakatos (1978) would describe it, there are a variety of 'scientific research programmes' that develop their own problems and solutions in parallel.

On the one hand, theories of natural law or 'natural rights' are still in place, studying law in relation to its moral content or purpose in an axiological sense. These theories typically focus on the substantive analysis of legal norms and their conformity with moral principles. The notion of justice is central to this view of law, as are various theses on the ultimate and transcendent foundation of law. Although the evolutionary view recognises the potential for the emergence of social, moral and legal norms to co-occur, and the possibility that legal rules may be informed by a 'moral heuristic', it does not contrast these with an external, objective morality. In essence, the morality that many evolutionary theorists refer to is a morality that emerges endogenously from individual interactions. These interactions involve rules of behaviour that produce certain satisfactory outcomes for the participating agents. These are not evaluated in the light of an external morality. Similarly, while these principles may give rise to certain legal rules (as discussed by Hart in relation to the minimum moral content of rules, 1997 (1961), p. 239), they do not serve as a standard for evaluating law. In other words, although certain legal rules or institutions may have arisen as a coordination or conflict resolution strategy from a moral principle, they are not obliged to maintain all their content or to be evaluated from their substantive aspects.

In contrast, other schools of thought attempt to explain the law from a logical or empirical perspective. Despite the differences between the main exponents of legal positivism (e.g. Hans Kelsen or H.L.A. Hart), the concept of law as a system of norms remains the focus. This school's approach is closely related to the emergence of nation states and the study of 'positive norms'—which are most often identified with the law of the state. The school proposes some methods for the identification, classification and systematisation of rules. Law is defined as positive norms deliberately created by organs with prescriptive powers and by different means, such as legislation or judicial decisions.

Consequently, respect for some formal meta-rules, such as the inclusion of a sanction element in their formulation, is established as a criterion for identifying and separating them from other types of rules (moral, social, etc.). This also leads us to the study of the validity of such rules, which are generally established as their conformity to certain formal requirements (procedure, competent authority, etc.) established by the same superior rules or meta-rules of the system. Law is therefore understood as a system of valid legal rules, organised in a specific, often hierarchical, manner. Finally, this system of positive rules can be studied by deploying a logical-analytical apparatus. In some cases, traditional logic can be used, while in other cases, a special logic, such as deontic logic, must be created to study this specific type of propositions.

While we consider that the evolutionary account of law could be complementary to some conceptions of positive law, such as that of H. L. A. Hart, with regard to positive norms, it differs with regard to the notion of the legal system as a whole. If we were to study law from this evolutionary perspective, we would see that individual expectations about possible sanctions for the violation of a legal norm are not only found by agents in positive norms, but also in a series of guidelines, principles, heuristics, etc., that have not necessarily been positivised to be conceived as law. We could even understand that the framework of law production, or even its 'rule of recognition', is more complex than the mere identification of an ultimate criterion or source to be resorted to whenever we want to identify what is 'inside and outside' the system.

Finally, the legal realism school of thought, as represented by American judges such as Oliver Wendell Holmes, Benjamin Cardozo and Jerome Frank, relates law to facts and actions. Despite the differences between each thinker, legal realism identifies law with actions performed by specific individuals, such as judges or lawyers, and with their consequences, such as judicial decisions backed by the power of the state. It holds that to ascertain the prevailing legal framework within a community, one must observe the practices within its judicial system. In this regard, they propose to utilise empirical methods for observing and predicting future judicial decisions. They also regard the judge as a pivotal figure within the legal system, entrusted with the role of law creation as opposed to the mere enforcement of legislated norms.

Another version of this school can be found in Scandinavian realism, represented by authors such as Olivecrona or Hägerström, among others. In this case, an attempt is made to explore the law in force not only from the perspective of the rules conceived or applied by the courts, but also from the perspective of society as a whole. In this case, there is a strong focus on the practical implications of legislation, state coercion, and the role of legal norms in motivating behaviour.

This naturalistic and anti-formalist perspective on law may be related, in certain aspects, to the evolutionary view proposed in this book. The key difference between them is methodological, particularly the confidence of many realist authors in the early twentieth-century conception of science. In this view, the evolutionary approach aligns with a more hypothetico-deductivist (and to some extent more falsifiable) vision of science, where hypotheses are constantly tested and discarded. From an evolutionary perspective, both agents in the field of action and scientists in the 'laboratory' possess limited rationality. They use heuristics and test hypotheses to identify the best explanations and solutions in each specific context.

Finally, we could establish several relationships between some of the derivations of the realist view in recent decades, such as the 'law and economics' school or its 'behaviourist' version, among others. The evolutionary view and these theories coincide in some points of their assumptions of human nature (although not in all, depending on the version of the theory) and also in their concern for the effects of legal rules on the motivations and expectations of individuals. In this regard, there is potential to explore a variety of bridges of communication.

In conclusion, this evolutionary account of law that we are proposing has been inspired by the 'classical evolutionism' represented by the Scottish Enlightenment—with notable figures including David Hume, Adam Smith and Adam Ferguson—and by Friedrich A. Hayek in the twentieth century. We have then proposed numerous conceptual connections between this classical evolutionism and a diverse set of new evolutionary theories in the social sciences, such as evolutionary psychology, co-evolution or evolutionary game theory. We consider that the intersection of these theories provides us with the most precise explanation of the emergence, stability and change of rules and institutions, as it allows for a deep understanding of legal systems in terms of their dynamics.

We also consider that this evolutionary account of law overcomes two current problems in the philosophy of the social sciences. Firstly, we propose a model of the agent with bounded rationality that combines a broad notion of self-interest (which can be varied) with the following of heuristics and social rules when the circumstances permit. It incorporates the latest findings from psychology and cognitive sciences on how the human brain works and how decision-making processes are in different circumstances. We add to this perspective the notion of the unintended consequences of human actions, providing a view of agents that is equidistant from the exclusionary models of 'homo economicus'and 'homo sociologicus'. Individuals are not viewed as maximising machines or blind rule-followers, but as agents with individual plans that respect rules derived from their own interactions and expectations.

Similarly, we are confident that the methodological dispute between methodological individualism and methodological holism has been resolved. The evolutionary view of law thus proposes a moderate individualism which, without denying the individual genesis of social facts, does not demand a strict translation of social terms into individual terms. It maintains that individuals, through their beliefs, actions, planning, and adaptation, have the capacity to influence and shape social phenomena. This understanding acknowledges the complexity of these phenomena and emphasises the necessity of studying them as integrated and dynamic systems, rather than as the simple sum of individual facts.

Consequently, self-interested individuals with the capacity to put themselves in the place of others, discovering that society is the best way to solve their natural limitations, interact and cooperate with each other. Law appears as the unintended result of these interactions, as a self-generated order composed of different kinds of rules, which allow, some more successfully than others, to overcome coordination problems. The concepts of classical evolutionism are now encapsulated in several models proposed by evolutionary game theory and agent-based models. These models share most of their assumptions and provide a more precise understanding of the dynamics of emergence, change and the stability of legal rules as more stable strategies in the long run. In particular, some of these agent-based models and learning rules provide insight into how individuals adopt, change or sustain strategies, and the heuristics that inform them. They also compare their performance and choose those that prove to be more successful in certain respects (e.g. allowing better coordination of individual plans).

In this way, we believe that we are making a contribution to legal theory by rethinking its object of study and its relationship and interdependence with other disciplines and fields of study.

10.5 Conclusions: Why Write a Book on an Evolutionary Account of Law Today?

Finally, we would like to make some concluding remarks on why it is relevant to us today to propose this evolutionary account of law. We will now set out our reasons.

It could be argued that this work does not propose a 'new' vision of law, since the evolutionary view has been proposed by many authors in the history of philosophical, political and legal thought. Indeed, the authorship of these ideas can be recognised in the work of renowned Scottish thinkers (e.g. Hume, Smith, Ferguson) and, more recently, in the work of authors such as F. A. Hayek. We have committed ourselves to this enterprise, however, as we believe that these works and authors contain the seeds of a way of explaining the processes of emergence, stability and the change of rules and institutions that have been developed, sophisticated and perfected to a great extent today. Presently, we have access to a range of new theoretical and empirical models that offer a greater degree of precision in analysing these processes.

Furthermore, it is crucial to note that within the field of philosophy of the social sciences, there has been significant debate for many years about both methodological and fundamental issues. We have observed, for example, that the sharp division which historically separated the social sciences from the natural sciences is slowly disappearing. These debates, new ideas and challenges do not seem to touch upon the general theory of law. We see that questions such as the structure of legal systems or the relationship between law and morality or law and politics continue to be discussed as if they were very distant fields that we have to bring closer together for some, or fields that overlap almost completely for others. All this as if the 'naturalistic or biological turn' in philosophy and social sciences had never happened.

Even in cases where we see an impact of these approaches on theories such as behavioural law and economics, it appears that these theories function by examining how individuals behave in the context of a given incentive framework or a 'given' system of rules. To summarise, these theories evaluate how individuals will act in response to specific rules, based on findings from neuroscience, decision-making or behavioural theories. However, they do not consider the specific way in which these rules arise. For instance, they do not address how individuals establish new rules or institutional frameworks, or the reasons behind discontinuing existing ones. They do not analyse the way in which incentive systems influence the emergence of these or other incentive frameworks, as well as the subsequent effect on legislators or judges, among other factors, and the interaction between all these levels.

We believe that the evolutionary perspective can provide a framework for exploring these questions and integrating the existing debates in the social sciences with legal thinking. We are optimistic that this initial step will be productive in this regard.

References

Alexander, J. M. K. (2007). *The structural evolution of morality*. Cambridge University Press.

Andreozzi, L. (2005). Hayek reads the literature on the emergence of norms. *Constitutional Political Economy, 16*(3), 227–247.

D'Arms, J. (1996). Sex, fairness and the theory of games. *The Journal of Philosophy, 1996*(93), 12.

Dworkin, R. (1978). *Taking rights seriously*. Harvard University Press.

Gigerenzer, G., & Brighton, H. (2009). Homo heuristicus: why biased minds make better inferences. *Topics in Cognitive Science, 1*, 107–143.

Gintis, H. (2006). Behavioral ethics meets natural justice. *Politics, Philosophy and Economics, 5*(1), 6.

Hart, H. L. A. (1961). *The concept of law*. Oxford University Press.

Hart, H. L. A. (1997). *The concept of law*. Oxford University Press. Original work published 1961.

Hayek, F. A. (1973). *Law, legislation and liberty* (Vol. I). University of Chicago Press.

Hayek, F. A. (1978). *The constitution of liberty*. The University of Chicago Press. Original work published 1960.

Hayek, F. A. (1983). The theory of complex phenomena. In *Studies in philosophy, politics and economics* (pp. 22–42). The University of Chicago Press. Original work published 1967.

Hume, D. (2000). *A treatise of human nature*. Oxford University Press. Original work published 1739–40.

Lakatos, I. (1978). *The methodology of scientific research programmes*. Philosophical Papers (Vol. I). Cambridge University Press.

North, D. (1990). *Institutions, Institutional Change and Economic Performance*. Cambridge University Press.

Richerson, P. J., & Boyd, R. (2006). *Not by genes alone: how culture transformed human evolution.* The University of Chicago Press.
Skyrms, B. (2004). *The stag hunt and the evolution of the social structure.* Cambridge University Press.
Vriend, N. (1999). *"Was Hayek an ace?" Queen Mary and Wastield college.* University of London.

Index

E. M. Santanatoglia, *An Evolutionary Account of Law*, Palgrave Studies in Classical Liberalism, https://doi.org/10.1007/978-3-032-12162-2

FSC
www.fsc.org
MIX
Papier | Fördert gute Waldnutzung
FSC® C083411

Kolibri 360 GmbH
Ferdinand-Jühlke-Straße 7
99095 Erfurt, Deutschland
produktsicherheit@kolibri360.de